COMMUNICATION AND ORGANIZATIONAL CONTROL

Communication and Organizational Control

CYBERNETICS IN HEALTH AND WELFARE SETTINGS

JERALD HAGE

A WILEY-INTERSCIENCE PUBLICATION

JOHN WILEY & SONS, New York · London · Sydney · Toronto

Library of Congress Cataloging in Publication Data

Hage, Jerald, 1932-
   Communication and organizational control.

   "A Wiley-interscience publication."
   Bibliography: p.
   1. Organizational research. 2. Communication
in the social sciences. 3. Hospitals—Administration.
I. Title. [DNLM:: 1. Communication. 2. Cybernetics.
3. Hospital administration. WX150 H141c 1973]

HM131.H228 1974   301.18'32'0141   73-19614
ISBN 0-471-33864-8

Printed in the United States of America

10 9 8 7 6 5 4 3 2 1

This monograph is dedicated to
Madeline Hage, my wife,
and
Emile Durkheim, my mentor,
who both taught an essentially
Teutonic mind the inner joys
of Latin intuitions

PREFACE

Books can emerge in many ways. This one had its origin in what was for me a fascinating experiment designed to improve the quality of patient care. Since completing my dissertation, which was based on this experiment, I have been searching for an orientation and theory that would generalize experience beyond the context of hospitals. First, I experimented with Weber's concepts but found them of little value for my purposes. About a year after completing graduate studies, however, I discovered and read Durkheim's *Division of Labor*. Not only did it discuss new problems, many of which were relevant to my study, but it represented an entirely new way of thinking for someone who, to a large extent, had studied Marx and Weber. Perhaps the most important impression left was that control or integration was problematical.

About the same time I met and married Madeleine Cottenet who had a similar impact on me by breaking some of the intellectual molds in which I had been cast. Together they led me towards new ways of thinking about the problem at hand and to them I dedicate this book.

Paradoxically, the introduction to cybernetics had occurred before this, when I was a graduate student. Johan Galtung suggested that Ashby's book might become very important in ten years and that perhaps I should study it carefully. I did but did not grasp its relevance for my work until I had been working on communication theory with my colleague Michael Aiken. Since this theory was developed by Cora

Bagley Marrett and him, these seemingly disparate pieces of my past began to fit together into a comprehensive whole. The title of this book has these key elements united: communication, control, and cybernetics. Having tried to write this monograph on some five occasions, I cannot describe the pleasure of finally feeling that what I have done is somehow right. For the first time I can feel that I have accomplished my goal.

In my different attempts at understanding, I have been much aided by the advice and criticism of others. Naturally, Michael Aiken and Cora Bagley Marrett have had many opportunities to broaden and extend the initial insights. Others who have enlightened me have been Charles Perrow, Gordon Whiting, James Price, and Gerald Marwell. They have supplied extensive criticisms and, in most cases, I have taken their comments to heart. To all of them I would like to express my appreciation for their feedback and socialization.

Seldom does one see discussions of the problem of financing research in prefaces and yet the patrons of research are frequently the real unsung heroes. In my case, the Department of Health, Education, and Welfare has been more than a benefactor. During my graduate studies, the experiment reported in this book was supported by the National Institutes of Health, allowing me to complete my Ph.D. while most other students had to drop out of school. It was not only a rare opportunity to study a serious problem in social change, but it amounted to a generous fellowship in the days when there were none. The second study is part of a larger one conducted by Michael Aiken and myself and supported by Social and Rehabilitation Services. Again it gave both of us a chance to test our ideas and organizations when we were still young assistant professors.

If there appears to be a concern for practicality in this book, it is because I view it as one way of expressing my gratitude for the kind of research support that I have received during the past 14 years. Neither the National Institutes of Health nor the Social and Rehabilitation Services are responsible for the opinions expressed in this book and may not even agree that professional control is a problem, much less that communication as feedback and socialization offer the ideal solution. Regardless, this book deals directly with what I perceive to be an important problem and attempts a solution.

It is my personal conviction that only theory can provide solutions to practical problems. The more one is concerned with changing the world the more one must develop a theory about what makes the world operate the way it does. In this connection, I am reminded vividly of one day in Community Hospital during a very stormy and conflictful period when one of the assistant administrators asked what I, as a professional sociologist, would suggest. I answered somewhat embarrassedly that the field had not yet accumulated enough knowledge to offer much advice, but added that, hopefully, studies such as I was doing would contribute to future solutions. This book represents my attempt to fulfill that promise.

This book is also intended to express my thanks to many professionals in the health and welfare fields with whom I had contact. I am especially appreciative of their patience with a sociologist who was trying to learn and who sometimes seemed to ask the same questions three times. Hopefully, all those hours spent in interviews and observations have borne insights that they themselves did not have about their organizations or their professions.

There have been a large number of research assistants and secretaries who have in various ways contributed to the success of these research projects and to this book. A full list would be almost impossible to make. However, I particularly want to thank Cora Bagley Marrett, who along with my wife and I, did most of the hard work on the coding of the communication scores and Gene Pullera who did most of the work that I dislike—operating the machines for the data analysis. Donna Peckett has typed more editions of this manuscript than she cares to remember. I appreciate her excellence in doing so. Neither the government, nor its agencies such as the National Institutes of Health and the Social and Rehabilitation Services, nor the many who have given advice necessarily agree with what is said in this book.

JERALD HAGE

University of Wisconsin
September 1973
Madison, Wisconsin

CONTENTS

PROLOGUE

THE GENERAL APPROACH AND A
SPECIFIC THEORY OF CYBERNETICS

I

Cybernetic Control in Organizations: Conceptual Approach and Analytical Problems

CYBERNETICS AS A SYSTEM OF THOUGHT has become increasingly popular with sociologists in general (e.g., Buckley, 1967) and with specialists in organizations in particular (Katz and Kahn, 1966; Litterer, 1963; Azumi and Hage, 1972; Blau, 1970). Most of its applications, however, have so far been metaphorical (see, e.g., Katz and Kahn, 1966). Words like input, information, and energy are frequently used as organizing devices around an unclear referent. No one has yet developed a formal theory of cybernetic control for organizations, nor has anyone tested such a theory.

Given the extended development of operations research—research conducted within the context of organizations—it is somewhat surprising that cybernetic analysis did not find a place in the thinking of organizational sociologists. There are relatively few explicit attempts to apply cybernetic concepts (Cadwaller, 1959, and Cangelosi and Dill, 1965, are exceptions) earlier. The meagerness is probably a reflection of the different measurement problems faced by operation researchers, who usually deal with production systems, material-flow systems, and certain mechanical systems whose variables are

3

known and measurable. Only recently has there been a growing agreement about what might be some critical organizational variables and how they might be measured (Price, 1972; Hall, 1972; Azumi and Hage, 1972). Then, too, the dramatic events of the 1960s—accelerating change (Toffler, 1970), deepening conflict (Corwin, 1969), and more frequent critiques (Gouldner, 1970)—have made organization analysts leave the relatively static concepts of structural-functionalism for the more dynamic process thinking of cybernetics.

Perhaps more than any others, Forrester and his group have demonstrated in a series of books (e.g., *Industrial Dynamics*, 1961, *Urban Dynamics*, 1969 and especially *Limits to Growth*, 1971) the power of systems concepts for organizing one's thought and for tackling seemingly intractable social problems. Although they may have generalized cybernetic concepts too much, and diffused much of the concepts' meaning, and although much of their success lies in the use of a special machine simulation program which handles nonlinear relationships, they have popularized cybernetic concepts and thinking. They have not suggested any formal theory of cybernetic control. Instead their emphasis has been more on developing models for particular problems, as reflects their training in operations research and engineering.

The purpose of this book is to propose a formal theory of cybernetic control—one for human beings. Hopefully, it will lead to a way in which systems thought in general and cybernetic analysis in particular can be extended and developed. Although the proposed theory deals specifically with organizations, the concepts and principles appear to be general enough to apply to a number of social collectives, especially to that most incomprehensible one—society. As the theory is first presented, then illustrated in a longitudinal case study of a community hospital, and then tested in a multi-organization study of mental health, rehabilitation, and welfare agencies, a number of cybernetic concepts and assumptions are explicated. This is particularly important because if cybernetic thinking is to take hold, the concepts must be as concrete as possible. Like Forrester and his group, my ultimate concern is less with proving the efficacy of a particular model or theory and more with demonstrating the utility of the concepts via the light they shed on social problems.

Much attention is given to the delineation of analytical problems. The real test of any proposed paradigm is its ability to help us see new issues and relationships. Therefore, the present studies indicate ways in which the analytical model has changed my perception.

Perhaps the most unusual aspect of the proposed theory of cybernetic control is its heavy emphasis on feedback with social-ization—via increases in communication as the regulatory mech-anism. Given the steady extension of reinforcement techniques, which are called sanctions in this theory, this may strike readers as strange. *Sanctions with programming and socialization with high feedback* are proposed as alternative mechanisms of control. A number of illustrations are given to show how socialization without the presence of sanctions can work as a mechanism, perhaps the most debatable aspect of the theory. Hopefully, these examples will make clear how this mechanism operates in many organizational contexts.

The present theory contrasts with the reinforcement theories of Skinner in two significant ways. *First,* the present theory focuses on how the members of organizations are controlled, not on how they control their clients. Reinforcement techniques have been widely applied to mental retardates, school children with behavioral prob-lems, and welfare clients and others in a relatively powerless position. The question is who controls the rehabilitation workers, teachers, welfare workers, and one might add psychologists, sociologists, and professionals in general. A system of control appropriate for their clients might not be appropriate for them. *Second,* the theory is more concerned with future systems of regulation and control rather than present ones. Socialization coupled with high feedback may only be applicable today to a small proportion of the present *adult* population, but fifty years from now it may be more widespread.

A theory that is not testable has, of course, little utility. For this reason, extended treatment is given to questions of measurement: how does one document the various mechanisms of control, how does one measure feedback, what is the relationship between communica-tions flow and feedback, what are the signs of a control system that has broken down, how does one measure networks of communication flow? While not all measurement problems are solved by any means, at least the difficulties and directions for further improvement are made clear.

There are several reasons why testing the adequacy of a theory is so important. Inevitably, one finds weaknesses in the light of data. And this cybernetic theory is no exception! Certain hypotheses are better substantiated than others when the theory is contrasted with alternative theoretical explanations. These need to be explicated. Perhaps more importantly, as one collects and analyzes the data new problems and new insights manifest thtemselves. The whole idea of studying how communication networks were constructed and how they evolved over time emerged in the process of data analysis; it did not spring from the theory although it is implied in it. Finally, for some readers a theory becomes much more convincing once evidence is presented to support it. Otherwise, one always has nagging doubts (see the critique of Glazer and Strauss, 1967, in this regard). Certainly my own opinion is that if the creator of the theory does not believe enough in it to test it himself, then I take his work less seriously.

In testing the adequacy of this present theory, I have employed an unusual combination of research methodologies, including both a longitudinal case study of a community hospital and a comparative one of mental health, rehabilitation, and welfare organizations. The first design has the advantage of reporting change across time and thus speaks to causal ordering—that is, does an increase in the rate of complexity (the number of specialists) lead to a change in the amount of horizontal communication rather than vice versa? The data was collected prior to the theory's construction, however, so that, at best, we can say that the case study is illustrative and not a test as such. In contrast, the comparative study of organizations was specifically designed to test the proposed theory of cybernetic control. As a consequence, considerable attention was given to the problem of measures of control mechanisms which can be employed in a variety of organizational settings. Furthermore, alternative theories of explanation were examined at the same time. This is a critical advantage of comparative research design, since, in many instances, one can imagine more than one cause or explanation for the particular effects noted. As Stinchcombe (1968) has observed, this is perhaps the most convincing way of evaluating the adequacy of a theory.

The combination of a longitudinal case study with a comparative one has other advantages. The former provides enough rich detail to make meaningful the abstract concepts of the theory. It adds concreteness and depth. This is especially important since many professionals will want to know how organizations can control their workers —particularly with socialization techniques in the absence of sanctions. This must be illustrated and explained, and at some length. The comparative study of several kinds of rehabilitation and welfare agencies explores some different issues more rigorously. Some attention is given to alternative pathways of evolution, something which could not be considered in a single case study. With a variety of organizations, it becomes possible to use more complex multivariate techniques such as partial correlational analysis. Together, the two research strategies provide a more exacting evaluation.

Since cybernetics imagery and the word system have so pervaded our scientific vocabularies, we must be careful with definitions. While I appreciate that it is deadly dull to start a book with a discussion of definitions, it is necessary in this instance. Feedback, cybernetic control, and system are words that have been employed so widely that they acquired a large variety of connotations which I wish to eschew. These should be explicitly eliminated. Hopefully, the process of winnowing away the excess weight will make the concepts more intelligible and convincing. One always wants to avoid jargon. The defining of concepts should not be considered an academic exercise: it is an important step in the construction of a theory. Buried in concepts are ways of perceiving the world; therefore, some attention to their meaning is worth the effort.

Perhaps the best way of illustrating this is to contrast structural-functional thought with cybernetic thought. Although Buckley (1967) has already done an admirable job of this, some review of the essential differences is necessary. Another way of illustrating how concepts provide a way of thinking is to explore a number of analytical problems which they imply. If cybernetic thought does provide a paradigm for sociology, especially the study of organizations— and I believe it does—then it should illuminate new insights and incisive problems.

THE MAJOR CONCEPTS AND ASSUMPTIONS
IN CYBERNETICS

The Assumption of a Production System

The first critical aspect of any cybernetic approach centers around the concept of a system. *Our first assumption is that there is a system of variables that interact in such a way that changes in one or more of these variables will result in changes in others.* The response of the human body during an attack of disease is a familiar illustration. The increased production of antibodies so that there is the destruction of virus or bacteria represents a set of variables where changes in one produce changes in the other. It also illustrates the important phenomenon of regulation vis-à-vis the environment, another defining characteristic of a system.

As Ashby (1956) has noted, an advantage of cybernetics is that one can make predictions about the behavior of very complex systems, such as organizations, without knowing all the variables that define the system. The simplest form of prediction is the input, throughput, output transformation. For example, we can predict how many fatalities will occur on a holiday weekend by knowing the inputs of cars, number of days, and the accident record for the same holiday the previous year. Or, we can predict, within tolerable limits, next year's GNP by knowing this year's investment, government expenditures, and savings. In the first example, we have a single system where much is known. In the second, we have a very complex set of variables where much remains unknown. By making the assumption of a system of interrelated variables, we need not identify all the links or even all the variables. A few will do as long as we can observe their interrelationships, for example, how does lengthening the weekend holiday from three to four days influence the number of fatalities.

Identifying which variables form the system is, however, not an easy task. Here, other concepts from cybernetics are at least an aid in locating what might be called the boundaries of the system. *Cybernetics starts with the simple assertion that the system of variables is a production process with inputs, throughputs, and outputs.* Locating the inputs and outputs and the kind of production process, or technology, thus becomes a criterion as to where the boundaries might be. In a community hospital, patients, physicians, fees, and donations represent inputs to the production of medical care. Variables such as the number of other hospitals or the per-capita income of the community are clearly not part of the system variables forming the production of medical care in a particular community hospital, although they have consequences for it. In other words, *that variables have cause and effect relationships does not mean that they are part of the same system of variables.*

Practically, when studying organizations, we find it relatively easy to locate the boundaries. They have names for their goals such as patient care, automobile production, manufacturing drugs, flying planes, and so on, which in turn suggest the production process and its inputs. Organizations are themselves relatively concrete units of analysis, usually having specific names. In contrast, with other kinds of social collectives, such as small groups or institutional sectors, where it is quite difficult to decide just exactly what are the inputs, throughputs, and outputs, we can at least begin to search for the variables that form the system and those that lie outside its boundary as economists have done with their analysis of the economy.

Even in organizations, the distinction between systems and subsystems is not always easy to make. For example, in studying a large university, we may desire to separate for our analysis the college of agriculture from the college of medicine because we want to work at this level and because we notice that these organizations appear to behave differently relative to some problem that interests us. (It goes without saying that the nature of the problem has much to do with which particular production processes we will consider.) The concept of a production process has buried in it a technological definition for separating out which variables belong where. In organizations, these different production processes usually have different names. Thus the medical student and the agricultural student not only learn different things but they learn them in different ways. At one level of analysis they are part of the higher-education production process, but at another level they are the production process for medical and agricultural education. Separate budgets and staff are additional justification for treating the two fields as two organizations which are part of a larger organization. From a research viewpoint, the main rule is: Be consistent! This will carry one a long way because there are systems within systems within systems, as is clear from our example of a university. As long as we can identify separate production processes at about the same level of abstraction, we will avoid most difficulties.

The Assumption of Feedback Control

Beyond the concept of system, which is, after all, nothing more than what any science would assume, *lies an assumption about some of the variables being regulated and controlled.* This assumption is most distinctive yet most frequently obscured by excess connotations. People sometimes confuse a production process with a control system. They have, as Buckley (1967) has noted, generalized the concept of feedback too far. The two ideas must be kept quite separate if the full force of cybernetic imagery is to be understood. In practice, the distinction is simple to make if not to maintain.

If we return to the example of predicting next year's GNP, we can see the difference between predicting it and attempting to regulate the growth of GNP. It may be considered either too slow as in Great Britain (less than 3 percent) or too fast as in Japan (more than 10 percent). A concern about the rate of growth and the resulting decisions to do something about it reflect regulatory attempts, whether or not they are successful. Here, GNP is the variable being controlled or monitored. It is also an example of a moving equilibrium regulation because the concern is not with the maintenance of a particular value of GNP such as one trillion dollars—a homeostatic regulation—but with its rate of change, that is, whether growth is higher than 3 and less than 10 percent. Government spending is in this instance both a cause of the growth rate and a variable frequently manipulated to control growth. But we should keep separate the idea of input, throughput, and output from the attempts to regulate the growth rate of that output. In an organizational production process, it is usually easier to see the difference between building a car and monitoring how well the car is built.

Another important distinction is between causal systems and control systems. Workers on an assembly line may experience fatigue because of boredom and their lack of control over the machines; some even say the workers are alienated (Blauner, 1964). We do not have a cybernetic system until we can demonstrate that worker boredom is being monitored, in measuring absenteeism, for example, and that this information triggers off an organizational response, such as job rotation. Here we observe that as we shift from a consideration of the causes of worker alienation to the monitoring of a variable such as absenteeism and the consequences of the feedback of information about its level, we tend to think in terms of different variables being linked together. This is not always the case, but it is typical of how the shift in imagery from cause and effect to feedback presents a different perception of the problem. Again, because the cause of the phenomenon can also be responses to information feedback, there is a tendency to think of the two kinds of linkages as essentially the same.

The distinction between causal thinking and feedback thinking has been well reviewed by Buckley (1967). The shift seems so small but the angle of vision is quite new and, I think, helpful. Perhaps the best way of seeing the difference is to study Figure 1.1 where a cause and effect relationship and two simple feedback relationships are diagrammed. If two variables have a cause and effect relationship as in Diagram I, then increases in one lead to increases in the other (Zetterberg, 1963). This is quite different from the notion of control. The success of the regulation is seen in the disappearance of the signal or the return of the homeostatic variable to its normal or typical ranges as pictured in Diagram II. Thus, if there is a university demonstration, a common danger signal of the 1960s, the response is frequently the heightened coercion of the police. The demonstration disappears and there is a return to normal operation. Again, it is worth observing that calling out the National Guard has nothing or little to do with the causes or reasons why students were demonstrating.

There are many more complex feedback curves, which have been well demonstrated and illustrated by Forrester in *Industrial Dynamics,* 1961. We have diagrammed a nonhomeostatic feedback or moving equilibrium control curve, such as in attempting to control the economy, so that it is understood that not all control and regulation processes are homeostatic. Although the proposed theory of cybernetic control is primarily concerned with this kind of regulation process, there are adjustment and adaptive processes as well.

In Figure 1.1, we illustrate the differences between production

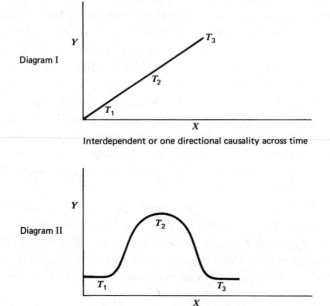

Diagram I
Y
X
T_1
T_2
T_3
Interdependent or one directional causality across time
Diagram II
Y
X
T_1
T_2
T_3
Feedback homeostatic control across time
Diagram III
Y
X
T_1
T_2
T_3
Feedback moving equilibrium control across time

Figure 1.1 Trace lines of two kinds of social causality (see Buckley, 1967, for an extended discussion).

processes and attempts to regulate them. Diagram I represents, let us say, the growth in the number of students being trained; the last diagram may represent attempts to regulate the growth in the size of the student body. Adding wiggles or curves, however, does not automatically mean that regulation or control is occurring. One could imagine that Diagram III might be the kind of growth pattern produced by a similar growth in the population. Here we would have a nonlinear cause and effect relationship without any demonstrable regulation. *We may assume that some variables are being regulated or controlled, but it is important to try to document this point as well.*

Practically, one begins to look for which variables in an organizational system are being regulated or controlled and which variables do the controlling. This does not mean conflict is ignored. Conflict in organizations is one of the variables frequently being regulated, as we shall see. What concerns us is the identification of the variables that regulate the extent and intensity of conflict. Heavy sanctions such as a loss of job and thus livelihood may control workers most of the time and prevent them from striking or engaging in other forms of conflict. But this does not mean they are less alienated. Controlling behavior does *not* imply that one has dealt with the causes of various forms of conflict or deviance. This is the reason one wants to keep the concepts of cause and effect, including reciprocal causation, and feedback quite distinct. It helps us appreciate that there might be latent conflicts which do not appear because of the use of control mechanisms, or what might be called repressive control.

The mechanism by which control or regulation occurs is information feedback. A signal of a malfunction or danger point is received, and, as a consequence, other variables increase or decrease to produce the necessary corrective. It is in this capacity that communication volume and direction become so important in ascertaining whether feedback is occurring. It goes to the heart of the idea of an information signal. Communication is by definition information and the more there is and in particular the more there is in specific directions, including the activation of an entire communication network, the more feedback occurs about what is happening in the organization in its various parts.

Our two assumptions that there is a production system of variables in which some variables are regulated via feedback of information are perhaps the major contributions of cybernetic thinking. It might also be useful to indicate what cybernetic thinking about organizations does not assume. To say that one analytical method is applicable to machine systems, biological systems, and social systems is not to say that the social system is machine-like. This is an important point because many sociologists recognize the fallacy of mechanical or of biological models. This is also why I state that attempts made to regulate conflict in organizations are demonstrations of the appropriateness of the assumptions. It does not mean regulation is as uniform and effective as in machine or biological systems.

Another way in which social systems are different from mechanical or biological ones is that frequently there is a wide variety of possible responses given the signal for the need for regulation. Cybernetics can easily handle multiple responses to danger signals, including some that represent the elimination of the system of variables (Ashby, 1956). There are points of no return where control breaks down. As yet, however, there have been few studies in organizations of this phenomenon. Similarly, cybernetics is helpful even with nondeterministic systems. One can study the probabilities of moving from one state to another. Relevant to this problem is the work of Cangelosi and Dill (1965), which suggests that organizations, like individuals, learn from previous mistakes. When one control response does not work, another is tried. If the second succeeds, it tends to become institutionalized, which only means that the next time it is more likely to be employed first. Here, our thinking is essentially probabilistic. No assumption of rationality intended. Organizations under certain conditions do *not* learn; they keep on making the same mistakes until they go out of business.

The Concepts of Differentiation and Equifinality

Katz and Kahn (1966), who first introduced system concepts to organizational study, also suggest some other key ideas. These are listed here with translations for organizational analysis.

Cybernetic Concept	Translation for Organization
1. Importation of energy	1. Resources, such as staff, money, and technology
2. Throughput	2. Production or treatment process
3. Output	3. What is actually accomplished, such as students trained or stereos built
4. Systems as cycle of events	4. Organizations repeat the production process often during a year

Cybernetic Concept	Translation for Organization
5. Negative entropy	5. Capacity for organizations to store unused energy for future use, such as in profits
6. Information and feedback	6. Variables, like conflict and deviance, are monitored and result in changes in the system when they become too high or too low
7. Steady state and homeostatis	7. Scores on particular variables represent conditions of stability even in changing environments
8. Differentiation	9. Organizations move in one direction as they change from one steady state to another, e.g., toward greater complexity in the division of labor
9. Equifinality	9. In the process of changing from one steady state to another, organizations have several pathways in terms of the variables that change first

The first four concepts are various ways of talking about the production process and thus locating the boundaries of the system. Concepts six and seven are ways of discussing what we have called above the second assumption of cybernetic analysis. However, some additional comments might be made about steady states and homeostatics.

Most readers probably have difficulty accepting the idea that in human systems such as organizations there are steady states of homeostatic variables. For example, Buckley (1967, Chapter 2) argues that this perspective is inappropriate, given modern adaptive systems. Yet, conflict and deviance would appear to be two variables that organizations and all social systems attempt to control. Here the word "attempt" may make readers feel more comfortable. As we have noted above, organizations do not work with the precision of a thermostat, the usual image that cybernetic control invokes. Control does break down and palace revolutions do occur. But the fact that social systems do not operate with mechanical efficiency does not mean homeostatic control is absent. No society will allow crime to increase indefinitely; it is controlled, although at times not very well. What interests us is the attempt to regulate this kind of human behavior. When these attempts are successful and when they are not is an important theoretical problem which has been largely ignored.

To suggest that there are some variables that are regulated or controlled homeostatically, that is, kept within certain limits, is not to say that modern systems are not adaptive. Adaptiveness involves, as we shall argue in the epilogue, other variables. There is more than one kind of regulation process, as we have suggested, and they should not be confused. The proposition that conflict is a homeostatic variable does not mean that there is no conflict in organizations. The beauty of cybernetic thinking is that it forces one to look at a series of questions, such as how high does conflict become before control is attempted, when does control break down, what mechanisms of regulation are used, and when. Cybernetic thinking is equally at home with the static imagery of structural-functionalism and the dynamic thought of conflict theory. It synthesizes the two in a more meaningful perspective.

In the concept of steady states there are a variety of scores which reflect stability of the system of variables. Equally important is the notion that other combinations of scores *on the same variables* represent instability. Thus they are two sides of the same concept, and a cybernetic theory should provide some predictions about states of stability *and* instability. As this is accomplished, one finds those critical thresholds where control processes do break down.

Concept eight, differentiation, has built into it a basic assumption with futuristic implications. We assume that social systems evolve towards more differentiation. This idea has been around a long time, long before general systems theory or cybernetic thinking was developed. It was an essential thesis of Durkheim (1933) and, before him, of Spencer (1898). The combination of this idea with systems theory really means that social systems, modern adaptive ones in Buckley's terms, are becoming more differentiated. The longitudinal case study of the community hospital documents this point quite nicely. *But the major analytical problem is to predict what system of cybernetic control is appropriate for highly differentiated systems as opposed to less differentiated ones.*

The last concept, equifinality, moves systems thought beyond traditional evolutionary thinking by noting that systems can evolve in more than one way. In the comparative analysis of mental health, rehabilitation, and welfare organizations, the proposed theory suggests (and the data tend to support this assertion) that organizations can evolve in more than one way. This concept allows for a richer synthesis of structural-functionalism and conflict theory, which we shall now discuss.

CYBERNETIC THINKING CONTRASTED WITH OTHER APPROACHES

To summarize particular theoretical orientations is always difficult. Each adherent to a specific perspective has his own distinctive viewpoint. Most individuals themselves evolve over time so that what was true for one period of their work is not true for another. Many of the arguments about Marx and what he said can be resolved by noting the date of publictaion. Likewise we slowly change our thinking in the light of new events and new paradigms. This has been particularly true in organizational analysis, Azumi and Hage, (1972).

Structural-Functionalism and Conflict

Most of the debates and critiques have focused on structural-functionalism as practiced in societies where, surprisingly, this perspective has not been much used. Little has been said about structural-functionalism in the organizational area where this approach has been a dominant one until recently.

In the area of organizations, the intellectual father was Weber (1947). Weber argued that a rational-legal form of authority, which we call bureaucracy, would gradually replace both traditional and charismatic authority—that is, it would survive—because it was more efficient. All the essential ingredients of a structural-functional argument are present. Aspects of the organizational structure—in this instance, largely the power structure—are seen as having consequences for either the organizational performances of effectiveness or efficiency. The structures that have more positive consequences will survive in the long run. The reader might note that aspects of social structure are related causally to key performances and outputs, which are either affected positively (functional) or negatively (dysfunctional). Furthermore, one can, as did Weber, put structural-functionalism into an evolutionary perspective by studying several different structural forms and arguing which has the most functional consequences relative to dysfunctional ones, or what Merton (1957, Chaper 1) calls the net balance of consequences.

Since Weber, most adherents of structural-functionalism have been concerned with elaborating the various structural variables and their corresponding performance variables that are important for the survival of the organization. Examples of this kind of thought are found in the work of Price (1967) and Hage (1965).

What is not usually considered in structural-functional thinking is control or regulation processes via information feedback process. They may be implicit but that is all. Control mechanisms are scarcely mentioned or considered in structural-functional theory, as my own previous work unfortunately illustrates. (An exception is the work of Price, 1967.)

The concept of adaptiveness has been important in functional thought, as a careful reading of Merton makes clear and as is illustrated in the work of Price and Hage, but here it is not conceived of as a steering process, as it is in cybernetics (see Buckley, 1967). The terms are the same, but the thinking is quite different.

These points of similarity should make clear how structural-functional thought can be easily incorporated into cybernetic reasoning. The latter is adding the essential ideas of a production system, of information feedback and of regulation processes. Feedback and regulation processes should be understood to be something more than the idea of double or reciprocal causation, however similar they appear to be in form.

As we have already observed, the many changes in the United States during the last decade required that organizational theorists rethink their intellectual perspectives and move in new directions. The major theoretical emphasis in the 1960s has been to examine the causes of the emergence of the structure. It is as if everyone took one step backwards and said if we know a little about how structure affects function and vice versa, we must now explain the cause of structure. In searching for this explanation, two possible causes have been examined: technology and size. Some examples of the former are Aldrich's (1972) reanalysis of Pugh et al. (1969a), Hickson et al. (1969), Woodward (1965), Perrow (1967), J. Thompson (1967), and Hage and Aiken (1969). Some examples of the latter are Blau (1970, and also see Blau and Schoenherr, 1971) and Pugh et al. (1969a).

With the exception of the Pugh et al. work, which is largely atheoretical, most of the new directions might be classified as a form of neostructional-functionalism. While it moved on to a new problem —what causes structure—the thinking is still largely functional. This is probably quite clear in Blau's and Perrow's work, the two who have been most theoretical in their explorations. But even in Woodward's (1965) work one finds the functionalist argument in the statement about the wrong kind of structure for the particular form of technology because this combination had adverse consequences for the overall success of the firm. The reasons are frequently given this kind of functional cast, that is, a particular variable has functional or dysfunctional consequences for efficiency or growth or some other performance variable. What is different is that the addition of technology and size has made the argument a much more complex and multivariate one and therefore a more interesting one.

Furthermore, in Blau's work (1970), one begins to see a movement towards the concept of feedback. Blau notes that dysfunctional consequences for efficiency will be observed and that they will have an impact on the existence of continued growth in size and structural differentiation. Here is the notion of monitoring a performance and the consequences of the feedback of information about that performance. This is, of course, the bridge between structural-functionalism and cybernetics.

The gradual movement towards cybernetic thinking as exemplified in the work of Blau and in others is a natural process. Its concepts are not antagonistic to the traditional ideas of structure and function; they built upon those ideas, adding new and important problems. The concept of a production process fits quite nicely with the technology perspective, and the concept of input is general enough so that both technology and size can be seen as inputs affecting some production process as well as the structure of the organization.

The conflict perspective has not been much emphasized in organizational research perhaps because of the dominance of Weber's models and their implied structural-functional thinking. Recently, again as a response to the problems of the 1960s, there has been some new research in this area.

Perhaps the major effort has been made by Corwin (1969) in his conflict study of high schools during the 1960s. He developed a variety of measures for conflict—a difficult task in itself—and then related them to various possible causes of conflict. Although there are few conflict studies in the literature, Corwin's is typical in that it is primarily concerned with the causes of conflict.

Cybernetics can easily incorporate this thinking into its framework. In fact, the concern for critical thresholds of conflict and the search for the various responses that might regulate conflict are helpful additions to any conflict perspective. While conflict in organizations may be endemic, its intensity varies, as Corwin has demonstrated. We must explain why this intensity varies over time. Control theory or cybernetic thinking is one part of the answer, albeit there are other pieces to this puzzle. Again, we must maintain the distinction between causes of conflict and the regulation or management of conflict, even if there is some overlap between them.

The Social Control and Integration Literature

The extensive social control literature in organizations has focused on the simple problem of identifying the basis of power rather than on the *process of control per se*. For example, Etzioni (1961) suggests that individuals obey because they are physically coerced, because they receive money, or because there are certain norms that give power to a particular person. French and Raven (in Warren, 1969) have five bases of power which are similar to those of Etzioni, except they distinguish between expertise and referent, which is Etzioni's normative. The phrase, basis of power, makes clear what a difference there is between this conceptualization of control and that found in cybernetics, where the emphasis is on the feedback of information.

Another distinctive aspect of this literature is that it is largely descriptive and not causal (for a possible exception, see Warren, 1969). In other words, various types or mechanisms have been proposed but not theories about when one or another control mechanism might be utilized. As one shifts his angle of vision from what are the bases of power to what are the mechanisms that produce conformity, a seemingly small shift, then some different possibilities come to mind, as we shall see in the next chapter.

Still a different literature is the work on task integration (as opposed to social integration), which has tended to be more relevant to the problem of coordination. Here little empirical work has been done until just recently. The most influential research is that of Lawrence and Lorsch (1967a and b). They have attempted to document a number of mechanisms: the emphasis on the right kind of orientations (intermediate), the right basis of influence (knowledge about the environment), the right modes for resolving conflict (confrontation). Most of the work on task integration has not emphasized feedback of information, although one can see it implied in Lawrence and Lorsch's discussion of committees as a mechanism for managing conflict.

In summary, cybernetic concepts are compatible with both structural-functional thinking, including the new technology and size perspectives, and conflict thinking. Furthermore, cybernetic thinking moves way beyond the traditional concerns found in the social control and integration literature.

ANALYTIC PROBLEMS IN CYBERNETICS

Cybernetics as a method of analysis has implied in it a large number of analytical problems that inform our thinking. In fact, one test of any mode of thought, and this is what cybernetics is, is to see how many relevant questions can be posed. The more worthwhile problems, the more fruitful the approach, and thus its greater likelihood of becoming a paradigm (Kuhn, 1962).

The first major issue in cybernetics, especially in the context of social systems, such as organizations, is the delineation of the coordination and control mechanisms. One essential difference between social systems and mechanical ones is that in the former more than one mechanism may be effective. Indeed, many are tempted to look for a variety of ways in which control is exerted. Etzioni (1961), Warren (1969), Julian (1966), Blau and Scott (1962), and others have explored several different conceptualizations of the way in which organizational control can be exerted. In the next chapter, two essential mechanisms of coordination and control—high feedback with socialization and programming with sanctions—are suggested with several reasons as to why only two may be necessary.

The longitudinal case study reported in Part One is an example of where a deliberate attempt was made to assert two kinds of control at the same time. The fact that only one kind was successful is informative. The organization, a community hospital, represents an increasingly common organizational model, what might be called the professional-organizational form.

The essential distinguishing characteristic of this kind of organization is that most of the work is done by members who belong to professions or occupations that require long periods of training and which place an emphasis on the acquisition of knowledge. Another typical organizational attribute is an emphasis on journal reading and on continued learning of new techniques and new skills. One simple test of the relative importance of journal reading is to look at the number of journal articles published by and for the professional or occupational group. The more journals, the more professionalized the occupation. More traditional definitions of profession have placed an emphasis on service to clients and the service "ideal" but this seems less important a factor in understanding the nature of professional organizations. Chemists are as much professionals as librarians, if not much more so. As a consequence, the problems of professional control are greater in a chemical laboratory than in a library. As one relies more and more upon the skill and expertise of the professional—and thus the importance of counting the number of journals because this is an indirect measure of this phenomenon— the more power they have and the more they will demand work autonomy. Among the more important kinds of professional organizations, that is, organizations whose professionals are responsible for achieving the goals of the organization, are universities, research institutes, hospitals, advertising agencies, welfare agencies, sheltered workshops, law firms, and management consultant firms. Many business organizations are becoming more and more professionalized as the proliferation of journals in the various specialties of management makes clear.

The case study illustrates in concrete detail the wide variety of ways in which one basic coordination and control mechanism, high feedback and socialization, can be manifested. Many ways in which control was exerted over the physicians suggest that they are applicable to a wide variety of professionals. The longitudinal study allows us to appreciate how the abstract concepts of feedback and socialization can be translated into concrete reality.

What kind of coordination and control mechanism is most acceptable to particular occupational groups? One of the essential aspects of any human system is that social behavior is regulated and that the members may resist it. This is one way in which social systems differ from mechanical ones. Any proposed theory of cybernetic control should consider this issue. Different mechanisms appear to be appropriate for different occupational groups. Professional occupations pose a great problem since professionals are most likely to resist social control. There has been a long tradition in sociology (Blau and Scott, 1962) of emphasizing the relative autonomy of the professional. This suggests that his behavior is not controlled or at least not as much as other kinds of workers. The proposed theory argues a certain paradox: the professional may be controlled more precisely as he is given more autonomy but only by more subtle means. This paradox needs to be explored at some length.

Since hospitals are among the most complex professional organizations and since the medical profession has been concerned with problems of control for some time now, the hospital's experience can provide a number of insights about what might happen in other professional organizations with different professional groups. While much work has been done on how to control the client—one reason for the success of reinforcement techniques—much less has been done on how to regulate the behavior of professionals. It is difficult to demonstrate, but probably, at least in part, the shift to cybernetic thinking makes one more aware of this issue. The essential problem of regulation in organizations is the regulation of the workers or participants. This becomes more problematical with those occupations that have power and prestige, as do most professions.

Perhaps the most critical problem in any theory of cybernetic control is the explanation of why one mechanism is employed as opposed to another. As soon as there are two or more possibilities, it becomes crucial to know which one will be selected by organizational elites. The prediction can come from a variety of intellectual perspectives. There are several theoretical orientations in organizational analysis. The approach advocated here is a structural one: the key variables for predicting what kind of control mechanism, or, more appropriately, what is the best mix, are inherent in the nature of how the structure is shaped. This is not to say that there are not other variables that determine how the structure is built, such as size and technology, but only to argue that in temporal ordering, the structure is the most direct link to the particular control emphasis. Part Two, for this reason, explores the efficacy of several different explanations, especially technology and size, for the various emphases observed.

Cybernetic theory illustrates an important point seldom emphasized in the systems literature: even the coordination and control mechanisms are moving adaptively. Buckley (1967) has rightly suggested that this is one of the most distinctive qualities of modern systems thinking. Social systems have the capacity to steer across time and learn from their mistakes. A simple example is the recent discussion of the relative emphasis on the technological gap in Europe. Several Western European countries were achieving new scientific breakthroughs less rapidly than the United States and thus were at a competitive disadvantage. Since they recognized this problem, they have been trying to alter their social structure to accelerate production of scientific information and new technologies. Diagram III in Figure 1.1 can be considered a representation of the relative emphasis across time on high feedback with socialization. Sometimes it does not change fast enough and sometimes it changes too much. An information signal is received and some response is made resulting in accelerations or decelerations in the growth process. This is an adaptive regulation process or steering across time. Even though we are primarily concerned with a more traditional regulation control process, homeostatic regulation, the theory illustrates that the appropriate regulation variables are involved in another kind of regulatory process, the adaptive process. Typically, one thinks of control or regulation maintaining itself as the system moves towards a new stability point. The thinking and evidence in this monograph indicates that as the system of variables evolves, so do the variables of the control system. Both Parts One and Two present evidence for this moving equilibrium of control and coordination.

No discussion of moving equilibrium is complete without a description of the states of stability and instability. The concern of structural-functionalism for the former and the concern of conflict theory for the latter, are united easily by having the same theory propose these as part of the same set of hypotheses. Again, although it is difficult to demonstrate, the imagery of states defined as particular scores on the systemic variables leads one naturally to this kind of synthesis. Implied in any set of hypotheses are combinations of scores that reflect different states of a system, some stable and others unstable. These implications are spelled out in the next chapter and then illustrated in Part One.

An essential theme of this book is that high feedback coupled with socialization is the future mechanism of control. In turn socialization occurs when communication networks are arranged in particular patterns. One of the major problems is determining how one measures organizational communication and specifies what these patterns might be, and especially with indicators applicable to a wide variety of organizations. Part Two explores this problem in considerable detail. Some attempt is made to determine which pathways of communication are most important as an organization evolves towards a network arrangement. All possible communication linkages between all parts of the organization are not necessary, although they are logically possible. More critically, there seems to be an inherent ordering in their emergence, which offers some key insights into how control systems evolve across time. We have already noted this essential assumption in cybernetic thinking—the concept of equifinality.

Since the source of explanation throughout this monograph is always structural, any cybernetic theory of control must be examined in the light of alternative interpretations of the data. While the combination of a research designs is a particularly powerful one for determining the plausibility of a theory, our interest in this specific cybernetic theory increases when we can safely rule out competitive interpretations. For this reason, Part Two tests four alternative explanations including size and technology. As this is done, some new insights about the theory of coordination and of control are obtained.

In the Epilogue, we briefly explore some other issues in the cybernetic perspective. One critical issue is whether the whole system of organizational evaluation is altered in the light of the movement towards cybernetic control via information feedback. A distinction is made between process regulation and output regulation and between quality control and quantity control. The importance of information feedback for quality control is emphasized.

The most distinctive aspects of cybernetic thought are the adaptive process and steering across time. Although most of the research reported does not bear directly on them (except to note the steering from one kind of coordination and control mechanism to another), the increasing emphasis on information feedback has implications for the adaptiveness of organizations. These implications are spelled out in the Epilogue.

Cybernetic thinking appears to be a possible paradigm for organizational analysis. As we noted at the beginning, one of the main contributions of Buckley, Forrester, and others is the suggestion that cybernetic thinking is a key tool for understanding modern social systems; it is rich in the number of theoretical problems it poses. Some of these new problems are suggested in the Epilogue.

II

A Theory of Cybernetic Control: Premises and Hypotheses

T HERE IS A WIDE VARIETY OF TASTES as to what a theory should include (Hage, 1972). A minimum requirement, however, is the specification of the basic premises from which are derived *testable* hypotheses. A major preoccupation of this monograph is the issue of measurement. It contains extended discussions of indices, examples and explorations of alternative operationalizations. A nontestable theory is not a theory. But a theory that does not also provide tentative explanations is only a theory fragment. Hypotheses, even those arranged in an elegant path diagram (Blalock, 1972) give predictions but only imply explanations. The latter is most clearly indicated by very general premises that can be critically examined, and, if desired, rejected. Therefore, our objective is to discuss at length several explanatory assumptions about organizational coordination and control. As this is done, some consideration is given to competing possibilities, such as the various proposals about the basis of control. Then hypotheses are derived and discussed. One reason for having a few very general premises is the possibility of deriving a large number of testable hypotheses. Part One, then, is an illustration and Part Two is an explicit test of the cybernetic theory.

27

THE PREMISES AND THEIR IMPLICATIONS

Our present premises and hypotheses are as follows.

Premises
1. All organizations require coordination and control.
2. There are two basic mechanisms for achieving coordination and control: Programming with sanctions and high feedback with socialization.
3. The greater the diversity of organizational structure, the greater the emphasis on high feedback with socialization.
4. The greater the differences of rank in the organizational structure, the greater the emphasis on programming with sanctions.

Derived Hypotheses
A. The greater the degree of complexity, the higher the rate of communication.
B. The greater the degree of complexity, the higher the rate of horizontal communication.
C. The greater the degree of formalization, the lower the rate of communication.
D. The greater the degree of formalization, the lower the rate of horizontal communication.
E. The greater the degree of centralization, the higher the rate of rewards.
F. The greater the degree of centralization, the higher the rate of punishments.
G. The greater the degree of stratification, the higher the rate of rewards.
H. The greater the degree of stratification, the higher the rate of punishments.

Our first premise in the cybernetic theory developed by the author in collaboration with Michael Aiken and Cora Bagley Marrett (cf. Hage, Aiken, and Marrett, 1971, where there are some differences from this and earlier formulations) is: *All organizations require coordination and control.* Coordination means integrating the various parts of an organization. As soon as there is more than one job in an organization, there is the question of how will the jobs be coordinated, as Lawrence and Lorsch (1967a and b) have noted. In more abstract terms, organizational theorists (March, Simon, 1958; Parsons, 1956; Victor Thompson, 1961; James Thompson, 1967) have noted that as soon as there is some differentiation of work into separate tasks, the tasks must be coordinated so that there is a common output.

Control taps the idea that, as soon as there is more than one person, we become concerned with whether or not the behavior of the human beings conforms to some standard. Simply put, do the men do their job? It does little good to coordinate two or more jobs if the job holders don't perform their tasks appropriately. Human systems, especially organizations, must have both processes.

How safe is our assumption about requirement? It seems next to impossible to imagine an organization not having at least some coordination and control. This does not mean that organizations will always have coordination and control or that they will always have the same amount. Regulation breaks down, as we shall see in the study of a community hospital. But, in general, it is also true that these are the exceptions and not the rule of organizational behavior. Where there is much more conflict than we may have realized, as some recent work indicates (Corwin, 1969), we may have not an absence of coordination and control but examples where the mechanisms are not too effective (Lawrence and Lorsch, 1967a and b). Therefore, our first premise appears to be a plausible one.

Mechanisms of coordination and of controls

In a few insightful pages March, and Simon, (1958: 158–169) suggest that there are two ways in which organizations can be coordinated: feedback and programming. Feedback represents the obtaining of information, especially new information; programming means the delineation of a detailed plan. James D. Thompson (1967) has called these ideas standardization and mutual adjustment.

When an organization is programmed, a detailed plan specifies what each occupational group in the organization is to do. In one sense, the behavior of individuals becomes ritualized. The plans can be quite intricate and involved, as military operation plans frequently are. Job descriptions are carefully worked out, rules manuals are prepared, and programs of action are developed for each contingency. The purpose of the master plan is, of course, to ensure that all of the parts of the organization are articulated in a team effort to produce a collective product.

Information feedback means that coordination takes place as a result of face-to-face interaction, on the spot, not by prior planning. Coordination is then a group process, occurring on a minute-by-minute basis.

In a different context, Parsons (1951) has noted that social control over individuals can be maintained either by socialization or by sanctions. In the application of these ideas to professional organizations, Blau and Scott (1962) have noted that professionals conform to organizational norms either because of peer pressures or because of rewards and punishments.

The concept of socialization has had a long history. Typically, it has meant the learning of norms and roles (Scott, 1971). Here the accent is more on the acquiring of knowledge, or, even more broadly, the receipt of information. With professionals especially the continuous acquisition of knowledge and information is critical. Although there has been some work done on adult socialization (Brim, 1968), this area has been ignored, especially within the context of organizations. The focus has been more on the learning of new roles in the life cycle rather than on the continuous learning required to perform in some occupations, especially professional ones. Most of the socialization literature has not emphasized that both individuals and occupations vary in how much socialization they receive. Everyone is seen as either being socialized or deviant and not as a matter of degree. Moreover, within organizational research, these questions have been totally ignored.

Most sociologists couple socialization and sanctions with norms (Scott, 1971; Parsons, 1951). If we disobey a rule, we receive punishment; if we conform to a norm, we receive a reward. This combination is somewhat misleading because it ignores anticipatory socialization and the importance of conversation or communication as a mechanism of learning. (Merton, 1957; Chapter 9). Some socialization occurs without much application of rewards or punishments. In other organizational contexts, there is little socialization and much reliance upon sanctions. In other words, we have here essentially a continuum with more or less emphasis at each end.

Since almost anything can be perceived as a reward (Homans, 1961), some examples are in order. Increases or decreases in salary, praise, or criticism relative to one's work, or reprimands or promotions are examples appropriate in the context of organizations. Explicit statements to and actions upon individuals and groups are designed to ensure their conformity, whether these statements are positive or negative. Social approval is a more subtle form of reward, and it explains much about social interactions and exchanges (Homans, 1961, and Blau, 1964). Criticisms and praises can be counted and observed; social approval is more elusive. It is rather difficult to determine whether social approval is operative even when there is no specific criticism or praise being made by either peers or superiors. This in a sense goes to the heart of what Blau and Scott (1962) meant by peer pressures. We must admit it as a possibility, although I am inclined to believe that it can be overemphasized. Certainly if there is an absence of explicit statements and actions such as those listed above — and it is a fairly complete list of what I mean by sanctions — then we can say that social approval if it is operative is a qualitively different kind of sanction. It might represent the middle ground between sanctions without socialization and socialization without sanctions, or what might be called socialization with mild sanctions.

The concepts of coordination and control are different, but their synthesis helps illuminate each idea. Both integration processes involve the articulation of a variety of task jobs and their occupants in a division of labor in which each fulfills his respective tasks. First, the activities of each job occupant can be programmed and then a system of sanctions can be utilized to ensure conformity to the basic organizational scheme. A clear blueprint of action would make departures from the plan immediately obvious and thus solve the problem of visibility (Merton, 1957, Chapter 9). Sanctions would provide the muscle behind the basic plan. Standards would leave little ambiguity about whom to punish and whom to reward. Second, organizations can rely more upon continuous and high flows of feedback with socialization as a method for coordinating the organization. Under this system, errors, when detected, are seen more as a problem of improper socialization or training and they can most readily be corrected with new information. Also implied in this approach is that pressure comes not so much from sanctions, in the strict sense of the term, but from peer pressures and inner standards of quality that have been developed through socialization. The first approach relies upon external control, whereas the latter is more concerned with internal control, or what is called self control by Parsons (1951).

It would be nice to have one word for both aspects of this phenomenon—usually cybernetic control will mean both coordination and control. However, because individuals have tended to think about coordination and control separately, it seems wise to employ both terms in the explanatory premises of the theory.

Our second premise, following March and Simon, 1958; Parsons, 1951; and Blau and Scott, 1962; is as follows.

There are two basic mechanisms for achieving coordination and control: programming with sanctions and high feedback with socialization. How justified are we to couple these two terms, programming with sanctions and high feedback with socialization? Are we not really making two assumptions in one premise? We cannot imagine a set of rules without some force or coercion behind it. If the rules are not enforced in some way, then there is no coordination or control being exerted. It may not be necessary to punish someone very often. The firing of an individual is a dramatic event; to be effective, it must be exercised rarely (Blau and Scott, 1962). More likely, there is a continuous application of positive sanctions whether via piece rates, bonus plans, profit-sharing, or simply praise to maintain conformity. But this is only successful when there are clear-cut standards or a program of action. Thus, the coupling of programming with sanctions appears justified.

The combination of high feedback and socialization is simpler. As is argued below, high communication rates measures these two phenomena simultaneously. The sheer passage of information is educative, and the more there is, the more this is true. Thus, there are not really two assumptions buried in one premise, but a single mechanism which operates in both ways simultaneously. We have kept the parallelism of coordination and control consistent throughout the premises in order to emphasize that we are synthesizing two distinct literatures and superimposing them on the cybernetic concepts.

In practice the two mechanisms—programming with sanctions and high feedback with socialization—get mixed together. We have a continuum on which most organizations are located, and we are emphasizing two ideal or extreme situations which seldom occur. The same institutional practice can be a mechanism of socialization and a mechanism of sanctions. An example of this is the practice of reviewing journal articles anonymously. The fact that the authors' and reviewers' identities must be kept secret tells us that professionals do worry about maintaining amicable relationships. The reviewers are more likely to be honest in praise and criticism when they do not know who the authors are. Some reviewers write with the idea of educating, or of turning the article into a publishable piece of work. Others enjoy the act of criticizing. The key test is to look at the content: there is a difference between saying something is wrong and pointing out how it might be done better. Although it is not always a valid measure, usually the sheer length of the review says much. Critical ones tend to be short and to be without reasons for their critical judgments, while educative ones tend to be much longer and offer suggestions. However subtle a criterion the length of the review may appear to be, it is the boundary line between the world of sanctions and the world of socialization.

Can socialization be effective without some sanctions? Some colleges have tried to eliminate the use of grades—a very effective kind of sanction. Although grades represent how well a student may be doing in a particular course, they are perhaps the major way in which a professor ensures that students see the world the way he wants them to see it. Thus grades are sanctions that ensure intellectual conformity. In their place has come a reliance upon information feedback as to how well the student is doing and in what areas he must work on. We are emphasizing here the relative emphasis on sanctions. As they are employed less frequently and less harshly, then we have some right to argue that the emphasis on sanctions is declining. The fact that many colleges, however, are moving away from grades as a sanction is itself instructive about their importance for future professionals, since most of them start their professional training or socialization in college.

The Structural Determinants of the Choice of Coordination and Control Mechanism

March and Simon (1958), Parsons (1951), Blau and Scott (1962) do not provide any suggestions about the structural concomitants of the mechanisms of coordination and control although March and Simon suggest that the uncertainty of the task may affect the choice. The internal structure of an organization should have an important effect on the most dominant form of coordination, and hence on the way in which communications are designed.

We assume that there are two major structural factors that affect the patterns of internal communication: diversity and rank distributions, the basic axes of organizational structure that Victor, Thompson (1961a and b) has noted. These can be utilized in the following premises:

> The greater the diversity of the organizational structure, the greater the emphasis on high feedback with socialization.
> The greater the differences of rank in the organizational structure, the greater the emphasis on programming with sanctions.

Thus there are essentially two structural forces that affect the selection of the coordination and control mechanisms. The third explanatory premise speaks to the heart of the problem of the coordination and control mechanisms which organizational participants select as the structure evolves toward greater differentiation. The answer is they rely more upon high feedback with socialization than programming with sanctions. This does not mean that the elites consciously select it as a mechanism of control. The choice gradually emerges through trial and error or learning. Different patterns are tried and found wanting. This is the idea of information feedback and of steering across time or adaptiveness. From this learning experience, high feedback appears to work better. The modern adaptive social system, to use Buckley's term, would have this kind of mechanism. Is there some rationale that explains in more detail what this third premise in our cybernetic theory is saying?

As the structure of the organization becomes more diverse, it becomes more and more difficut to program a successful blueprint for the organization. As the variety of tasks in an organization increases, the number of potential connections among parts increases even more rapidly, the articulation of organizational parts by a set of predetermined rules becomes more complicated, and the application of sanctions becomes more difficult because each must have a different set of standards. As the jobs themselves become more complicated, with a greater variety of tasks, requiring greater skill, it becomes increasingly difficult to apply concrete and unambiguous standards. Quality standards in particular have this characteristic. Furthermore, the more complex the judgment, the more one must rely upon others with the same training and same experience. How many people can accurately evaluate the quality of surgery done in a heart transplant? This is one argument that professionals use to justify the norm of professional autonomy.

Consider the case of a dean or university president with a background in a specific discipline such as agriculture. He does not have the expertise to evaluate the appropriateness of the teaching methods of a large variety of fields such as medical education or business administration. He must rely upon the advice of those in those disciplines. Under these circumstances, it becomes difficult to apply sanctions. The manipulation of social approval does not appear to be an option available to him. In the University of Wisconsin, which does not have a fixed salary scale, yearly salary increases and promotions are voted upon by the entire senior faculty in each department relative to the individual concerned. The increases and promotions voted are the basis of the recommendations to the dean for individual's salary increases and promotions. The recommendations are seldom denied or altered, and one easily understands why. Denial requires a clear reason, which is difficult to assert.

The decision-makers in such organizations are likely to be forced to rely more upon continuous feedback mechanisms than upon infrequent reports. This whole process is enhanced if the nature of most jobs in the structure is very complex and involves a variety of activities, which is often the case with professionals. The complexity affects the intensity of communication flow and its direction. The variety of tasks, not necessarily uncertainty, is the important factor. The two may be related, however (Duncan, 1972).

As the tasks become more complex, the problem of *correct and complete* socialization becomes greater and greater. Making mistakes becomes both more likely and more understandable. If the job is highly programmed into a series of simple tasks, such as on the assembly line, then mistakes are less understandable. As the tasks become more and more complicated, they need more and more monitoring in order to be sure that they are done properly. As mistakes become more understandable, we desire to impose fewer sanctions and more socialization.

We have used the word diversity rather than structural differentiation, a term that is well planted in the empirical literature (see Blau and Schoeherr, 1971). We want our premises to be as general as possible. Organizations can be diverse in more ways than the standard measures of structural differentiation, which are: the number of job titles, the number of authority levels, and the number of departments or divisions. Production processes as well as jobs can vary in the diversity of tasks.

Great differences in social rank among job occupants in an organization are likely to inhibit the level of information feedback. As distance between organizational levels increases, the flow of information is slowed. Similarly, the threat of sanctions from the top discourages the frank discussion of problems, and, therefore, organizational decision-makers are unlikely to learn of diffculties until a crisis has developed, as Blau and Scott (1962) have suggested and as Barnard (1946) explicitly argued.

As differences in rank increase, those who are at the top, the eltie, are more likely to want to use programming and sanctions. Many of us like to rely upon the use of blueprints, rewards, and punishments —when we use them on others. But most of us are unlikely to want to employ the same methods on ourselves. Therefore, it is not surprising that professionals will use reinforcement techniques with their clients but they will be quite upset when anyone suggests that they themselves be controlled in the same way.

The increase in organizational diversity propels the organization toward attempts to coordinate and control through information feedback and socialization. Differences in rank propel the organization toward attempts to coordinate and control through programming and sanctioning. Together, they influence the probabilities of the adoption of either programming and sanctioning or feedback and socialization—or more precisely, the particular combination, since each of these factors can be operative at the same time. We assume that organizational elites attempt to program some interaction in the form of regular reports. Even when they have made a conscious decision to rely only upon a high feedback mechanism of coordination, there will always be some feeble attempts to rationalize parts of the organization via programming. What is critical here is the differential emphasis on coordination and control via information feedback or programming. The theoretical question is whether structural diversity and differences in rank explain this varying emphasis on different types of coordination and control processes.

THE HYPOTHESES AND THEIR IMPLICATIONS

These few and relatively simple premises about the nature of coordination and control suggest a wide number of testable hypotheses.
They are diagrammed in Figure 2.1. Before we discuss this path diagram, we need to consider carefully how task communication can be
at once high feedback and socialization.

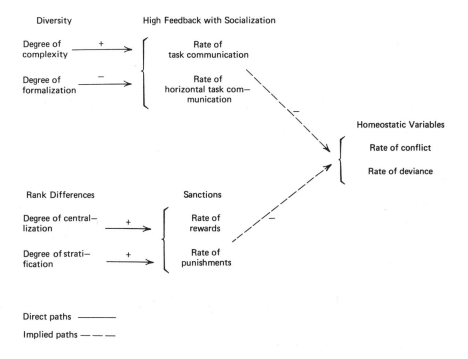

Figure 2.1   The implied path diagram of the cybernetic theory of coordination
and control.

High Task Communications Rates as High Feedback

Perhaps the most critical aspect of any cybernetic theory is the
inclusion of feedback. Usually this is just assumed to occur. For us,
the key to this difficult problem lies in measuring the task-communi-
cations flow in the organization generally and in specific directions.

The communications literature has made a distinction between horizontal and vertical communication flow (Landsberger, 1961; Guetzkow, 1965). Likewise, Burns and Stalker (1961), working independently, suggested a hierarchy of communication and control as a mechanical model and a network of communication as an organic model of an organizational system. These distinctions are helpful and indeed critical to our attempts to unite the cybernetics and structural-functional literatures.

Essential to the concept of high feedback is the notion that information is received from all parts of the organization. Through what channel are these signals being transmitted? Written reports and memos are one channel, but, in point of fact, more words and information can be spoken in a minute than one can write. Futhermore, only verbal communication about tasks allows for quick information feedback, the give-and-take of question and answer. Both participants to the communication are learning, and both are taking corrective action at the same time. A simple example is a social worker discussing a difficult case with her supervisor. The supervisor asks whether several approaches have been tried. The social worker then explains that they have failed. In this instance, the supervisor has learned a piece of information where clearly there have been no sanctions as we have defined them. We doubt even that supervisor would blush at discovering that the suggestions were wrong because we are making the assumption that this was a difficult case to handle. Certainly supervisors in family therapy expect to make mistakes in their suggestions to their workers. The supervisor, after this conversation, may meet another supervisor who handles the same kind of case load, and in passing may note that technique X may not work in case Y. The two supervisors may discuss why this is so. Likewise the social worker will share experiences with others in the same department and in other departments. Through trial and error, the members of professional organizations learn not to do certain things just as much as they learn how to do them. This is socialization and it is high feedback relevant to the problem of quality service. It occurs through verbal communication about specific tasks where difficulties arise or in the periodic checks built into the organization. What is distinctive is that the supervisor can learn from the worker as much as the worker can learn from the supervisor. In the example we have taken one of the professional situations where there is an explicit supervisor-subordinate relationship. Many other professions and professional organizations do not have such an explicit hierarchical relationship.

As organizations attempt to monitor all aspects of their various production processes, they are forced to rely more and more upon verbal task communications as the major channel of feedback. It allows for a quick response and solves the problem of correct socialization at the same time. In this regard, it is interesting to note that even in highly programmed organizations, when there is an emergence of a new kind of problem, there is a shift to verbal communication (Crozier, 1964; Ronken and Lawrence, 1952). Again, it is important to recognize we are discussing only human systems, where there is increasing reliance upon or demand for verbal feedback. Reports are still employed, probably in greater quantities, but the proportion of verbal communication increases even faster because it can handle a larger volume more quickly.

Information flow comes from all parts of the organization. Not only does verbal communication increase, but it is increasing faster in horizontal rather than vertical pathways as a network of communications is institutionalized.

We are only interested in communication rates relative to the tasks of the organization. This represents another frequent distinction made in the communications literature, between what Price (1967) calls instrumental versus expressive communication. Here, we prefer to use the term task communication, that is, verbal communication relative to the job of the individual or the objective of the organization. A much more extended discussion of how one actually measures task verbal communications is in Chapter 8.

The Derivation of the Hypotheses

In our premises we have used extremely general terms such as "diversity," "rank," "socialization," and "sanctions." The word diversity includes a number of variables but most importantly the degree of complexity, which we shall define as the diversity or variety of occupations in any organization. We hypothesize first that as organi-

zations become more complex, there will be an increase in the rate
of communications directed in a horizontal direction (Thompson,
1961). This seems to be one of the critical aspects of the meaning
of a communications network, to use Burns and Stalker's (1961)
term. (The problem of how to measure a network is the focus of
Chapter 9.) Secondly, we hypothesize that formalization, another
structural variable and one that indirectly taps the idea of programming, represents an attempt to eliminate variety (Frank, 1958).
Specifically, we define formalization as the codification of jobs.
Therefore, the greater the formalization, the more the decrease in
the rate of communication, especially horizontal communication,
and the greater the amount of upward or vertical communication.
If the plan or blueprint of the organization is a good one, there is
little need for much communication except an occasional report or
a question about a rule or regulation. This naturally reduces not
only the volume of verbal communication, but, presumably, changes
the direction as well, since most individuals are likely to check rules
with their peers (Blau, 1955) or their immediate superiors.

There are other ways in which diversity could be tapped. Complexity refers to the division of labor; it does not necessarily include
the idea of complex jobs. We can easily imagine an organization with
a complex division of labor having considerable differences in the
complexity levels of particular positions or occupations within it.
Although this has not been measured in either of our studies, we
would expect differences in the rates of task communication of those
with complex jobs and those with more simplified jobs.

Likewise, the formalization of jobs, at least as reported in the
comparative study, does not represent the standardization of the
work process. This is another variable and involves two more hypotheses which can be derived from the same explanatory premises.

There appear to be two major ways in which jobs or job occupants
can be ranked within an organization (Parsons, 1956; Barnard,
1946): either by the distribution of power or by the distribution of
rewards. Here we mean both salary and prestige, formal and informal
rewards. The two variables that tap these attributes of the organizational structure are the degree of centralization and the degree of
stratification. The former is defined as the extent of differences in the
rank of power or participation in decision-making. The latter is the
extent of the differences in the rank of rewards or the distribution

of salaries, fringe benefits, and prestige. Thus, as centralization and stratification increase in an organization, we expect increases of rewards and punishments used as sanctions. There might be some confusion since we have said that the degree of stratification represents the distribution of rewards and that sanctions implied the application of rewards. This is not tautological. In the first place, there is a difference between how rewards are distributed and whether or not they are employed as sanctions. Civil service is an example of where there are relatively fixed salary levels, where the stratification system remains somewhat rigid. However, by promoting people or praising them or even by changing the location of their office—a question of prestige—we can sanction them with a view of controlling their behavior as well as that of others. We can easily imagine that different organizations under the same civil-service code have varying degrees of emphasis on sanctions. Another difference is in measurement. With the distribution of rewards, we compute a ratio between department head salaries and work salaries (Palumbo, 1969). We can also compute a lorenz curve. When measuring rewards, we compute a rate, that is, how many times in a year was someone in the organization promoted or demoted, praised or criticized, fired or given a raise. This reward is a process variable and not a structural one. In practice, we would anticipate, as our hypotheses state, that as the total sum of wages becomes concentrated in a few elite salaries, these elites will employ salaries as a basic mechanism of reward. Where there is high stratification, raises would also become a very powerful sanction. Conversely, if everyone has about the same salary, a condition of equality more typical of professionals working in professional organizations, then the sanctions assume less importance to individuals.

Rewards have also been used in another sense, the sense of what people strive for. Marx made much of the fact that capitalists will strive to maximize their profits, one kind of reward. People strive for other kinds of rewards, or goals. They strive for recognition or fame, for power, even for the good of others. This meaning of rewards should not be confused with sanctions or the distribution of rewards, or stratification, as we have defined these concepts. In a particular community hospital, some physicians may work to maximize their salaries by trying to get as many patients as possible; others may be more concerned with doing a good job. A variety of motives may be present. The question here is, can particular control mechanisms be effective? Is socialization effective with professionals, for example, even though some of them are working to maximize their salary?

Beyond these basic hypotheses, others are implied as well. Perhaps the most important ones are the effects of complexity and formalization on rates of rewards and punishments and the effects of centralization and stratification on rates of communications, especially in a horizontal direction. Since Premise 2 suggests that programming with sanctions and high feedback with socialization are alternatives, complexity should be negatively related to the use of rewards and punishments. An absence of formalization should have the same impact. Conversely, centralization and stratification should inhibit communication, as has been suggested by Blau and Scott (1962); Ronken and Lawrence (1952); and Crozier (1964). In our discussion of the explanatory premises, we suggested reasons as to why this is so. These effects are diagrammed in Figure 2.1 as well.

It should be noted that much is made of Landsberger's (1961) notion of horizontal communication in our hypotheses. This is because this communication pattern is most likely to have the content of feedback and socialization. However, we also expect that the volume must increase. This means that communication increases in all directions but especially horizontally.

Our several premises have generated a number of derived hypotheses. These several ways in which diversity and status differences, and feedback and socialization, can manifest themselves and provide us with many opportunities to test the adequacy of our reasoning. But this is not our only check, another is the capacity to combine both structural-functional and conflict orientations. In the previous chapter, we suggested that a good cybernetic theory should stipulate states of stability and of instability. These implications are considered below.

States of Stability and Instability

One important problem for any theory of cybernetic control is the definition of steady states, or points of equilibrium. With the exception of the basic motivation model of March and Simon (1958), in the organizational literature there have been relatively few attempts to make explicit the system of variables and what their equilibrium points are. The following table contains the predicted scores for two steady states, the mechanical and the organic, and two unstable states, the anomic and the anarchical.

The theory suggests, along with some other works in organizations (Burns and Stalker, 1961; Hage, 1965; Perrow, 1967), that as organizations evolve toward greater complexity or differentiation, they need to alter their mechanism of coordination and control. Their social structure moves toward more decentralization, less reliance on formalization, and less stratification. As long as all these variables move together, which is the meaning of a moving equilibrium, then conflict and deviance, two variables, which are homeostatic in the sense that organizations attempt to keep them within tolerable limits, are regulated without difficulty.

But organizations seldom move ever onward and upward toward greater differentiation without some missteps along the way. As we shall see in the next few chapters, organizations can move into various states of instability. There is some question whether heightened conflict represents a state of disequilibrium or instability (Pondy, 1967; White, 1961). Although small amounts of conflict are likely to be omnipresent, we are focusing on more extreme forms of conflict such as the threat to leave the organization or the strike.

One kind of instability we have labeled the anomic, essentially following Durkhim's (1933 and 1951) imagery. Instability occurs when complexity increases at too fast a rate for the other structural variables to alter. A series of power, role, and status conflicts occur and coordination and control mechanisms, especially the old ones, break down or prove to be ineffective. This state lasts until communication rates increase. Centralization decreases and the other variables alter in the predicted direction. Or—since there is always more than one way to solve a problem—the organization can decrease the degree of complexity. This option, however, is usually not selected because of the strong evolutionary trend towards greater differentiation which we have already noted.

Another kind of instability is created if an organization decentralizes too much relative to a low level of differentiation in the division of labor. While democracy appears to be desirable and wanted, sometimes organizations have difficulty in adjusting to this state of affairs. McCleery's (1957) study of a prison is one such example.

There can be too much decentralization as well as too little, especially if combined with little complexity. We might call this anarchical instability because the problem is one of too little rather than too much concentration of power.

> *Mechanical Steady State*
>   Low complexity—low communication
>   High centralization—high coercion
>   High formalization—low conflict
>   High stratification—low deviance
> *Organic Steady State*
>   High complexity—high communication
>   Low centralization—low coercion
>   Low formalization—low conflict
>   Low stratification—low deviance
> *Anomic Instability*
>   High complexity—low communication
>   High centralization—low coercion
>   High formalization—high conflict
>   High stratification—high deviance
> *Anarchical Instability*
>   Low complexity—low communication
>   Low centralization—low coercion
>   High formalization—high conflict
>   High stratification—high deviance

The two different kinds of evolution—examples of our concept of equifinality—are implied in our premises and hypotheses. Since there are two basic structural factors that affect the choice of coordination and control mechanisms, there are two distinct ways in which organizations can become unstable. Furthermore, since there are four structural variables, we could argue for many more combinations of scores. We have chosen not to because complexity and centralization appear to be the more important variables, and we appear to have identified the most typical states.

Looking for states of instability is an important way of testing a theory. *If we find the exceptions to our hypotheses are associated with high rates of conflict, then we have a strong argument for accepting the theory.* Our empirical exceptions then prove our theoretical rules about the interrelationships between the structural and coordination/control variables. Equally critical is the idea that the best way of demonstrating the existence of a system that has regulation is to observe what happens when regulation is lacking; that is, when feedback does not work and instability emerges. The instances of lack of regulation should be infrequent, but they are decisive tests of cybernetic thinking and its utility. If the breakdown of control is infrequent, then we know we have some justification for arguing for homeostatic variables being maintained within certain limits or boundaries. A simple way of uniting structural-functional thought and conflict thinking is to shift the question from whether conflict exists to how frequently does it occur and with what intensity. Once this is done, the argument between these perspectives largely vanishes. Likewise the problem of whether conflict is a state of disequilibrium should be resolved.

Additional states of instability can be specified. For example, one might imagine organizations having high rates of both communications and coercion, and thus, an overly controlled and regulated system. This should manifest itself in a complete absence of conflict or deviance, probably itself a sign of future difficulty in the organization. We might call this state a meta-stable one, since it has the appearance of stability and yet is probably not stable.

Appropriateness of Coordination Mechanisms for
Different Occupational Groups

Implied in the theory are some hypotheses as to what kinds of coordination and control mechanisms are likely to be appropriate to different kinds of occupations. If the occupation's work is simple, routine (Perrow, 1967), and of low status, then all other things being equal, we would anticipate that sanctions would be accepted as an appropriate mechanism of control. In a contrast, if the job or occupation is complex and of high status, then all other things being equal, we would anticipate that socialization would be preferred. In the former instance, we might talk about task specialization, to use Victor Thompson's (1961) term for work on an assembly line, and in the latter situation, person specialization. Professionals in particular represent a major grouping of occupations who resist any attempt to institute a system of sanctions. Armed with their norm of autonomy, they will prevent attempts to rationalize the coordination of the production or treatment process, that is, the man-man system, by programming.

The problem of which system of cybernetical control is acceptable is a practical one. Given difficulties in an organization, it is one thing to say that there should be more coordination and another to say how this should be implemented. This problem represents still another check on the adequacy of our cybernetic theory. If we find that attempts to institute the inappropriate mechanisms lead to resistance, we have increased confidence that our theory is tapping some essential aspects of organizational life.

The idea that professionals can be controlled is itself a paradoxical one. There is a relatively large literature that discusses how professionals fight against the notion of supervision and for the right to work autonomously (Blau and Scott, 1962). One is left with an idea of individuals who are left free to do what they please. In part, this is a correct image, but it is only half complete. The mechanism of socialization, especially when seen as a continuous process that never abates, means that control is being exerted. It may be self-control, but it is control nevertheless. As we have already indicated, what is critical about socialization is that there is probably much more control over behavior and attitudes than is true of a system of sanctions.

CONCLUSIONS: ORGANIZATIONAL EVOLUTION

The premises and their derived hypotheses allow us to tell a story about organizational evolution, or what system theorists would label the problem of the moving equilibrium between one steady state to another. In organizations without many occupations, especially professional ones, and with a simple division of labor, it is easy to program the entire production process. Standards of production, or quantity standards, are easy to specify and to enforce with a reward system. There is a small elite who makes the decisions about how rewards are distributed and to whom. They reward themselves a great deal so that there are great differences in power and status between themselves and the workers. The workers accept this control system provided they do not have much education or are not required to do complex tasks. This is a mechanical steady state. It contains a hierarchical pattern of authority, communications, and control. There is some feedback but only relative to the volume of production.

The process of control is a simple one. If a worker breaks a rule, he is swiftly punished either with a loss of pay or work privileges. The plan or blueprint makes easy the detection of nonconformity. The punishment of one deviant is an example to everyone else so that punishment is not necessarily frequent. Rewards are tied to how much people produce within a given period of time; they create a motivation to conform to work standards. Likewise, the threat of losing a job or pay depresses conflict, such as strikes, except for major causes. Indeed, the infrequent appearance of strikes testifies to how well this system of control functions.

Organizations can change from a mechanical steady state in two ways. This is an example of equifinality, the possibility of several different pathways by which a system of variables moves to a new steady state. One is a decrease in differences in rank. Under these circumstances the inhibitions against communication break down and the amount of feedback increases; there are greater rates of interaction across several status levels. We begin to see workers conferring directly with the executive level rather than going through the chain of command. This is one kind of intermediate steady state —there is a mixture of programming and feedback, sanctioning and socialization.

Another evolutionary pathway is for the division of labor to become more complex. As organizations become more differentiated, to use Katz and Kahn's (1966) term for it, it becomes increasingly more difficult to develop a simple set of standards by which the behavior of all members can be regulated. The production or treatment process—the throughput—becomes more diverse and therefore more difficult to program. As a consequence, there is a movement away from the reliance upon rewards and punishments as the mechanism of cybernetic control. More and more effort is placed on developing communication links between various parts of the organization, and more critically, the skilled occupations involved in the production or treatment process. This represents the second pathway towards an intermediate steady state of programmed interaction.

If the rate of change in the division of labor is too rapid, the system of variables does not have an opportunity to adjust and the mechanism of control and coordination break down into a series of conflicts. The conflicts do not have to be strikes but can be frequent verbal arguments, collective threats to resign, or refusals to do certain things. Likewise, the rules in the program are likely to be ignored and old standards of production no longer accepted. We have called this particular condition an anomic state of instability. Although the rapid differentiation of the division of labor is the most likely way for an anomic state to occur, it can also be created by a decrease in the formalization of the organization which is too rapid to allow other variables to alter in appropriate ways. Coordination and control are not exerted and we again have instability.

More typically, we would expect organizations to evolve slowly from a mechanical to an organic steady state. As diversity grows, differences in rank should diminish. The reasons have been given elsewhere (Hage, 1965). If both structural conditions are fulfilled, then there is a steady evolution or moving equilibrium in the proportion of sanctions and socialization employed. In professional organizations, the prototype of an organic steady state, the professions are coordinated via a large number of committees. Considerable emphasis is placed on continuous learning, and a variety of socialization procedures are established to keep the professionals abreast of current technological developments. Usually, however, the professionals teach each other and thus are controlled even more than they would be by a system of sanctions. As long as they are given work autonomy, professionals accept socialization as desirable, and their behavior is in effect monitored and modified when found wanting. Socialization works well with quality standards, which are diffuse and shifting, but which the public demands more and more. Thus, for many reasons, high feedback with socialization appears to be the control mechanism of the future.

We have thus identified the variables that form an organizational system, and we have indicated which are controlled or regulated and by what other variables. In the process of meeting these two basic assumptions in system analysis, we have also indicated how many of the cybernetic concepts have content within the context of organizational analysis. Now we shall illustrate the cybernetic theory in a study of a community hospital where there was a deliberate attempt to institute both high feedback with socialization and sanctions although the attempt was not conceived of in that way.

PART ONE

AN ILLUSTRATION OF A CYBERNETIC THEORY: AN ORGANIZATION IN VARIOUS STAGES OF STABILITY AND INSTABILITY

III

A Proposal for Improving Professional Control

FOR SOME TIME in the late 1950s and early 1960s there appeared increasing evidence that professional control in a large number of hospitals was not operating. An extensive study of medical care in the Greater New York Area was published by Trussel et al. in 1961. Trussel, a physician, worked with a team of top medical educators, also physicians. Among other findings, the study indicated that about 50 percent of the hysterectomies, an operation which removed the female organs of reproduction, were, on the basis of the medical charts, unjustified. The results were published in *The New York Times, The New York Herald Tribune,* and other major newspapers, and caused a considerable public outcry. The American Medical Association condemned the study, noting that it was self-evident that all doctors provided good medical care!

Without reviewing the entire research study, several findings are of special interest. As one might expect, of those doctors who had received advanced training in some specialty (called a residency) and who passed examinations (called boards), board-certified specialists provided better medical care than general practitioners and specialists who had not passed their boards. As one might not expect, the overall quality of care of the board-certified specialists varied accord-

51

ing to which hospital they worked in; it was best and generally quite good in the university hospitals, next best and not so good in community hospitals with training programs, and worst in community hospitals without training programs. Since the medical educators examined the charts of over 400 cases in some 100 hospitals, the findings have a number of implications. University hospitals, that is, hospitals associated with medical schools, usually, but not always, attached to a university, account for only 5 percent of the patient care in the United States. The next category, hospitals with education programs for the training of specialists and internships, the education programs for general practitioners, accounts for about 35 percent of the patient care in the United States. The bulk of patient care, about 60 percent, is handled in either community hospitals without training programs or proprietary hospitals, hospitals operated for the profit of the physicians as opposed to the welfare of the community.

In speculating about the differences in the quality of care, at least across the various disease entities examined, the team of investigators suggested what they called a "loose medical organization." They did not explicate what this meant or what its causes were. We can reinterpret their terms by saying there was little organization coordination and professional control.

The problem of the quality of care in community hospitals was well known, and numerous attempts were made to devise a better system. This study reports one of these attempts, perhaps one of the more interesting ones. The Butler plan for improving the amount of professional care described below is applicable to a large number of different professions. Although the medical profession has moved much farther in the direction of developing a wide variety of control mechanisms, those developed were not operating effectively primarily because they relied upon sanctions. The various control mechanisms in the Butler plan allow us to understand concretely how socialization can operate as a control mechanism. In some respects, it seems strange to say that physicians need more socialization because they are the most highly trained professionals. Likewise, the medical profession has done so much to attempt to improve its standards that one would think there would be little need for more professional control, regardless of how it was achieved. Yet, as the Trussel et al. study made clear, there were problems, and some better system of coordination and control had to be devised. The fact that this was necessary for physicians perhaps only underlines the need for new ideas as to how professional control might be effected.

THE PROPOSAL

The Proposed Remedy of More Professional Socialization

How does one improve the quality of patient care in a community hospital with a training program? One cannot fire all of the physicians, or even those who are providing the worst patient care because there is a physician shortage (Colombotos, 1969). In any case, the power of the American Medical Association is such that hospital administrators are not in a position to do this. Somehow, one must work with the doctors who are available to develop better control and coordination. To attempt to restrict fees or privileges, that is, to use sanctions, is not an available alternative. The solution has to be found elsewhere.

Dr. Butler, as a result of his experiences as a director of medical education in community hospitals with training programs, developed a plan for altering the social structure and control processes of the typical community hospital with training programs. His plan proposed adding several key characteristics of a university hospital production system to community hospitals with training programs (Jeghers, O'Brien, and Butler, 1956; Butler and Hage, 1966). The plan had two major ingredients. The first was to increase the complexity in a community hospital by adding several new medical specialties: medical subspecialists and assistant directors of medical education. The second was to add a number of socialization mechanisms: teaching rounds, grand rounds, subspecialty rounds. (All these terms are defined and illustrated in the next chapter.) The major purpose of the medical subspecialists was to add specialized skills not normally found in community hospitals that have training programs; for example, hematology, endocrinology, infectious diseases,and neurology. The medical subspecialists were expected to hold subspecialty rounds and thereby detect unrecognized diseases within their areas of competence and, at the same time, supervise and educate the doctors, the house staff, who were in the training programs, and, through them, the practicing physicians, or the active staff.

Other activities of the medical subspecialists included conducting highly specialized laboratory tests and providing consultations for difficult cases within the immediate regional area of the hospital. It was hoped that the medical subspecialists would assume responsibility for the administration of the clinical laboratories and thereby improve the quality of work in them.

Assistant directors of medical education were to be added to each of the major clinical departments, that is, medicine, surgery, obstetrics-gynecology, and pediatrics. They would hold teaching rounds, giving suggestions about improvements in patient care. *Thus, one critical ingredient of the plan was to provide continuous socialization to the house staff who, in turn, would do the same for the active staff.* It was hoped that the assistant directors of medical education would eventually assume the administrative duties of service, and thus, in the future be able to apply sanctions if needed.

A crucial element in the entire plan was the quality of the house staff. Dr. Butler anticipated that the new specialists would make the training program attractive and thus the hospital would acquire a full complement of American trained interns and residents. The house staff would then be able to provide complete patient coverage in the hospital. It would also provide the communication pathway by which the medical specialists could supervise patient care and educate the physicians attached to the hospital. An excellent house staff would also stimulate the physicians to read more and take more interest in medical education. Finally, a full house staff of doctors in training would increase the hospital's prestige, thereby making it more likely that the program would become permanent. As its fame spread, it was hoped that the plan would become institutionalized in other community hospitals with training programs, and the general level of patient care improved in the United States as a consequence.

The Theoretical Implications

Certainly Dr. Butler was not thinking in sociological terms when he devised his plan for improving the quality of patient care in community hospitals with training programs. He proposed increasing socialization via the addition of communication links as a major way in which to control physicians' behavior. This does not mean that he was uninterested in the use of sanctions but only that he viewed it as a long-term objective, not immediately realizable. His proposal to increase the complexity of the hospital by adding specialists is of interest as well. Although the division of labor has been an important variable in the sociological literature since Durkheim's (1933) famous work (written in 1898), it has seldom been studied as an explicit plan for change, even less for the improvement of the functioning of an organization. Thus, the plan has two features of interest, namely the manipulation of a structural variable, complexity, to improve the quality of patient care, and the increase of the communication rate, to achieve the same objective.

Although Dr. Butler anticipated resistance, he did not conceive of the hospital as a set of interrelated variables, a social system. As a consequence, the possibility of other kinds of changes were largely unanticipated. In some respects, these changes, as discussed in Chapter Seven, are of special interest because they demonstrate how an organization is usefully viewed as a set of interdependent variables.

Another point to note is that this is essentially a cybernetic control system, although Butler did not conceive of the plan in these terms. To make this clear, we can liken the treatment of the patient in a hospital, the basic production process, to an assembly line. Although the imagery may make most readers wince, it is an appropriate analogy. Patients in hospitals are wheeled around to various rooms for X-rays, special tests, and operations. Various specialists come to the patient and do work upon him. What Butler proposed adding was not only new specialists with new tasks but a variety of checks on the quality of the work being done. In other words, he proposed a high feedback system that would provide quality control. The main function of the assistant directors of medical education was to act as inspectors of the work being done on the production line of patient care. The gauges are in the form of teaching rounds (where a physician takes interns and residents around to study what other physicians are doing with their patients), an independent diagnosis (where an intern and resident diagnose the patient's problems without the knowledge of the practising physician's diagnosis), morning report (where a physician checks on what has happened to patients during the night and, implicitly, on what interns and residents have been doing), and subspecialty rounds (like teaching rounds except more specialized in particular areas of patient care). The corrective was largely a considerable increase in the amount of socialization. The interns and residents were hearing about the newest drugs and latest discoveries from the medical educators, and, in the context of patient care, they would pass this information on to the physician. If the resident's and physician's diagnoses were different, they needed to to be reconciled in some way, with both learning in the process. If the result of the teaching rounds was the opinion that the physician might be making a mistake, then he would receive recommendations and reasons for them. Other key communication links were added. General rounds (where difficult cases were discussed once a week by all the physicians, interns, and residents in the same department) provided another vital link where the latest discoveries and advances could be discussed. The subspecialists added still another kind of socialization channel. The rapid growth in medical knowledge was felt to be so fast that it was impossible for even a specialist to keep up with all the new information in his area. Therefore, it was hoped he would call in the subspecialists as consultants on difficult cases and in the process learn more about another aspect of medicine appropriate to his case load. Thus, implicit in the plan was the addition of many more communication links which, in turn, allowed for much higher levels of feedback and of socialization.

In more general theoretical terms, Butler's plan can be summarized as saying that professional organizations should create specialists who would have the time to read journals and who would transmit their knowledge to students who, in turn, would educate the other professionals who work in the organization. How much this increases the volume of communication is easily seen.

THE RESEARCH STUDY

With a plan for action, Dr. Butler had to find a hospital willing to conduct the experiment and a researcher willing to study it. A hospital was found, and the author became involved as the principal investigator to report what occurred.

The Organization: Community Hospital

The name is, of course, a pseudonym, as are all names reported in Chapters 3 through 7. Approximately one-fourth of the active staff of Community Hospital were board-certified, one-third were general practitioners, and the rest were specialists, but not board-certified. These ratios, except for board certification, are about the same as those that prevailed in the United States as a whole in 1960 (Health Manpower Source Book). This ratio of board certification is less than that of the community hospitals with internship and residency programs in the Trussel et al. (1961), study of patient care, and presumably the level of patient care was the same or less. (It might be noted that the Trussel et al. study was conducted in the same geographical area as the case study hospital and therefore the comparison is reasonable.)

Community Hospital had approximately 400 beds. Again, this is an average size, only slightly larger than the average for community hospitals with training programs (Directory of Internships and Residencies 1965). All told, 1,000 personnel, including some 200 physicians, cared for an average of 1,000 patients per month. The physical plant covered a city block and included a diagnostic wing, a school of nursing, and quarters for interns and residents as well as the patient wards. The diagnostic wing is unusual for community hospitals with trainng programs and was quite modern, having been built just before the commencement of the present experiment. Community Hospital had about 35 interns and residents just prior to the initiation of the Butler plan. The hospital had approved residencies or training programs in medicine, pediatrics, obstetrics-gynecology, pathology, and cardiology. This is better than the average for community hospitals with training programs. The interns and medical residents accounted for two-thirds of the house staff. Two-thirds were from foreign medical schools, and one-third were foreign citizens, again a very common pattern for this kind of hospital. Thus, in general, one can say that the organization was as typical as one could expect under these circumstances.

The Research Design

Although this is a case study of a single organization, it is quite different from the usual one in the literature (Blau, 1955; Crozier, 1964; Gouldner, 1954; Guest, 1962; McCleery, 1957; Ronken and Lawrence, 1952; Price, 1967: 6–7). First, it is an experiment involving the changing of a major structural variable, and of a major control variable. Most others have not involved as much change. The work done by the human relations group at the University of Michigan is the major exception. Second, the description of events represents a period of four years. The data collection in most case studies covers about six months or less. Third, the research design combines participant observation with a three-wave panel of interviews. It is rare to have a panel study in an organization, and even more rare to combine it with observational data (Barton, 1961; the major exception is Seashore and Bowers, 1963). These particular design features allow us to study the causes of physician resistance in some detail and to document the overall changes in the organizational system.

Since the data were collected prior to the development of the theory described in the previous chapter, this study can only be considered as illustrative. Perhaps what is striking about it is that there were no a priori hypotheses; instead, the hypotheses emerged as the organization moved from one steady state to another. One limitation of this, however, is that particular variables were not measured with hard data as such but simply observed. This is the inevitable consequence of doing case studies. On the other hand, while the measures are not as exacting as in comparative work, the time ordering of changes in the variables is very clear. Furthermore, the longitudinal study allows us to see the actual process of change in all its detail.

The most exciting part of the research design is that it was an experiment. Two variables, degree of complexity and communication rate, were manipulated, allowing one to observe all the consequences for the variable system. It is somewhat analogous to putting dye in the water and watching where the currents carry it. Likewise, the system of organizational variables revealed itself largely by these currents of change in the system.

The Data Collection

The first wave of interviews occurred when most of the new medical specialists had just arrived and before they started trying to introduce control mechanisms. The waves were scheduled one year apart since there was little likelihood of the doctors consenting to be interviewed more frequently than this. Fortunately, the last wave of interviews occurred when all attempts at exerting more controls had stopped. Needless to say, this could not be planned, but was a "lucky accident." The interviews were designed to measure the causes of resistance, the analysis of which appears in Chapter 6. Although the physicians on the active staff of the hospital were generally uncooperative with the Butler prescription for better patient care, they were cooperative with the research. (For a more complete description of the sample, design, and interview schedules, see Hage, 1963.)

The participant observation started just before the hiring of most of the new medical specialists (see Figure 3.1). Retrospective inter-

	First Year				Second Year				Third Year				Fourth Year			
	1	2	3	4	1	2	3	4	1	2	3	4	1	2	3	4
Observation																
Interviews						First Panel Wave				Second Panel Wave				Third Panel Wave		
Arrival of specialists						Cook Fine Sloan				Abel						
				Bacon	Shore	Donald				Larry				Strong		

Figure 3-1   Research Design

views were used to cover the period of time prior to their arrival. This was supplemented with a number of official documents.

Observation was accomplished by sampling particular days and attending most of the important committee meetings. This was felt to be not only the most accessible place to study the workings of the hospital, but probably one of the more critical vantage points. Observation was supplemented with informant interviewing. Together, they were used to measure the social structure and the processes of change, conflict, and control. Most of the data reported in Chapters 4, 5, and 6 was obtained by this method.

Some Methodological Problems

Despite the theoretical advantages, there are methodological difficulties with an experiment of planned social change (Blalock, 1967; Zelditch and Hopkins, 1961). One of the major problems is whether any definite conclusions can be drawn. Why would some hospitals be more interested in adopting Butler's plan? Does their willingness imply some hidden variable which is related to all the others being examined? Is the process likely to be quite different because it is planned or managed as opposed to occurring "naturally"? Admittedly, these questions are hard to answer, but they should be asked because they indicate possible limitations on the inferences that we can draw.

Perhaps a more disturbing methodological issue in experiments such as this one is that they frequently accelerate in a short period of time what normally occurs over a much longer time period. The Morse and Reimer (1967) experiment, for example, did in one year what, under "natural" conditions, would take place over 20 years as a result of many incidents and minor controversies. In this longitudinal study, eight new specialties were added in less than three years. This is a considerable acceleration of the normal process of structural differentiation, and it raises the intriguing issue of what impact it had on the observed consequences. Hopefully, the major impact is only an acceleration of their magnitude and not a qualitative difference. Thus, conflict decreases in intensity when it is spread out over a longer period of time. If this is true, then planned experiments may be likened to the running of the film at a fast speed; it allows us to see what happens in a relatively short period of time. This methodological problem of how natural the experiment is should be studied much more before we can be certain about the results that are obtained. However, since our major concern in this part of the book is with illustrating the cybernetic theory, it is not an important limitation.

IV

A Mechanical State of Stability

THE CYBERNETIC THEORY PREDICTS a basic continuum of steady states, ranging from the mechanical pole to the organic. Community hospitals with training programs, as professional organizations, are closer to the organic end of the continuum. If we think in relative terms, Community Hospital can be categorized as moderately complex and centralized. What is distinctive is that given this structural arrangement, there was a low volume of communication and as a consequence little information feedback. The hospital had problems but they remained largely undetected by the elites and especially the administration as a result of its structural arrangement.

Like any profession, doctors have developed a whole specialized vocabulary which at times is hard to decipher. When a medical student graduates from medical school, he receives the title of doctor, but he must still take a year's practicum in a hospital. This is called an internship. Upon completion of this training, he can practice as a general practitioner. He may decide to specialize in one of the four major areas of medicine (excluding psychiatry): internal medicine, which treats adults with drugs; pediatrics, which treats children with drugs; surgery, which operates on both adults and children; and obstetrics-gynecology, which handles the special problem of birth and female disorders. These specialized training programs are called residencies. Doctors who are taking their internships or residencies comprise the house staff. Upon completion of several years of residency, a doctor can practice as a specialist. He does not need to pass an examination to do so. However, if he does, he becomes a board-certified specialist. It is this kind of physician who played an important part in the analysis of the Trussel et al. study. A doctor who continues his training beyond two to three years of residency usually goes into some subspecialty in one of the four areas of medicine. Most of this training is done within university hospitals. Most doctors start to practice and to study for their board examinations.

Once a doctor starts to practice, he needs a hospital. Typically, he applies for affiliation. The doctors who are already affiliated decide if he is competent to practice. If the admissions committee recommends that he be affiliated and the recommendation is accepted by the executive committee of physicians, then the doctor can send patients to the hospital. Normally a doctor starts as an assistant attending, moves up to associate attending, and then senior attending. These doctors are called practicing physicians, attendings or active staff. We shall use all these terms in our discussion because each term was used by a different group in the hospital.

The particular methods of socialization and sanctions used in hospitals will be defined later in the chapter. For now, the main task is to understand how the physicians, active and house staff, that is attendings and interns and residents, were organized.

THE SOCIAL STRUCTURE: MODERATE COMPLEXITY AND CENTRALIZATION

The Degree of Complexity

Community Hospital had a moderate amount of medical specialization, and, especially when contrasted with a university hospital, a complex organization. At the same time, it was typical of many of the community hospitals with training programs in the United States as far as its degree of medical specialization, the size of the active staff, the number of hospital beds, and other indicators of the complexity or differentiation of the professional social structure (Blau and Schoenherr, 1971). As we have already noted, only about one-fourth of the active staff were board-certified specialists. In the Trussel et al. (1961) study, 80 percent of the active staffs in university hospitals in this same geographical region had this level of qualification.

Most of the attendings were assigned to one of the four major departments, called clinical services. Thus specialists in treating adults, or internists, were assigned to the medical department; pediatricians, to the pediatrics department; surgeons, to the surgical department; and obstetricians and gynecologists, to the obstetrician-gynecological department (hereafter, this specialty will be called ob-gyn, the abbreviation used in most hospitals).

The house staff, or the doctors receiving formal training, were attached to the particular department where they practiced medicine. Thus a doctor taking a residency in internal medicine was assigned to the department of medicine. Most of the residents were in this department, several were attached to pediatrics, and several to ob-gyn. The interns had what was called a rotating internship, that is, they spent several months in each of the four major departments.

The size of these clinical services or departments varied considerably within the hospital. In general, most of the general practitioners were assigned to either the department of medicine or surgery; there were none in pediatrics, and only a few in ob-gyn. Besides the four major clinical services, there were a number of minor departments, corresponding to the various surgical and medical subspecialties. Community Hospital, like most community hospitals, had very few of these medical subspecialties. Cardiology, dermatology, and allergy were represented. In contrast, all the major and common surgical subspecialties were represented.

Hospitals are not only places where patients are treated by physicians, they are also hotels with a vast array of specialized services. In this sense, one can say that the modern hospital is indeed a complex organization. There were, at the time the study began, about 700 employees. And, like most community hospitals, most of them were nurses. The rest were in the business, laboratory, dietary, and house-cleaning departments.

Most of these employees were not trained specialists and there was little variety of job titles. Most of the nurses did not have specialized training. There were few highly trained laboratory technicians. The same was true throughout the hospital. Most of the general occupational groups found in a hospital were represented in Community Hospital, but not much structural differentiation had occurred within them.

The Degree of Centralization

As to the distribution of medical power in this hospital, there was absolutely no question that the power over medical matters resided in the hands of the physicians or active staff (see Figure 4.1). The

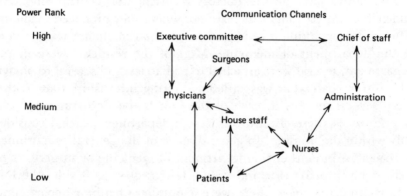

Figure 4.1   Power and communications structure in Community Hospital.

administration had little or no say in the area of medical matters. One could say that the hospital's structure was relatively centralized. However, the situation among the doctors was more complicated.

Ostensibly, the active staff is a colleagual group with few differences in rank. Distinctions are made, however, among senior attending, associate attending, and assistant attending. These distinctions are determined by the physicians on the active staff. With these distinctions come certain privileges. Only senior attendings can vote for the key positions on the executive committee and other important committees. In practice, the distinctions in rank did not make much difference except in the department of surgery where the senior attendings insisted that one of them had to be present at every operation. This point was later to become a major issue in the conflict between the assistant directors of medical education and the department of surgery.

The physicians were actually a coalition of groups. Power resided generally in the senior attendings, the only physicians who vote for members of the executive committee, which supervises and regulates physician behavior. Since a majority of the senior attendings were surgeons or surgical subspecialists, they were the most powerful group within the active staff. The ob-gyn specialists and the surgical subspecialists who could vote usually supported the surgeons. For a number of years the president of the active staff and chairman of the executive committee, an elected position, was occupied by a member of the surgical department. Usually he was, surprisingly, a general practitioner and not a specialist.

The most influential man on the executive committee was the chief of staff or medical director. (An indicator of his power is that the cardiology department was the best-equipped in the hospital.) Since requests were most frequently channeled through him, his power was augmented by his control of the hospital's communications hierarchy (McCleery, 1957). He was a major articulation point between the medical profession and the administration and could play one off against the other. The chief of staff's sources of power derived not only from his formal position as a liaison, but also from his adroit handling of the executive committee. Minutes were never kept, nor were votes taken. The chief of staff, Dr. Andrew, once remarked after one meeting: "They didn't even know they had approved that."

But why did the doctors in general have so much power, especially vis-à-vis the administration? One key factor was the patient, and therefore, hospital income. The major source of patients for any community hospital are referrals of the physicians. When a doctor wanted something, he would frequently tell the senior administrator that he would transfer his patients elsewhere if his request were not met. This was not an idle threat in Community Hospital, which was located in a large urban area with a number of competitors. Most of the physicians had multiple hospital affiliations and could easily transfer their patients. The administration would purchase extra equipment, fail to enforce hospital regulations, and accept all recommendations of the executive committee in their desire to placate the physician.

One consequence of the centralization of power, especially among the physicians, was that board-certified specialists were leaving the hospital. In other words, the general practitioners were able to maintain their power position by not giving privileges they had to men who had qualifications! Indeed, in the several years preceding the commencement of the experiment, the size of the active staff actually declined. Many of those who left were board-certified specialists. This was particularly true in the department of surgery where most of the senior attendings were general practitioners. The administration was unaware of this trend or of the reasons for it, mainly because of its lack of communication with the active staff.

Patterns of Authority

The ownership and operation of the hospital by a group of nuns means that the basis of authority is somewhat different than it would be in a nonsectarian hospital (Julian, 1966; Peabody, 1962; Warren, 1969). An order from the sister administrator carries double weight; obedience to the order rests on her position as the administrator and her position as mother superior. As a consequence, she enjoyed enormous respect from both physicians and personnel. At the same time, the religious vows of charity, in many cases, interfered with the hospital's operation. The sister administrator was reluctant to fire anyone for incompetence. She once commented: "I don't like to make anyone unhappy." She was usually under considerable pressure to attempt to please everyone. In particular, the religious training made conflict abhorrent, and this usually resulted in attempts to suppress it, thereby reducing the administration's effectiveness in gaining power.

The actual distribution of power described above does not represent the formal lines of authority as stipulated in the hospital's constitution. It is perhaps commonplace in sociology to note that an organization does not follow its blueprint, that is, it is not arranged as it should be (Barton, 1961). According to the constitution, the executive committee and board of trustees advise the sister administrator (see Figure 4.2.) The chief of staff and two assistant administrators are responsible for the administration of the medical and administrative departments, respectively. The former included the four major clinical departments of medicine, pediatrics, surgery, and ob-gyn, and those of the medical and surgical subspecialties. The latter included the major administrative departments of personnel, accounting, laboratory, housekeeping, dietary, nursing, etc. Below the chiefs of the clinical departments were the physicians or attendings, and below the administrative heads were the paramedical occupations or employes.

PROCESSES OF COORDINATION AND CONTROL

For Burns and Stalker (1961) as for Weber (1947), a hierarchical pattern of power and authority, which is, indeed, the pattern of Community Hospital at this time, was associated with a similar pattern of control and coordination of a relatively simple division of labor. The fact that there is a hierarchical distribution of power does not mean that there is necessarily effective coordination and control. Indeed, if the hierarchy of authority is among professionals, it may result in the *absence* of any control being exerted. We have already noted that the administration was unaware that specialists in surgery were leaving the hospital. There were other difficulties as well.

Sanctions and Socialization

The power of the executive committee was usually demonstrated more in the absence than the presence of action, particularly in the regulation of the professional behavior of the physicians. Although a hospital regulation requires prompt completion of medical charts, many physicians were months behind. The executive committee never reported to the administration any infractions of rules. Once, when the administrator did hear of healthy tissue being removed from a patient, she asked what was being done with the physician responsible. A surgeon and a member of the executive committee told her that these were professional matters and were being handled. The tissue committee seldom indicated any unjustified operations in

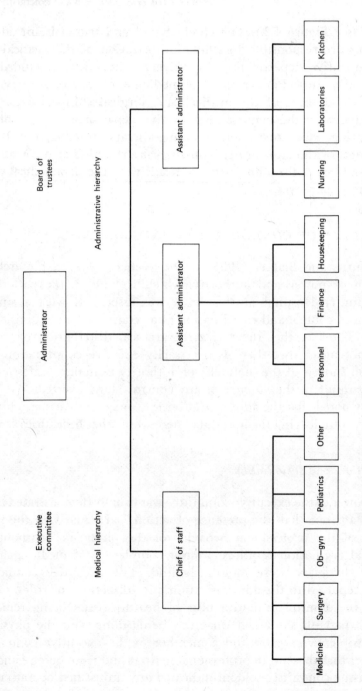

Figure 4.2   The formal authority structure in Community Hospital.

its reports to the executive committee and yet one could expect a certain percentage as a normal occurrence.

The following incident illustrates how professional power and professional control were related in Community Hospital. A chief of service discovered that a general practitioner in his department was taking needless risks with patients (verified by specialists). Instead of being able to stop this practice by his own authority, the chief was forced to ask the executive committee to reprimand the doctor concerned. It should be noted that the chief of service thought in terms of applying a sanction. The executive committee did nothing, even though the chief of service threatened to resign. The chief of service left the hospital for a period of time and later returned. The general practitioner remained in his department and continued to take needless risks.

The active staff never lost their staff privileges. The chiefs of service could not discipline the attendings because they lacked authority. The medical committees—that is, tissue, records, credentials—which are designed to exert control, did not function in this capacity. (The tissue committee examines reports of the pathologist as to whether healthy tissue has been removed, the records committee checks the adequacy of the patient records or medical charts, and the credentials committee passes on whether a physician can be admitted to the staff and receive certain key privileges, such as access to the operating room, and the designation of assistant, associate, or senior attending.) A number of hospital regulations were largely ignored by many of the physicians. There were few grand rounds, or conferences where difficult cases are discussed by all physicians and where deaths and mismanaged cases, especially in medicine and surgery, are analyzed. Attendance tended to be low. The physicians seldom attended the outpatient clinics as required by another hospital regulation.

Therefore, in general, we can say that for the physician, sanctions were seldom applied. What is instructive is that they *cannot* be applied, given the fact that one is dealing with professionals and especially a profession as powerful and technically specialized as the medical profession. What is distinctive about the medical profession is that it has developed, at least in university hospitals, a large number of socialization and feedback techniques. These are listed below.

Mechanisms	*Definition*
1. Teaching rounds	1. Visits made at the bedside, usually every day with the house staff and a teaching physician, charts are checked, questions asked, treatment suggestions made; one for each service
2. Subspecialty rounds	2. Same as teaching rounds, except held once a week and conducted by a subspecialist on very special cases; one for each subspecialty
3. Grand rounds	3. Once a week in which cases difficult to diagnose are discussed or special lectures are presented; this is for the entire active and house staffs on a particular service
4. Morning report	4. Early (usually 7 A.M.) discussion of the progress of every patient during the night by the house staff on duty with an attending physician
5. Independent diagnoses	5. House staff do workups and diagnose patient independently of attending physician's diagnosis; the two are then compared

All of them result in a constant monitoring of the patient's treatment and at many points in the process. All the specific mechanisms involve verbal communication, which represents both socialization and feedback of information. It is not necessary to reprimand a house-staff physician; instead, the intern or resident can be told what to do. Likewise, in grand rounds or when the resident discusses a case with the appropriate attending physician, he is continuously learning. Correspondingly, his behavior is modified. All these mechanisms together provide coordination and control.

As one might expect, most of these mechanisms of feedback and socialization were absent. There were no teaching rounds, that is, physicians taking residents and interns around to patients' bedsides, asking them questions about the patients' illnesses, diagnoses, and courses of recovery. The residents never made independent diagnoses. The education program consisted of a resident accompanying a private physician when he went to see his patients. As a consequence of this informal arrangement, each house staff physician gravitated toward a physician who took a personal interest in him. It was basically an apprenticeship. If the physician was knowledgeable, then the resident could learn a great deal. But it was still far less than would have been possible with a formal program of scheduled teaching, grand and subspecialty rounds, supplemented by lectures and reading in which the knowledge of all physicians in the hospital is pooled, the pattern found in university hospitals. (Subspecialty rounds are like teaching rounds but in a highly specialized area, such as hematology).

While Community Hospital had some mechanisms of professional control, they were not effectively utilized. The house staff, who spend a much longer time in the hospital than the private physician and who are largely responsible for the day-to-day patient care, received little supervision. Patients admitted during the evening hours were often kept waiting until the next morning when the interns took a history and physical. The residents worked every sixth night, with the consequence that patient coverage was very thin during the evening. Frequently, many of the house staff did not come to the hospital on Saturday mornings. The house staff received even less supervision in the out-patient clinics where the private physician seldom met his hospital obligation by coming.

Feedback and Programming

Another consequence of the power distribution was the absence of horizontal communication channels (Landsberger, 1961) between the administration, active staff, and house staff, as indicated in Figure 4.1. This low communication volume was the result of a number of factors. The major cause was the centralization of the professional staff. This inhibited the free flow of information between the two hierarchies of authority, medical and administrative. The absence of a number of socialization mechanisms had much the same consequence. Doctors, whether active or house staff, did not have regular meetings where they could discuss common problems. As a result, each doctor was largely isolated except for whatever physician friends he saw on a regular basis. The administration and active staff received their information about each other from the chief of staff. While this enhanced chief of staff's power, it did not increase coordination of the division of labor, perhaps the most critical consequences of this form of coordination. The house staff complained that they never saw the sister administrator. And, many physicians felt that they never knew what was happening. Thus the lack of feedback was causing another problem, namely lowered morale among the physicians. In turn, the absence of feedback also meant that the organizational elite was unaware of this difficulty. As we noted in Chapter 1, causal analysis and feedback analysis are not usually the same. Here is an instance of where they were the same.

Why should physicians be upset about not knowing what was happening in the hospital? As people are trained more and become professionals, they develop expectations about their rights in other areas. They want more information and they seek it (Hage and Aiken, 1967b). Thus a moderate degree of complexity and centralization produced some problems, such as lowered morale, among at least the active and house staffs.

But our theory of cybernetic control suggests that, given the moderate levels of complexity and of centralization, there were no forces pushing the organization to establish horizontal pathways of communication. The differences in rank between physician and non-medical personnel inhibited upward communication. A number of doctors on the active staff complained that they never knew what was happening. Many of the house staff also felt that they were not informed about what was happening. Thus, some signs of disequilibrium were appearing in the form of complaints, but they had not been detected as such by the administration. Likewise, another danger signal, the leaving of board-certified specialists—was undetected by the administration. In fact, four years later the administration still blamed the new medical subspecialists and the assistant director of medical education for this problem. Low feedback means little knowledge about what is happening; problems go undetected until they reach crisis proportions. Thus, mechanical stability is not a coordination and control system with much feedback, making it highly vulnerable when changes occur to upset the equilibrium of the system.

Another observation is that if social approval did operate in this instance, it did not work to control the behavior of the physicians in their work to provide better patient care. Certainly the obstetrician working on the wards was not concerned about the social approval of his chief of service. This incident also illustrates that, given a lack of sanctions, such as being able to restrict hospital privileges, social approval does not necessarily fill the vacuum.

THE PRIMARY GOAL: QUANTITY PATIENT CARE

Although all hospitals are designed to treat patients, it is not neces-sarily their major goal. All organizations have several goals; this is especially true in the case of university hospitals and community hos-pitals with training programs. What is more problematic is the meas-urement of what these collective goals are (Zald, 1963). Instead of interviewing individuals or reading the constitution (Zald, 1963; Perrow, 1968), one is wiser to study which priority is paramount when goals are in conflict. Still another approach is to look at the basis of decision-making regarding the allocation of scarce resources. As is well-known, hospitals are always short of money, and as we have noted, this one had a large annual deficit.

Community Hospital mentioned three goals in their constitution: patient care, medical education, and medical research. There was a fourth goal—perhaps an obvious one, and therefore never mentioned —the number of patients. This goal received the highest priority and, in part, contributed to the power of the surgeons and, in part, reflected their own power position (Perrow, 1963).

Several examples can illustrate this point. When a chief of service complained to the administrator about the quality of care provided by a general practitioner, she noted that the physician sent a number of patients to the hospital. After weighing all factors, she decided not to intervene. When the credentials committee recommended that a physician with dubious qualifications be admitted to the active staff, the administrator questioned him. She was told by a senior attending in surgery: "This hospital depends on general practitioners; it should take care of them." After weighing the factors, the sister administra-tor allowed the doctor in question to become affiliated. (The consti-tution of the hospital also made a point of stating that a physician's affiliation depended upon his supply of patients.)

The hospital was losing $300,000 a year during this period; this increased concern about finding more patients. At times, the hospital had difficulty in meeting its payroll. The bishop and the board of trustees were concerned about reducing the deficit and, therefore, increased their pressure on the administration to worry more about enough patients to reach some break-even point in fiscal operation.

Usually the goals of medical education and patient care reinforce each other, but quality patient care and quantity patient care are incompatible, unless the hospital has a large enough staff to maintain its quality while it increases quantity. Education and quantity care are also incompatible. The compatibility of medical research with the other objectives depends on the circumstances. Education and patient care are usually compatible because increased education— whether for the house staff, active staff, or nurses—translates immediately into improved patient care. In contrast, any increase in the equipment for patients, while promoting patient care, raises costs. Thus, there is built into an organization with multiple purposes a series of dilemmas and goal conflicts. Their resolution says something about the power of various groups within the organization.

CONCLUSIONS: THE STEADY STATE OF MECHANICAL STABILITY

We see here a picture of an organization in a mechanical steady state. Perhaps the most disinctive feature is the hierarchical structure of control, authority, and communication. And yet, this structure did not exert much control or impose coordination. One of the most obvious reasons is that the group in power—the general practitioners —were not interested in exerting control over themselves. This is always likely to be the situation when there is a small group in control, that is, when the power is relatively centralized. Elites do not like to discipline themselves—punishment is for someone else. In this regard, the physicians are no different from any other professional group or from any other elite for that matter.

The mechanical model of hierarchical control, authority, and communication cannot function very effectively with a professional group. The norm of autonomy is too strong. The principle of election is too well institutionalized. The sense of a colleagual body is too ingrained to expect this to work in this kind of organization. The election of the executive committee is more a manifestation of this phenomenon than a cause of a lack of professional control. The most important reason why coordination and control via sanctions and programming cannot work is that there is a relatively complex division of labor.

Our cybernetic perspective makes us look at the amount of information feedback and socialization via communication as a key variable. We noted that there was little. As a consequence, problems remained undetected. The administration did not know that specialists were leaving the hospital nor that its active staff felt uninformed. The physicians did not know what was happening and their morale suffered. Few people were aware that the quality of patient care was low. That the house staff did not receive much training was a problem that went unrecognized.

Cybernetic theory tells us that if we look at the combination of variables, we can predict some states of disequilibrium. One combination is moderate complexity with centralization. In short, the hospital was overcentralized, especially among the professionals, and this led to many of the problems noted above. There was no professional control via either communication or rewards and punishments. One might say that Community Hospital was already moving toward an anomic state of instability. Although no conflict or deviance was manifested, there were certainly signs that it existed. Hospital regulations were not followed. Inappropriate techniques were used with patients, and knowingly so. We have noted that the hospital had a goal, at least one the elites pursued, of emphasizing the quantity of patients treated rather than the quality of their treatment. This was to be expected given the centralization of power and the lack of horizontal communication. The administration could not know what was happening on the wards, nor could most members of the organization. Under these circumstances the administration is likely to pursue its own values, which are an emphasis on efficiency and thus the quantity of patients being served. Again, it is a sign of a mechanical steady state.

V

Processes of Change and Conflict:
The Period of Instability

WHAT PRODUCES AN IMPETUS toward change? The answer to this question illustrates how critical information feedback is for making an organization adapt to changing circumstances. Community Hospital, like all hospitals with training programs, participates in the intern-matching program, where hospitals and interns express their prefences. There are more internships than interns, and some hospitals are left with unfilled internships. Since the results are published throughout the country, failure is highly visible. As a consequence, the Butler plan, which had as a key element the attraction of interns, became of interest to the hospital administration. This element became one of the more compelling arguments to convince the active staff to accept the plan despite some of its more controversial features.

The introduction of the Butler plan into Community Hospital disrupted the normal stability described in the previous chapter. As soon as one adds new specialties to a social structure, there is an anomic situation (Durkheim, 1951), at least, temporarily. Each new specialty must get a job description, so to speak, a set of activities which defines what its occupants are to do. Role conflicts occur because the new specialists may perform activities that were part of someone else's job description, implicitly, if not explicitly. Gradually defining what the new specialist does, however, usually results in the *addition* of new responsibilities or activities for others in the organization. The organization becomes complex in more than one way. In other words, the addition of new specialties often results in a greater variety of tasks for many of the occupants of other positions with whom they interact.

By social conflict, we mean disagreements. Various stages of disagreement are worth discussing. The simplest level is an argument that is eventually resolved. At a more advanced level is, of course, shouting and screaming. Still more advanced is a strike or refusal to work. In Community Hospital there was not only plenty of screaming and shouting, but whole departments of physicians threatened to pull out of the hospital, the professional equivalent to a strike.

Another aspect of any definition of social conflict should include a separation between interpersonal conflicts and group conflicts, the psychological level and the sociological level. So far much of the organizational conflict literature has tended to emphasize the former (Pondy, 1967; Corwin, 1969; Schmidt and Kochan, 1972). Those that have focused on the latter have usually looked at interdepartmental conflict (Watton and Dutton, 1969). While studying interdepartmental conflict is a useful approach, it is more likely to tap those endemic hostilities that do not represent states of disequilibrium, and which White (1961) observed. An important distinction is between the levels of intensity and another is the number of people involved (Corwin, 1969). When groups have conflicts, the reasons are probably less in the clash of personalities and more in the structure of the situation. In Community Hospital, the conflicts were frequently between whole departments, usually the department of medical education and one of the clinical services. The issues were usually rank, power, and status. In general, we would expect complexity to be negatively associated with the degree of centralization and stratification (Hage, 1965); however, this association comes about through a series of struggles which alters the distribution of power. Another kind of conflict we have noted is role conflict (Kahn et al., 1964; Schmidt and Kochan, 1972)—attempts to regulate the jobs of particular individuals. Still a third kind is conflict over goals and policies. In practice, it is hard to separate this from the others.

At first there were conflicts over whether there was a need for the specialty, as is described in the first section (Dalton, 1950; Goode,

1960). Then, there were a series of conflicts—described in the second section—over defining the newly created positions as the assistant directors of medical education (D.M.E.'s) attempted to introduce mechanisms for sanctioning and for socializing the active staff physicians. Of course, buried in these fights were questions of power and status, as became clear from interviews with many physicians. Throughout all of these conflicts was the basic underlying value conflict about the most appropriate goals of the hospital: quantity of patients or quality of patient care. The department of medical education was fighting for better patient care. Many doctors were more concerned about how many patients they handled. What was morally imperative to the medical educators was superfluous, and, worse yet, the beginning of "socialized medicine" to many of the attendings on the active staff. Implicit in these conflicts were disagreements about goals or priorities, although everyone gave lip service to the idea of quality patient care as the dominant objective. There were also verbal disagreements over the relative emphasis on medical education.

The conflicts in Community Hospital were unusual in their large amount over such a short period of time. The introduction of too many changes too quickly allowed us to perceive more easily the weaknesses in the control and coordination processes and their causes.

A critical point is that much of the conflict could have been resolved if there were more communication and information feedback. Since there was so little communication, the elite found out about crises after they came to a head. The conflict, however, generated by the addition of the medical educators, gradually led to the recognition of the need for more mechanisms of coordination, especially horizontal communication, a point to which we shall return in Chapter 7. Thus, we see how stability breaks down and gradually re-emerges in a new steady state. In this way, we can combine structural-functional analysis with conflict analysis.

GAINING ACCEPTANCE FOR THE NEW SPECIALISTS

Dr. Bacon, who had exactly the same viewpoints as Dr. Butler, was appointed director of medical education in Community Hospital and given the responsibility for introducing the Butler plan on an experimental basis. His appointment was made by the chief of staff and the administrator. The plan was expensive, and Dr. Bacon's first task was to find foundation support for it. Once financing was accomplished, his next problem was to recruit physicians for the new funded positions. The physicians started arriving in Community Hospital about a year and a half after Dr. Bacon. (See Figure 3.1) Then started the period of change and conflict.

The problems of obtaining approval for the initiation of new specialties varied according to where the new specialty or occupation was located in the hospital's structure. The addition of medical subspecialties, in most cases, affected few physicians directly. The addition of assistant D.M.E.'s in each of the clinical departments involved many of the attendings or active staff.

The addition of an endocrinologist was a relatively simple matter. Only one or two internists were even remotely connected with this medical subspecialty. The hematologist was also a relatively easy addition. In both instances, Dr. Andrew, the chief of staff, who was also chief of the medical service, was very much in favor of the addition of these full-time men. This was also true for the infectionist position. Again, no one in the hospital had any training in this subspecialty. It is seldom found in community hospitals with training programs in the United States. These subspecialists in medicine have no counterparts in surgery. Like allergy or dermatology, they are separate areas of medicine.

One consequence of the addition of these three full-time professional positions in the medical subspecialties was that the new subspecialists supervised the clinical laboratories. At the time, the pathologist was responsible for their supervision, as in most community hospitals. The administration supported the transfer of authority, even though the pathologist opposed it because he had seldom supervised or administered these laboratories. In fact, one nun commented: "The pathologist is no help; we have to do all the work."

Another problem connected with the addition of full-time physicians in the laboratories was the reallocation of other resources. The medical subspecialists needed office and research laboratory space in the new diagnostic wing. With some reluctance, the administrator finally agreed to convert several rooms next to the clinical laboratories into offices and research laboratories. Several nuns and nurses thereby lost their spaces, and they resisted this loss of status. The administrator was, as usual, in the middle. She once commented: "He (Dr. Bacon) just keeps requesting more and more space; there seems to be no end of it. He'd have the whole hospital if he could." The redefinitions of power and status in the laboratories were in reality easily made because few physicians were directly involved.

Equally simple was the addition of a full-time assistant D.M.E. to the department of pediatrics. The chief of service and attendings were in full accord with the idea. Similarly, the addition of a cardiologist went smoothly because Dr. Andrew, the chief of staff and chief of medicine was very much in favor of it, although the cardiac surgeons were opposed.

While the addition of the full-time positions in the clinical laboratory was relatively uncomplicated, the addition of some of the other full-time positions were more difficult. Dr. Andrew, the sister administrator, Dr. Bacon, and the senior attendings in the department of surgery met to discuss the advisability of creating an assistant D.M.E. for the surgical service. Prior to the meeting, Dr. Bacon had talked to the chief of surgery, Dr. Andrew, and the sister administrator about the problems of this change in order to prepare them. During the meeting, one of the senior attendings stated;

> What does this mean for the attendings? I don't want any institutionalized medicine. Strange things keep happening. You clarify what a physician is supposed to do and then later he is doing more, and you are left out in the cold.

This reflects a concern over status and the possible loss of income. The physician, a general practitioner, cited examples from other hospitals. Dr. Bacon pointed out that this was unlikely to be the case at Community Hospital since the surgical teacher would be under the control of the senior attendings.

The attendings then discussed the importance of hiring someone with the "right personality," so that he would "belong to the community of doctors." Dr. Bacon suggested that the senior attendings could conduct the interviews for the candidate whom he proposed.

The meeting also included a discussion of the definition of the duties of the assistant D.M.E. in surgery. The senior attendings agreed that he should be given the charity cases, and that he should not have consultation privileges. They wanted to be sure he would not acquire a private practice in the area!

The objectives of the plan were frankly discussed at the meeting and Dr. Andrew emphasized that one advantage of having assistant D.M.E.'s would be to attract a full quota of American-trained interns. He mentioned that he personally found it difficult, with the demands of a private practice, to keep abreast of the rapid advances in the field of medicine. He therefore looked to the new specialists to learn more about his specialty of cardiology. The senior attendings agreed that a good medical education program was very important. Thus, there seemed to be some acceptance of a crucial component of the Butler plan. On the other hand, the meeting concluded with the decision that an assistant D.M.E. position should be created, but it would have no authority over administration; all decisions would be made by the senior attendings.

The next meeting involved the creation of an assistant D.M.E. position in the ob-gyn department. The participants were Dr. Andrew, the sister administrator, Dr. Bacon, and the chief of ob-gyn. The chief stated that he was not concerned about himself but about his associate and assistant attendings lest the new man might gain too much power. It was agreed, therefore, that the individual hired would be under the authority of the chief of service and that his outside practice would be limited, thus defining the status of the new position. During the course of the discussion, the chief commented, "It was not so bad as it seemed."

One accomplishment of the meetings was to reduce a lack of knowledge about the plan and dispel erroneous ideas. The meetings also served to increase communication between the major occupational groups in the hospital, something that seldom occurred. Here we see how increases in the volume of communications, especially of a horizontal nature, can act as a coordination and a control mechanism. in this case reducing if not eliminating conflict. Thus, some of the initial disruption was smoothed over because this variable was increased. As we shall see, however, this initial success was not reinforced by repetition.

The general themes varied slightly from meeting to meeting; *during the initiation stage, the main issues were power and status.* This was clearly indicated in an interview with a senior attending in surgery, one of the most powerful men in the hospital. He said:

> Some of the men on the active staff have a fear of those teachers. They feel it is a prelude to the full-time physicians doing the hospital work. I don't have that fear. Some of the men who have not kept up do have this fear. These men will not limit my work. Referrals to me will continue. By constant reading and keeping up with the newest things, I have kept abreast of what's going on and I have no fear of being squeezed out.

Since all attendings in community hospitals are private physicians, they depend upon referrals from patients or other doctors as their source of income. Each new doctor represented a potential competitor and therefore a threat. If a full-time physician were paid by the hospital, as is the practice in university hospitals, he might provide patient care at lower cost, creating competition for the attendings.

How could such a change for the average community hospital finally be accepted, despite so many concerns on the part of the physicians? A partial answer lies in the methods used by Dr. Bacon. He had many prior conversations with the senior attendings, the men with power. During the group discussion of his plan, the physicians were permitted to define both the power and the status of the new specialists. For example, they set limits on consultation privileges and the size of private practice. The senior attendings or chiefs were assured of their authority over the full-time teachers, thus largely eliminating much of the administrative responsibilities, which was one of the original objectives of the Butler plan.

In addition, the goals were made overt. They were phrased in terms of the values shared by the active staff, for example, the importance of attracting a full quota of American-trained interns. The previous conversations with the two key individuals, Dr. Andrew and the administrator, resulted in their support of Dr. Bacon's proposal and their active participation in conversations with dissident physicians.

Each of the departments represents another example of the efficacy of using group discussion, prior conversations with powerful individuals, two-sided presentations, etc., as a method for introducing controversial changes. This, again supports the efficacy of the human-relations strategy of change (Coch and French, 1948; Greenblatt, York, and Brown, 1955; and Seashore and Bowers, 1963). The following table makes more explicit some of its elements.

Methods Creating Resistance	*Methods Creating Acceptance*
Flat or command	Discussion with those affected
Nonparticipation in planning	Participation in planning
Lack of consultations with informal leaders	Prior consultations with informal leaders
Nonutilization of recognized experts	Utilization of recognized experts
Covert objectives	Overt objectives
Offered as permanent changes	Offered as experimental changes
Values of participants not stressed	Stressing of participant values
Only good points stressed	Emphasizing the good and the bad

Dr. Bacon was able to gain approval for the creation of new positions, but he paid a price for it. The assistant D.M.E.'s, especially those in the surgical services, did not have much authority or status. They did not, for example, have power to coordinate their department. These compromises were to hamper the men who became assistant D.M.E.'s when they attempted to implement a series of changes involving increased professional control.

ATTEMPTS TO ADD MECHANISMS OF COORDINATION AND CONTROL

It took Dr. Bacon from one to two years to recruit specialists for the newly created positions. He was looking for individuals who would be willing to accept professional positions whose power was not clearly defined and whose duties were not specified. The individuals who accepted these new professional specialties were left with the task of building their own jobs. Dr. Bacon was also looking for individuals who had achieved excellent academic records in the leading university hospitals, such as Harvard, Yale, Columbia, Chicago, and Cornell Medical. Most of those recruited arrived in one summer (see Figure 3.1), and shortly thereafter started to make changes in their respective departments or clinical services. Since there were differences in the intensity of the conflicts generated within departments, the two-year priod of implementation is described separately for each of them.

The Medical Department

Before the arrival of the other specialists, Dr. Bacon had been successful in establishing grand rounds—a major mechanism of socialization. Few physicians in the department, however, attended them. Even attendance at the required monthly meetings was low. Dr. Bacon turned his attention to increasing participation in these meetings. As a first step, he increased the quality of grand rounds. He instructed his senior resident to select difficult or mismanaged cases. Gradually, the quality of case presentation by the house staff improved. Audiovisual aids and mimeographed accounts of the pertinent facts were introduced. The medical subspecialists and the assistant D.M.E.'s from the other clinical departments were invited to attend. Occasionally, professors from university hospitals presented lectures. Participation started to improve.

As a second step, Dr. Bacon attempted to increase attendance so that this feedback and socialization procedure would reach the main target, the private physician. He convinced Dr. Andrew, who was also chief of the medical service, that attendance-taking was necessary. The records of attendance indicated that during the first six monthly meetings after the arrival of most of the new specialists, participation was generally less than one-third. Dr. Bacon asked the administration to send a letter to the members of the department, requesting their cooperation. In the following six-month period, the attendance rose by 25 percent.

Dr. Bacon instituted the morning report, a practice common to university hospitals. This is a report on the condition and diagnosis of every patient admitted during the previous 24-hour period, as well as a report on patients who showed any significant changes. It provides a regular check on the process of patient recovery.

At the end of the first year after the arrival of the full-time teachers, Dr. Bacon accepted a position in a university hospital. He maintained liaison with Community Hospital in order to continue implementing the Butler plan for improving the quality of patient care. At this time, Dr. Cook, who had been recruited as a hematologist the previous year, was promoted to the position of Director of the Department of Medical Education.

In the medical department, the major thrust during the second year of implementation was to obtain more participation in teaching rounds from the physicians. At a department meeting, Dr. Cook asked for volunteers for teaching rounds. He explained their importance and, after some discussion, received nine volunteers. Since the medical subspecialists were also making rounds, this was enough for an effective program. However, it represented less than one-fourth of the attendings in the department.

The other changes in the medical department were far more subtle, but nonetheless important. There was a continued increase in the quality of teaching and grand rounds. The standards for patient care by the house staff were raised toward the end of the second year of implementation, when the impact of the changes on the recruitment of the house staff became evident. The large complement of American trained interns had a considerable influence not only on the residents, but also on the attitudes of the active staff toward the whole program. (See Chapter 6 for an analysis of their attitudes.) Dr. Cook made more demands on the house staff during the morning report and patient care was improved. The American-trained interns helped to improve case presentation in grand rounds, which resulted in some dissemination of knowledge to the active staff and it stimulated all the professionals in the hospital.

The Pediatric Department

Dr. Shore, the pediatric assistant D.M.E., arrived about a year after Dr. Bacon. Dr. Bacon advised Dr. Shore to wait six months before implementing his training program because of the resistance he himself had already encountered. Dr. Shore profited from this advice. He spent the first few months becoming acquainted with the attendings, nurses, and social workers, and with the operation of the hospital.

Once most of the new specialists had arrived, Dr. Shore started adding responsibilities and duties. As the first step, he started a monthly conference at which changes in the pediatric service were discussed. The meetings served as an effective communications pattern; they increased the integration between the pediatric senior attendings and their house staff. Prior to these meetings, Dr. Shore held private conversations with individuals before making any proposals in an attempt to estimate the degree of opposition. As a consequence, most changes were approved when proposed. If the opposition appeared to be great, the change was not suggested.

Dr. Shore started to hold his own teaching rounds with the house staff and to supervise them in the clinics and wards. He organized a series of lectures for the residents on the behavioral problems of children. In addition, he implemented a number of administrative changes. He began to formalize the procedures of the department by having them mimeographed. He changed the forms used in the clinics and on the wards by adopting those used in university hospitals.

Dr. Shore succeeded in altering the undesirable work habits of the house staff. He considerably changed the differentiation in work between the first- and second-year residents in order to provide a sequential training program. He altered the night-rotation policy to conform with that used in the medical department, a change that had been made by Dr. Bacon the previous year. He created a position of chief pediatric resident with responsibility for the scheduling of the work and supervision of resident performance. He also supervised the residents' work and insisted on more complete workups and prompt handling of admissions. The amount of work performed by the house staff was increased considerably as a consequence of these changes. Complicating the relationships among the full-time teacher, Dr. Shore, and the periodic attendings was the intense dissatisfaction of the newly recruited American-trained residents. They were demanding more and better teaching rounds, with a more comprehensive education program. They were highly critical of the quality of the service provided by the pediatric attendings, almost all of whom were specialists. This was the best demonstration of how the mechanism of higher communication rates results in greater feedback, including negative reports on the quality of care.

In a small department, such as pediatrics, this type of dissension produced a much greater strain on relationships than it would have produced in a larger one, such as medicine. At the beginning of the second year of implementation, the discontent of the American-trained residents manifested itself in a series of complaints to Dr. Cook, who had just replaced Dr. Bacon as the Director of Medical

Education. The pediatric attendings also held several secret meetings in an attempt to limit Dr. Shore's status and power. They were particularly concerned about his morning report and his separate teaching rounds because they felt these activities reflected adversely on them as physicians. In other words, the pediatric attendings decided it best to eliminate the mechanisms. After a large number of meetings, most of the items contained in the memorandum prepared by the pediatric attendings were not implemented; on the other hand, they were successful in eliminating both Dr. Shore's morning report and his teaching rounds, thereby reducing his effectiveness. This lessened his impact on the quality of patient care and medical education. The paradox is that the attempt to improve the quality of the house staff, which had been successful in pediatrics, was too rapid for absorption and led to less effectiveness.

The last major change attempted by Dr. Shore very nearly proved the undoing of the entire Butler plan. At a meeting of the pediatric attendings, Dr. Shore suggested some changes, including the reorganization of the pediatric residency and the establishment of a teaching ward service. (At the same meeting, Dr. Cook criticized the department.) These approaches for introducing changes produced considerable resistance. Although the chief of pediatrics had been advised of the proposal prior to the meeting, he remained silent during the meeting. The pediatric attendings held their own meeting and threatened to resign in a body if the administration did not replace Dr. Shore. This crisis resulted in a flurry of extra-organizational conferences within the administration and among the administration, house staff, full-time teachers, and pediatrics attendings. Communication channels were not opened until much after the crisis had matured.

Although the administration supported Dr. Shore, his effectiveness had been largely negated. He reverted to half-time in the hospital. A special committee was formed on the pediatric service in an attempt to introduce changes in the department. *This meant that one of the by-products of the conflict over change was a new arrangement that facilitated the discussion of changes, particularly administrative ones* (Coser, 1964). However, none of Dr. Shore's specific proposals were ever acted upon; they were lost in the attempt to maintain him as a full-time teacher. Nevertheless, *the conflict had made the administration much more aware of the problems in each of the clinical departments, and thus led to more attempts to increase feedback from the various parts of the organization.* The administration interviewed the house staff and began to realize the extent of its difficulties. It became more aware of the necessity for making future changes.

The Surgical Department

Dr. Donald, the surgical assistant D.M.E., had been informed of the many difficulties encountered by Dr. Bacon, and he therefore expected considerable resistance from the department of surgery. The nature of the department made it difficult to implement changes. It was completely controlled by the senior attendings who made decisions informally. The chief of the department seldom sent patients to Community Hospital and therefore was in the hospital infrequently. The department's attending physicians placed emphasis on being a member of the professional community; they looked distrustfully on strangers. For these reasons, the nature of the relationship between Dr. Donald and the senior attendings would have a considerable impact on the likelihood of changes, especially those involving new mechanisms of social control. Dr. Donald did not recognize this and attempted to implement his program through the chief of surgery and Dr. Andrew.

At the beginning, Dr. Donald tried to define his own duties and responsibilities. In this respect, he started with more difficulties than did either Dr. Shore or Dr. Bacon. Dr. Donald had a private practice in another city and wanted operating room privileges at Community Hospital, mainly as a symbol of status. He would normally have expected to receive them immediately because of his long residency and the nature of his teaching duties. Obtaining operating room privileges for Dr. Donald consumed three to four months of negotiations among Dr. Andrew, the chief of surgery, and Dr. Bacon. The question of consulting privileges was so sensitive that it was not even discussed for almost a year. These privileges were finally granted, but not in writing. They were not discussed with the other senior attendings, and, in the process, the credentials committee was completely by-passed. For the first few months, Dr. Donald had to call the chief of surgery every time he wanted to perform an operation. This procedure created considerable confusion in the operating room. It resulted in embarrassment for Dr. Donald because he was never sure whether he could instruct the surgical residents in operating techniques. All this resulted in reactions of distrust and resentment from the surgical senior attendings who were left to discover that Dr. Donald was using the operating room. It substantiates, in reverse, the consequences of the change tactics as listed above.

Dr. Donald instituted other activities defining his role relatively quickly. He started his own teaching rounds. At first, he held them only on the patients of the chief of the surgical service. Gradually, he extended them to other physicians' patients. He supervised the work of the house staff in the clinics and on the wards. Since the surgical residency was a new one, Dr. Donald had only one resident and two interns. Thus, one of the key mechanisms for socializing the staff, the teaching rounds, was not as effective as it could have been because of the small house staff. The patient coverage was not as complete as it was in the other departments, and there were fewer opportunities to communicate with the private physicians. Dr. Donald established a number of teaching conferences, including work in pathology. He was granted the right to assume responsibility for the monthly conferences at which deaths were discussed.

Where Dr. Donald attempted to redefine the activities of the active staff by establishing some new mechanisms of sanctioning, he created a considerable number of role, power, and status conflicts. He tried to reorganize the tumor board and to establish a teaching-ward service. He started to implement this change almost immediately after his arrival in the hospital, hoping to educate both the active and house staffs at the meetings of the tumor board. Not unexpectedly, the surgeons did not allow this to happen. They did agree to a compromise. After a series of conferences about the tumor board, several of which were held with its chairman, the composition of the board was altered to include three full-time teachers, including Dr. Donald. The chairman, however, was not replaced. Although the chairman agreed to schedule regular meetings, he never did. This was one critical committee that did not function as intended.

The second change aimed at placing all of the charity patients in a single geographical area on the surgical wards. Several of the associate attendings, who were board-certified surgeons, agreed to assist Dr. Donald in supervising the residents by holding teaching rounds. The purpose of the separate service was to provide the house staff with more autonomy in patient care, and, at the same time, more opportunity for learning under qualified supervision.

After a series of conferences among Dr. Andrew, Dr. Bacon, and the chief of surgery, the three agreed about the need of a teaching-ward service and they agreed about who should implement it. The administration also concurred and then held a series of conferences with the senior attendings, who were unalterably opposed to the plan. One of them even threatened the hospital with a law suit. During the course of these meetings, the chief of surgery withdrew his support. The president of the staff, also a senior attending in the surgical department, continued his opposition to the proposal. The administration worked out a compromise whereby the senior attendings would schedule rounds and treatment on the teaching-ward service, but Dr. Donald and some of the associate attendings woud participate in it. Again, as above, the senior attendings never scheduled any rounds.

It became apparent during the course of the many conferences and discussions that the prime source of resistance was not financial but concern over the loss of authority. One surgeon summed up the situation in the surgical department as follows:

> One, Donald is taking over where he has no right to. There's a rule here that no man should do surgery unless he has one year of observation. He hasn't and is doing it. He should be under the supervision of the staff. Two, Donald is wrecking the morale of the whole surgical staff with the power he has. I don't know who is permitting him to enforce this power. Three, we are the laughing stock of the city because Donald is telling everyone he's teaching us, and it's a standing joke— when you meet another doctor, he asks if Donald is teaching you surgery.

During the second year, Dr. Donald, worn out by a year of conflict, attempted few changes except to increase the number of surgical operations in which the interns could participate, and to increase participation in the teaching rounds. But no one agreed to participate and thus the major socialization mechanism was largely nullified.

The Ob-Gyn Department

The ob-gyn assistant D.M.E., Dr. Sloan, was appointed at the same time as his surgical counterpart. He had previously been a member of the active staff in Community Hospital. This had a number of consequences. He understood the hospital, especially its informal arrangements. He had both organizational friends and enemies; generally, he was perceived as a member of the local community. His problems of status and power were therefore diminished in comparison to those of Dr. Donald, who was a newcomer. The question of a private practice and consultation privileges did not become an issue, although he did agree to a financial limit on his practice.

Unlike the pediatric and surgical departments, the chief of the department exercised considerable authority over his attendings. The department was relatively small in comparison to either medicine or surgery, but still twice the size of pediatrics.

When Dr. Sloan wished to introduce some changes, he would discuss them with many of the senior attendings. He did not always discuss them with the chief of the department, which created some friction between them. Dr. Sloan's first changes were designed to define his own position. Since the residency program was fairly adequate, he proceeded to supplement it with a series of basic science courses. He established in his office a special library for the department, he started a journal file, and he took over the monthly conferences. Weekly grand rounds were added as well as a morning report. Dr. Sloan supervised the house staff, both in the clinics and on the wards, along with those senior attendings who were interested in teaching. Outside of the house staff, Dr. Sloan did not attempt to redefine the activities of the active staff or any other group in the hospital during his first year.

In general, there were conflicting attitudes about Dr. Sloan. One senior attending had this to say:

> I think they've [meaning Dr. Sloan] taken too much for granted as far as power is concerned. For example, a doctor [Dr. Sloan] was ready to deny renewal of next year's residency to one man because he thought he lacked compatibility without discussing this first with the chief. This, to my way of thinking, is assuming too much power.

Another senior attending had this opinion:

> I've just completed the month of service and the first time I had the assistant D.M.E. [Dr. Sloan] around, i.e., the one for ob-gyn. As it now stands, it could be an ideal arrangement.

Not unexpectedly, the same men with whom Dr. Sloan had difficulty before he became an assistant D.M.E. were those that did not accept him in his new position.

The Medical Subspecialists

The situation encountered by the two full-time teachers who were medical subspecialists and who arrived at the same time as Drs. Sloan and Donald was entirely different from those in the clinical departments. They did not have the difficulty of attempting to exert as much control over physician behavior. Their main concern was to start their new job, which consisted primarily of adding subspecialty rounds. Since they were subspecialists—Dr. Cook was a hematologist, and Dr. Fine was an endocrinologist—they offered little potential competition. They were not in private practice. While they did give consultations, they offered knowledge and skills that were largely lacking in Community Hospital.

The medical subspecialists created their own specialized laboratories, a radioactive isotope laboratory for the endocrinologist, and a blood laboratory for the hematologist. Both taught some new skills to the lab technicians. They started rotating medical residents through the laboratories. Besides their subspecialty rounds, Drs. Cook and Fine attended teaching and grand rounds in the department of medicine, thus considerably augmenting the scope of the education program on that service. They prepared special lectures. They were frequently asked to participate in pediatric teaching conferences and rounds, which they did. Finally, they instituted hematology and endocrinology clinics in the outpatient department.

Just as the full-time teachers' role definition resulted in changes for the active staff's role, so the subspecialists changed the job descriptions of the laboratory staff. They supervised the work of the laboratory and assumed responsibility for recruitment and assignments. It had previously been the joint responsibility of the pathologist and a nun.

Dr. Larry, the neurologist, worked at the hospital about one-sixth of the time and he therefore had little impact on the number of neurological cases in the hospital. There was little increase in the number of recorded neurological cases and almost no referrals, although Dr. Larry gave subspecialty rounds and read the EEGs. Since there was little increase in the number of neurological cases, there was not enough teaching material. Dr. Larry received virtually no consultations from the neurosurgeons who resented his presence in the hospital. Dr. Able, the cardiologist, joined the already well-established cardiac program. He was well received by the internists but not by the cardiac surgeons. Dr. Andrew placed him in charge of the catheterization team. Dr. Able managed to introduce standard cardiac forms and increase the effective use of catheterization tests. He became involved in several research projects, delivering a paper at the national meeting of the A.M.A. He also participated in cardiac teaching and grand rounds, which had been instituted by Dr. Andrew, and participated in the teaching and grand rounds in internal medicine.

Dr. Strong, the infectionist, arrived toward the end of the second year. Like Drs. Cook and Fine, he was in a medical subspecialty without a surgical counterpart. And, like them, he established a specialty lab and became involved in research. As a consequence of the addition of Dr. Strong to the medical department's teaching rounds, bacteriological tests and cultures were more extensively used. He started his own subspecialty rounds and outpatient department clinic. He also organized for his specialty a series of lectures by university professors.

DIFFERENTIAL SUCCESS IN IMPLEMENTING CONTROL

A constant theme that runs through all of our discussion is the greater resistance by the surgical physicians than the medical ones. In the next chapter, the attitudes of these physicians at the beginning, middle, and end of the change and conflict period are quantified and analyzed. Our task is to see how successful each specialist was in defining his role and those of others in the same department. We hope to discover whether certain kinds of mechanisms of professional control are more acceptable than others.

In general, the medical department accepted most of the proposals of Drs. Bacon and Cook. The pediatric and ob-gyn departments accepted some of the changes proposed by their clinical full-time teachers. The surgeons rejected almost all the proposals made by Dr. Donald.

Successful implementation depended, in part, on the particular change. When the change represented a definition of the duties of the new specialty, for example, educational activities, it was much more readily accepted than when it involved the definition of the active staff's duties, for example, grand rounds. However, *the relative rate of successful implementation between the clinical departments remains the same, irrespective of whether the change involved the definition of the assistant D.M.E.'s responsibilities or the attending physicians'*. Personality factors therefore may not be that important. For example, Dr. Donald had to be circumspect about when he performed operations and whose patients he held rounds on—problems not encountered by Drs. Sloan, Shore, or Bacon. Similarly, the definition of the authority rank of the assistant D.M.E.'s tended to be much more sensitive than other definitions, including status. Again, the situation was more sensitive in surgery than in any other department. While the type of change affected the likelihood of implementation, there was still variation among the clinical departments.

The specific methods or tactics of change probably had an effect on acceptance independently of the nature of the proposals and whom they affected. Drs. Bacon and Shore appeared to have the most effective approach. They instituted conferences to discuss changes. If resistance seemed great, they would talk to everyone affected by the proposals, including the nurses. The other two assistant D.M.E.'s and Dr. Cook, when he became D.M.E., usually worked only through their chiefs. Where the chief was powerful, as he was in medicine and ob-gyn, this approach was effective. Where the chief had little power vis-à-vis the senior attendings, it was not effective. (See Table 5.1.)

It is difficult to estimate the importance of the power of chiefs of service to the acceptance of various attempts to exert professional control. Dr. Shore, in pediatrics, was able to implement some changes without an influential department head, but the senior attendings blocked his plans concerning the teaching-ward service. In general, it appears that the power of the chief only influences the individuals with whom the innovator must work and not the actual acceptance. If the chief has power, then he must be consulted; if he does not have

Table 5.1 Differential Success in Implementing New Specialist Work Activities

1. D.M.E.'s Activities	Clinical Department			
	Medicine[a]	Surgery	Pediatrics	Ob-Gyn
a. Teaching rounds	yes	yes	yes	yes
b. Conferences, lectures	yes	yes	yes	yes
c. Clinics	yes	yes	yes	yes
d. Private practice	no	yes	no	yes
e. Research	yes	yes	yes	yes
f. University teaching	yes	no	yes	yes
g. Morning report	yes	no	no	yes

2. Attending Physicians'	Proportion Participating			
a. Teaching rounds	many	none	many	some
b. Grand rounds	many	none	many	some
c. Clinics[b]	little	little	little	little

3. Medical Subspecialists'	Medical Subspecialties[c]			
	Hematology[d]	Endocrinology	Neurology	Cardiology	Infectious Disease
a. Subspecialty rounds	yes	yes	yes	yes	yes
b. Conferences, lectures	yes	yes	yes	yes	yes
c. Subspecialty clinics	yes	yes	yes	yes	yes
d. Private practice	no[e]	no	yes	no[e]	no
e. Research	yes	yes	no	yes	yes
f. University teaching	yes	yes	no	yes	yes
g. Subspecialty laboratories	yes	yes	no	yes	yes

[a] The full-time teacher in medicine was also Director of Medical Education, and, therefore, had a number of administrative responsibilities the others did not have; he was also the hematologist.

[b] Few attempts were made in this area. This is used as a basis of comparison with areas where attempts were made.

[c] The neurologist was on one-sixth time, others were on full time.

[d] He became D.M.E. during the period of change, and therefore, had additional administrative duties.

[e] An occasional private patient, but this was rare.

power, then it is necessary to determine who does and obtain their support. In this respect, Dr. Donald made a serious error by not ignoring the chief of surgery and chief of staff, Dr. Andrew, and dealing with the surgical senior attendings who had influence in the department.

When the four departments are examined in terms of one important change—attempts to increase participation in teaching rounds, an important mechanism of socialization—some interesting differences emerge. This change was successfully implemented in the medical department with little resistance. On the pediatric service, there was some resistance, but there too it was easily implemented. In the two surgical services, little was accomplished, and what little there was occurred in the ob-gyn department. *Thus, resistance is patterned by department and by the nature of the professional work.* The reasons for this are specified in the next chapter.

The medical subspecialists were able to implement their programs relatively rapidly. However, the laboratory subspecialists were able to accomplish more than those in the medical subspecialties who had surgical counterparts.

At the end of the period, during which the new specialists attempted to implement the Butler plan, the medical subspecialists had generally well-defined jobs as teacher-administrators, and had some status and authority. This was not true for the assistant D.M.E.'s.

CONCLUSIONS: INSTABILITY AND TENDENCIES TO RESTABILIZE

The momentum established during the first year of implementation slowed down during the second year, until, at the end of that year, very few changes were being suggested by the specialists. By then, they had ceased to be a group of innovators and became a group of consolidators. During the first year, the assistant D.M.E.'s spent a considerable portion of their time debating and discussing among themselves various proposals and plans which might improve the quality of patient care. During the second year, the clinical full-time teachers spent a large amount of their time attempting to maintain what they had already accomplished. Since they were hampered in their efforts to change Community Hospital, they gradually allocated more of their time to research and administration.

Why did the specialists stop implementing the Butler plan? The crisis in the surgical department at the end of the first year resulted in the reluctance to propose changes for fear of further conflict. The full-time teachers still hoped to make progress in the medical departments. When the pediatric crisis occurred toward the end of the second year, the assistant D.M.E.'s lost hope. Thus, group conflict leads to fewer attempts to institute social change, which is the cause of conflict. Instability, we can see, is difficult to tolerate.

Here we see an illustration of how feedback operates to restore an organization to stability. The assistant D.M.E.'s learned that changes were producing conflict and so they stopped making changes. While the system is simple and the point obvious, it illustrates how cybernetic thinking moves one in the direction of process analysis.

Besides the failure of the surgical teaching ward and the pediatric crisis, there were several other factors which contributed to the loss of the momentum gained during the first year. Dr. Cook became the new D.M.E. at the end of the first year of implementation. He was interested in improving the relationships between the department of medical education and the active staff. He therefore recommended avoiding controversy. This meant not making any changes, which eliminated one of the major sources of conflict between the department of medical education and the active staff.

Another factor probably contributing to the slowing of the momentum was the achievements made during the first year of implementation. Attempts to change the behavior of others require a considerable amount of effort. Since there are few studies of change in organizations (Hage and Aiken, 1970, Chapter 3), it is difficult to estimate how long individuals can remain innovators, particularly when they are experiencing not only resistance and hostility but conflicts such as those described here. (Loy, 1969, suggests little relationship between innovation and perseverance.) The assistant D.M.E.'s lived in a situation of continued conflict, never knowing when a new controversy might develop. This is debilitating at best.

Thus, the period of change ended, not by design, but by circumstance. The price paid by Dr. Bacon, the curtailment of authority, hampered the achievement of the eventual objective of the assistant D.M.E.'s as full-time chiefs of service. But it would seem that without this price, some of the new specialist positions, and thus the Butler plan itself could not have been even started, given the nature of Community Hospital and its centralization of power. The period of conflict reduced the momentum until there were no new proposals for change. But again, the conflict was inevitable since it was the price for the creation of new coordination and control mechanisms.

As we shall see in Chapter 7, the irony is that they became exhausted just as acceptance of the Butler plan and their power was increasing.

If we visualize an organizational structure as a mobile with various parts, one for each power or occupational group, it is easy to see how the addition of several more parts upsets the balance or steady state of the entire structure. The new professional occupations must be given some status, power, and responsibilities. In the process, the status, power, and responsibilities of at least some of the other positions are redefined. The many meetings when the new medical specialists were added make this clear. The absorption of one new part only produces minor adjustments, but the addition of several at the same time inevitably means a shaking of the entire mobile via conflict until a new balance is negotiated between the various occupations and centers of power and thus a new steady state of stability is established. The fact that the conflict is greater in some parts of the organization rather than others does not make this less true. As becomes clear in Chapter 7, a new structure did emerge with new mechanisms of coordination and control.

Conflict is clearly not a normal state of affairs. The best signs of this are all the attempts of the new D.M.E., the administration, and the assistant D.M.E.'s to eliminate it. Anyone who has lived through an organizational crisis similar to those that occurred in the pediatrics and surgical services knows that heightened conflict is indeed a variable that can only be tolerated within certain limits. It is thus different from interpersonal conflicts or endemic departmental hostilities studied by others (White, 1961; also note the change in correlations when the conflicts are major in Corwin, 1969).

Although none of the participants had ever read any cybernetics literature, each group, in their own way, attempted to reduce the conflicts that were occurring. The new specialists gradually abandoned the Butler plan. The response of the new Director of Medical Education was a natural one given the many conflicts of this department. The administration opened new channels of communications, a change that was to prove decisive, and the active staff reluctantly accepted some of the mechanisms of control as a *fait accompli,* thus aiding in their own way to the redefinition of the social structure. It was a gigantic power struggle in which each group lost something and gained something. We seldom get to see these struggles, and only observe the final product—the structure *qua status quo,* that is when balance is achieved and there is stability. But here, everything is laid bare as we observe conflict as process over time. The conflicts make the basis on which social structures are built crystal clear. This is the great advantage of studying organizations during periods of instability.

What was the most important factor causing the instability? This is the critical question because we want to predict under what circumstances an organization becomes anomic. *The answer is the rate of change in the degree of complexity. Too many specialists were added in too short a period of time.* If, for example, only two per year were added and if, in particular, the surgical assistant D.M.E.'s came later, then the hospital could have absorbed more easily the disruptive effects. The administration, active staff, and medical educators all felt that they were in a state of war. This heightened the resistance to change and made each new change loom larger.

The new specialists themselves moved too fast. It would have been better to add only one socialization procedure each year under a kind of five-year plan of implementation. This would have provided opportunities to use more appropriate strategies of change, such as those suggested by the human relations group. The fears of change would then have had an opportunity to subside. Under these circumstances, the administration would probably have been more willing to support the medical educators in time of crisis, if there were major conflicts.

One kind of instability is caused by a rapid acceleration in the process of structural differentiation. It produces high conflict because there is no time for centralization and stratification to decrease. As we can see, new specialists demand power and status. Those who have it are unwilling to give it up, at least quickly. But the existing coordination mechanisms, namely the hierarchical pattern of control with the low levels of feedback, was incapable of handling the problems generated by the addition of the new specialists. If there had been *more communication, especially horizontal communication among departments, there would have been more feedback and quicker remedial action.*

Given a state of instability, an organization can move in one of two directions: reduce its complexity, which would here mean firing the new specialists, or change the distribution of power, which would mean perhaps losing some physicians unwilling to give up any authority. If the second direction is followed, new mechanisms of coordination and control must be established. A change from one steady state to another is not only a change in the scores of various variables but an adaptive change in the kind of mechanisms of regulation, a movement towards an emphasis on feedback. This is why we call it a cybernetic control system. Before we consider which way the organization went and why, we need to explore in some depth the causes of conflict.

VI

The Causes of Conflict

IN THE PREVIOUS TWO chapters, we have been most concerned with illustrating the cybernetic theory, first, by looking at one steady state, and second, by looking at how the process of change created instability. Throughout we have been talking about the importance of feedback and socialization: as a mechanism of control which was largely absent in the steady state, as a process which reduced the extent of change and resulted in the reestablishment of equilibrium and stability. We suggested that both structural-functional and conflict thinking could be united in the same cybernetic theory. We found that too rapid a change in one variable does not allow for the others to change and the system goes into disequilibrium. Control and regulation processes break down, only to reemerge later. In this chapter we shall continue to explore the problem of conflict from the vantage point of our theory. We shall see if the theory tells us which physicians were opposed to the addition of new medical specialists and teachers and their mechanisms of socialization, and which physicians were more accepting. As is clear from the previous chapter, there were considerable differences between departments and groups of physicians.

What were the occupational bases of the conflict? As we have seen

in the previous chapter, the themes of professional status and responsibilities emerged in discussions about the addition of new specialists.
The reader may therefore conclude that the answer is one of vested
interests. But this is too simple an explanation. If this were the case,
all the doctors would have been opposed to the Butler plan; although
they all had something to lose, it is clear that not all physicians were
resistant to these changes. We must search elsewhere for the differential acceptance of the various feedback and socialization mechanisms.

Our essential premises are repeated in summary form as follows.

Premises
1. All organizations require coordination and control.
2. There are two basic mechanisms for achieving coordination and control:
   Programming with sanctions and high feedback with socialization.
3. The greater the diversity of organizational structure, the greater the
   emphasis on high feedback with socialization.
4. The greater the differences of rank in the organizational structure, the
   greater the emphasis on programming with sanctions.

Derived Hypotheses
A. The more emphasis placed on feedback and on socialization in the work
   of the professional, the more likely he is to accept changes designed to add
   these mechanisms of control.
B. The more emphasis placed on differences in rank in the work of the professional, the more likely he is to resist changes designed to add mechanisms of feedback and of socialization.
C. The less emphasis placed on diversity in the work of the professional, the
   more likely he is to resist changes designed to add mechanisms of feedback
   and of socialization.

This time we are deriving hypotheses about the kinds of professional work and its consequences for resistance to various professional
control mechanisms. Essentially we shall explore two main hypotheses about the nature of professional work and its predisposing
consequences for attitudes about the changes described in the previous chapter. Our derived hypotheses and their reasoning is quite
simple. *First,* we would expect, just on the basis of consistency, that
if professionals were already accustomed to high communication
levels, they would be quite tolerant and accepting of these kinds of
changes. Conversely, if professionals did not have experience with

this kind of control system—which we have called a cybernetic system because of its emphasis on feedback and monitoring of individual performances via communication—then understandably resistance would be greater. *Second*, we would expect that work situations with an emphasis in authority and status should lead to a resistance to feedback and socialization mechanisms. It would be nice to derive still another kind of hypothesis, one about the complexity and variety of professional work. But with physicians it becomes very difficult to discuss measures that are fine enough to detect differences. The work of a doctor is already very complex and varied. To measure differences between various specialties is a task that must await future development. It might only be noted that this kind of hypothesis is also derivable from the theory (for a discussion of the derivation of hypotheses, see Hage, 1972).

PROFESSIONAL WORK STYLES AND CONFLICT

The essential differences between the work of a medical physician and a surgical physician are well known. The former, whether an internist, pediatrician, medical subspecialist, or general practitioner largely interested in medical treatment, cures his patients by drug therapy. This means that he watches his patient and is more willing to ask the advice of others. The latter, whether a surgeon, obstetrician-gynecologist, surgical subspecialist, or a general practitioner largely interested in surgical treatment, cures patients by operating. This means that he must be quick, decisive, and more willing to assume complete responsibility. The medical physicians rely more upon their colleagues in treating patients than do surgical physicians. Studies of community hospitals have indicated that medical physicians are more likely than their surgical counterparts to use consultants, allow house staff to treat their patients, and to explore their patients' social and emotional problems (Kendall, n.d.). In other words doctors who cure by drugs are, because of the nature of their work, more interested in communication.

In the operating room there is one man, the head surgeon, clearly in command, and there is little time for consultation or seeking of advice from others. Thus, the surgical man sees himself as solely responsible for his patients, while the medical man is more apt to preceive himself coordinating a number of people. The necessity for quick decision and pinpointed responsibility means that an operating room functions very much like a military unit in combat. There is high centralization and greater stratification. These differences have created different social structures on the surgical and medical wards in the clinical departments as well. The former have much greater differences in authority and status between the attending and the house staff and nurses than do the latter (Perrow, 1965).

Given these different work styles, it becomes clear how medical physicians would accept mechanisms of feedback and socialization much more readily than the surgeons. It is inherent in their pattern of work. They rely more upon communication and they place less emphasis on authority and on status. Given the great emphasis on differences in rank, the physicians who do surgery of one kind or another resist attempts to add mechanisms such as teaching rounds or morning reports.

Similarly, there is a basic difference in the way in which medical physicians and surgeons gain expertise. The medical physicians, who treat with drugs, learn about them through reading and conversation with others, that is, through communication. There is always a new drug or diagnostic technique to learn. The surgeons learn by practice. Experience is the crucial mechanism of education. The nature of their professional work means that medical physicians must use their minds more than their hands, while surgeons rely more on dexterity than on thought. Needless to say, we are only speaking relatively about professionals with the same level of training and the same degree of qualifications, the board-certified specialists.

There is a parallelism between what professionals do and what they can accept. Emphasis on continued reading is a recognition of the necessity for continued socialization; emphasis on practice is almost a denial of the need for continued socialization. To tell a surgeon he should learn more is quite threatening because one is suggesting that he is not doing adequate surgery. To tell a medical man he must learn more is to be commonplace.

The general practitioner is more likely to see himself as responsible for the total care of the patient. As the division of labor progresses, that is, as work is divided into professional specialties, the necessity of consultants becomes more apparent. The specialist knows he is an expert, but in only one area, and therefore, is more likely to rely the advice of other specialists, that is, on horizontal communication. The general practitioner does use consultations, but his work style encourages him to assume as much individual responsibility as he possibly can. Similarly, *the specialist who has studied longer is more likely to put an emphasis on the importance of reading and continued education—socialization—than the general practitioner.* The latter is more likely to emphasize learning by experience.

These basic differences in professional work styles between an emphasis on technique and individual responsibility, an emphasis on advice and collective responsibility, an emphasis on learning by practice and learning by reading are applicable to all professionals, and therefore, are of general interest. They affect the likelihood of resistance to the addition of feedback and socialization mechanisms.

The basic differences between drug and surgical therapy raise the question of whether the concept of work style is nothing more than a new name for technology. Increasingly in the last few years, this perspective has become more and more popular as a way of predicting how organizations are structured (Fullan, 1970; Hage and Aiken, 1969; Hickson et al., 1969; Perrow, 1967). The differences between drug and surgical therapy are clearly technological. By technology, we mean nothing more than an emphasis on tools, physical artifacts, or what Hickson et al. (1970) call materials technology. However, the client work style of the professionals is described here as either consultative or individual responsibility, and as either learning by reading or learning by practice. Has the accent been placed on the wrong factor? It is difficult to know. These techniques may affect work styles, but it is not at all certain. In any case, these basic work styles are more general than the distinction between drugs and operations, and therefore, are to be preferred. But before we can be sure that we have chosen the correct explanation, we need to study social workers, teachers, and other kinds of professionals. This explanation is, however, derived from more general premises which seem to explain under what conditions one will find an emphasis on feedback and socialization.

Patterns of Resistance

Two questions were used for measuring the physician's resistance to the changes:

1. From *your point of view*, do you think these full-time teachers are desirable or undesirable?
2. From the *viewpoint of the hospital*, do you think these full-time teachers are desirable or undesirable?

The phrase full-time teachers was used because it was the phrase most often used in the hospital. The answers were combined into a five-point index, with acceptors classified as three or four, and rejectors as all other scores. Immediately after this question, the respondents were asked why they answered as they did. The responses were used to ascertain what values were most important to the physicians. Indeed, the reasons provided give a number of insights into how work styles affect ideology. The open-ended, as opposed to the fixed-alternative format, was preferred so that the doctor would expound, mentioning examples and anecdotes. (It was also used as a way of providing contrast in the interview schedule and avoiding too many fixed-alternative questions.) In the third wave of interviews, a fixed-alternative question about the perceived consequences for the physicians and for the hospital was added to the supplement of the analysis. (For a more detailed description, see Hage, 1963.) The physicians' attitudes were measured three times, once a year. The last wave of interviews occurred about five months after the pediatric crisis described in the previous chapter. The resistance rate for the physicians, classified by basic work style is reported in Figure 6.1.

The work style, whether medical or surgical, whether general or specialist, had a persistent impact on resistance to the addition of new specialties. As can be seen, the medical specialists accepted this change, while the surgical general practitioners resisted it. The impact of the work styles on resistance to change, at least of the kinds discussed in the previous chapter became more apparent in the second interview, which occurred about two months after the crisis in the department of surgery. Initially, many physicians were not

Figure 6.1 Proportion of Acceptors Among Physicians Classified According to Their Work Styles[a]

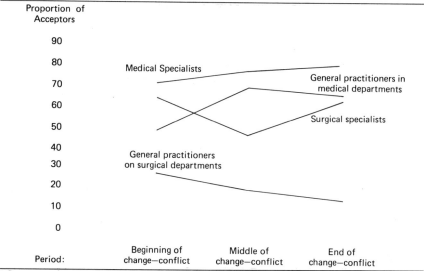

[a] Seventy-nine percent of the selected samples were interviewed all three times so that the distortion, due to refusals, is minimal. On the second and third measurements, most of the refusers were surgeons, specifically the specialists, so that the rate of acceptance in this subgroup may be an overestimate of the true proportion.

[b] An index of acceptance was constructed on the basis of answers to two questions: one regarding the benefits of the new specialties for the hospital, and the other regarding the benefits for the physician.

sure of their attitudes toward the addition of full-time teachers. By the second interview, attitudes had crystallized. The interview took longer, although the same questions were asked each time, as physicians went into some detail expounding on their reasons. The proportion of "don't know" responses declined. The events previously described reinforced the influences of the work styles on attitudes about the addition of new specialists.

The more doctors rely upon consultative patterns of work the more accepting they are of the addition of new professional specialties. In contrast, a sense of individual responsibility leads to the opposite reaction. The factor of a potential competitor probably becomes more important, as was suggested in the quotes from the interviews reported in the previous chapter.

Other factors were considered as possible explanations of the different rates of resistance. Age is frequently mentioned as a cause of resistance to any change, whether caused by an increase in the division of labor or not. When work style, medical versus surgical, and general versus specialist, are held constant, age has little effect on attitudes. At least here there was no generation gap. Where a physician was trained was also considered. It had some effect prior to the changes reported in the previous chapter, but once attitudes had crystallized, it had none. The rank of the physician, that is, whether he was a senior, associate, or assistant attending, was also explored. There was some correlation with resistance during the middle of the implementation period, but this disappeared in the third wave, nor was the effect consistent.

Since the general practitioner usually had less education than the specialist, it is possible that the differences in attitudes might be a consequence of the amount of education. However, when length of residency training was explored, it had no consistent relationship with acceptance or resistance. The number of patients and the number of other hospital affiliations were also explored on the speculation that attendings with few patients in Community Hospital would be unaffected by the addition of full-time teachers. Again no correlation. *Instead, it is the work style as such that appears to be more important than these other possible causative factors.*

There are four classifications of physicians reported in Figure 6.1. Two of them, the medical specialists and the general practitioners in the surgical departments (surgery, obstetrics-gynecology, and the surgical subspecialties) have consistent work styles in terms of the above line of reasoning. In contrast, two of these groups, the surgical specialists and the general practitioners, have inconsistent work styles. Their work has conflicting impacts on their acceptance or rejection of the addition of full-time teachers. To use a term common in sociology, they are under cross-pressures. As is to be expected from our argument, the acceptance rate of these work styles is in between that of the medical specialists, who are very much in favor of the addition of new specialists, and the surgical general practitioners who are very much against it. This ordering of the professionals provides additional confidence that our speculations about work styles and their impact on resistance are correct.

That the general practitioners in the medical departments (internal medicine and pediatrics) and surgical specialists are under cross-pressures is also demonstrated by their attitudinal swings durings the three waves of interviews. Their attitude is less firm and therefore more vulnerable to current changes and conflicts. The surgical specialists resistance rate increased after the crisis in surgery over the teaching ward service. Similarly, the general practitioners in the medical departments were probably affected by the pediatric crisis, although none of them were assigned to this clinical department.

The net figures in Figure 6.1 do not indicate the many gross changes in attitudes that occurred among specific physicians. Most of these fluctuations occurred in the two classifications of physicians who were under cross-pressures from their work. In other words, their attitudes were less stable, again supporting our interpretation that their opinions were being influenced in contradictory ways. Many of the attendings who changed from rejection to acceptance during the second year of implementation, or vice versa, had the opposite shift in attitude during the previous year.

The Specification of Learning Work Styles

We would like more precise measures of work style than a physician's assignment to a particular department. This is especially important, given our desire to generalize beyond the medical profession. One important theme running through the idea of reading as opposed to practice is an orientation to continued learning or socialization. (It is worth remembering that this is a critical element in the Butler plan, as well as a major mechanism of professional control.) This was tapped with the following question. Each member of the active staff was asked to select two topics which would have the most interest for him from the following list:

Group practice—pros and cons
Office treatment of thyroid disorders
Lipid metabolism
How to avoid malpractice suits
Stimulants and sedatives
The role of serotonin in the gut

These topics were representative of three different kinds of information which might interest a physician. Lipid metabolism and the role of serotonin in the gut represent the most advanced and theoretically oriented medical topics; group practice and how to avoid malpractice suits reflect a different kind of knowledge, having little to do with the treatment of patients. (The topics were chosen so that they had equal relevance for both medically and surgically oriented physicians, Kendall, n.d.)

When the proportion of physicians who expressed a personal interest in the more advanced medical knowledge, classified by type of practice, type of service, and acceptance of the new positions, is examined, the variations in the work styles between the four kinds of professionals are observable. (See Table 6.1.) The specialists are much more interested in these topics than the general practitioners; the medical men, that is, those doctors who treat with drugs, regardless of type of practice, are more interested than the surgeons. Furthermore, the choice of one of the two academic topics is related to acceptance of the assistant D.M.E.'s, except among the general practitioners in the surgical departments, where only a single physician was interested in them. *The work patterns reflect different orientations toward continued socialization, and when this is measured*

Table 6.1 Acceptors, Regardless of Work Style, Are More Likely To Be Interested in Continued Socialization: Proportion Stating a Preference for Advanced Medical Knowledge

| | General Practitioners | | Specialists[a] | |
	Medical[b]	Surgical[c]	Medical[b]	Surgical[c]
Rejectors	— (6)	6 (17)	(1)[d] (7)	11 (19)
Acceptors	21 (14)	— (3)	45 (29)	27 (33)
Total	15 (20)	5 (20)	39 (36)	21 (52)

[a] Defined as those with 90 percent of their patient load in a particular area of medicine; they may not have had any formal training in a residency; less than one-half were board-certified specialists.

[b] Defined as someone who is assigned to the department of medicine or pediatrics and treats most of his patients with drugs.

[c] Defined as someone who is assigned to the department of surgery, obstetrics-gynecology, or one of the small surgical subspecialty departments and treats most of his patients by operating.

[d] The total is below 10 and, therefore, too small for percentaging.

independently, it is found to be related to acceptance of new specialists.

Another way of looking at the interest in continued socialization is to see which communication channels the physician relies upon. This was measured by asking the physician to rank the first three channels he used most frequently to learn "about unusual or new drugs and medications." The list provided included:

Detail men (drug salesman) or bulletins from pharmaceutical houses
Research reports in medical journals
Postgraduate medical education lectures
Your hospital's formulary and printed additions to it
Full-time teachers
Attending physicians in private practice (active staff)
House staff (interns and residents)

The selection or use of these different channels implies many things about the doctor. Physicians who rely primarily on detail men or drug salesmen as the first source of information are more likely to provide poor patient care, at least as indicated by the Peterson et al. (1956) study of general practitioners in North Carolina. The use of drug salesmen as the primary source of information suggests that there has been little critical evaluation of the drug. Research reports, or even the reports of the physicians (whether teacher-administrators, active staff, that is, practicing physicians affiliated with a hospital, or house staff, that is, interns and residents), are much more likely to be critical. More importantly, the use of drug salesmen from the major pharmaceutical manufacturers as the first source suggests that the emphasis is placed on the ease of effort and the availability of information as opposed to its amount and the accuracy of communication.

The specialists and medical men are much less likely to utilize drug salesmen as their primary source. (See Table 6.2.) To put it another way, the selection of channels substantiates our generalizations about the importance of continued socialization in the professional's work style. Most physicians who treat with drugs rely upon consultations and are interested in continued learning. If a medical

Table 6.2 Acceptors, Regardless of Work Style, Are Less Likely to Use Detail Men as the Primary Source of New Drug Information: Proportion Stating They Use Detail Men as Their Primary Source

	General Practitioners				Specialists			
	Medical		Surgical		Medical		Surgical	
Rejectors	(3)ᵃ	(6)	65	(17)	(1)ᵃ	(7)	42	(19)
Acceptors	29	(14)	(1)ᵃ	(3)	10	(29)	30	(33)
Total	35	(20)	60	(20)	11	(36)	35	(52)

ᵃ The total is below 10 and, therefore, too small for percentaging.

specialist does use drug salesmen, contrary to the typical work style for this professional category, then he is likely to resist the addition of new professional specialties. These exceptions substantiate our interpretations of the major factors in professional work which help shape attitudes.

Another way to explore the relationship between the use of detail men and acceptance of the full-time teachers is to examine what proportion of the four basic work groups select drug salesmen as a first, second, or third communication channel. Since the physicians were offered seven possibilities, there was an opportunity to avoid the choice of detail men completely. The difference does not disappear when the first three communication channels are considered. The medical specialists in particular provide a sharp contrast to the other three professional categories within the active staff; only 53 percent of them, as opposed to 85 percent of the surgical specialists, are likely to select detail men as one of their three choices.

Another important aspect of continued professional socialization is the number of communication channels used for continued socialization. This is a crude measure of the communication volume. The comments of some physicians, especially the general practitioners on the surgical services, suggest that they did not rely upon some channels available to them because they did not think they could learn much. The active staff was asked whether they felt they had learned from the medical specialists. None of the rejectors, regardless of work style, felt that they had gained new knowledge from full-time teachers.

The physicians were also asked whether they had ever learned much from the house staff when they helped treat their private patients. (The word "much" was used in order to determine if this was a salient mechanism of socialization.) The medical physicians and the general practitioners were much more likely to report that they did learn from the house staff than the doctors who were being trained and therefore lower in status and authority. This is a particularly important finding, given the basic Butler plan. Since it emphasizes this indirect mechanism of socialization, it is important to know if it is an effective communication channel. It might be expected that the general practitioners would be more likely than the specialists to state that they do learn from the house staff, but this is not so. Again we see the paradox that it is the physicians with the most training who say that they are learning more and relying more on communication channels. Thus the specialists are most likely to have high volumes of communication, especially of a horizontal nature—considering the residents as equal or lower in status and authority than the general practitioners.

The mechanism of socialization, including preferred content and the number and the kinds of communication channels, helps specify the meaning of the work styles of the medical specialists, the surgical specialists, and the medical and the surgical general practitioners. It is clear that the specialist places much greater emphasis on continued education and that this emphasis is associated with his greater acceptance of new specialists. As we have already suggested, this is largely a matter of consistency between work and attitudes towards change.

The Specification of a Concern About Authority and Status

Another basic difference in work styles is the willingness to allow others to share in the treatment of the patient. An emphasis on consulting with others implies a certain degree of control over one's own behavior, a willingness to accept feedback of information. This was probably an important factor in the demise of teaching-ward services in surgery and pediatrics. A concern with authority and status, on the other hand, leads to an unwillingness to give up control over patients or, more correctly, to share control with interns and residents.

The active staff was asked whether they felt the house staff should be given fairly complete control of charity cases. Again physicians in medical departments were more willing to delegate authority than were physicians in surgical departments. The acceptors were much more likely than the rejectors to believe that the house staff should have fairly complete control and that only limited supervision by the physicians of the active staff should be employed. As might be expected, the specialists are more willing to share their authority than the general practitioners, but the differences between the medical and surgical services are greater than those between specialists and generalists. (See Table 6.3.)

Perhaps the most sensitive measure of the saliency of authority is the physicians' attitudes about private cases. While one-half of the active staff were willing to give fairly complete control on charity cases, this proportion is only 4 percent for private cases—that is, almost no one (See Tables 6.3 and 6.4.) Only 24 percent of the active staff in Community Hospital was willing to give even partial control. The differences between the clinical departments are revealing. Even though medical physicians are much more willing to give partial control, there is a considerable difference between the two medical departments. More importantly, the acceptors are much more willing to share authority than the rejectors. *This sensitivity to sharing authority represents one of the crucial reasons for conflict with the new specialists.* But since most new positions involve some change in the distribution of power, the theoretical question is why some men are willing to share authority and thus, in the process, allow more control to be exerted over their own behavior. Veblen's concept of vested interests suggests that those who have power or status will resist changes because the latter affect those rewards. Likewise, one could misinterpret Marx to be saying that everyone who has money will resist attempts to take it away. This is not the case.

Table 6.3 Acceptors, Regardless of Department, Are More Likely to Give Fairly Complete Control to the House Staff on Charity Patients: Proportion Stating Fairly Complete Control

	Medical		Pediatrics		Surgery		Ob-Gyn		Surgical Sub-specialties	
Rejectors	58	(12)	(1)[a]	(1)	—	(11)	(4)[a]	(6)	37	(19)
Acceptors	71	(34)	(8)[a]	(9)	50	(12)	(7)[a]	(9)	27	(15)
Total	67	(46)	90	(10)	26	(23)	73	(15)	32	(34)

[a] The total is less than 10; therefore, percentages were not computed.

Table 6.4   Acceptors, Regardless of Department Are More Likely to Give Partial Control to the House Staff on Private Patients: Proportion Stating Partial Control

	Medical	Pediatrics	Surgery	Ob-Gyn	Surgical Sub-specialties
Rejectors	17 (12)	— (1)	— (11)	— (6)	5 (19)
Acceptors	62 (34)	(3)[a] (9)	— (12)	(1)[a] (9)	20 (15)
Total	50 (46)	30 (10)	— (23)	7 (15)	12 (34)

[a] The total is less than 10; therefore, percentages were not computed.

The study of Community Hospital implies a modification of this point of view, namely, that *professional work style influences the relative importance or saliency of power or status to the professional, whether he has it or not.*

Work Style and Ideology

What professional values or goals are important to physicians who have these different professional work styles? To measure this, the attendings of Community Hospital were asked to report why they accepted or rejected the new medical specialists. Their answers reflect basic differences in values as to what is most important, and these answers were systematically patterned by their work behaviors.

If the doctor's work were characterized by consultations and reading, that is, if he were either an internist or pediatrician, he was likely to value education and quality patient care as most salient. One physician commented:

> They [the full-time teachers] will probably be an inducement for more residents and interns to make applications to the hospital. It would add to the education program . . . also help the busy practitioner in the evaluation of patients.

An internist said in his interview:

> Since they [the full-time teachers] are here most of the time, they are the ones the residents and interns can get information from and discuss the case. If a question comes up in the afternoon and no one is around,

they help by making suggestions. There will be more research and papers coming out of Community Hospital, which improves the quality of education and service.

The emphasis on teamwork and the reliance on continued reading of journals were reflected in the answers of many of the medical physicians who were pleased with the addition of the assistance of D.M.E.'s One senior attending in the pediatrics department had this to say:

> Because they [the full-time teachers] have a ready fund of highly specialized knowledge, it greatly improved the quality of medical service, as well as the quality of medical education.

Those physicians whose work is characterized by individual responsibility and learning through experience, that is, the doctors on the surgical services, were most likely to feel that the loss of power and status were the most salient consequences of the new specialties. An associate attending in obstetrics-gynecology mentioned the power of the assistant D.M.E.'s when he said,

> They walk around like they control the patients.

An assistant in the same department commented,

> They should not set policy for various departments for patient care. This should come from the chief.

An associate in surgery reflected concern over referrals when he said,

> I think that they [the full-time teachers] will gradually start treating patients who could normally come to me. They represent a form of competition, subsidized by the hospital.

One surgeon said,

> The goal of many hospitals today is to get rid of the attending staff. This would give a greater income to the hospital. The have men at their beck and call and wouldn't have to call upon the private physician. [X] Hospital has already done the same thing.

The specialists were apt to emphasize the value of intellectual stimulation that could come from the D.M.E.'s. One pediatrician said,

> It certainly enhances the educational program. It means a higher standard for the care of the patient. It's stimulating to men who have private patients here. Every doctor needs a stimulation now and then or they get into a rut.

The general practitioner was likely to perceive no need for them whatsoever. One general practitioner had this to say,

> I think it [full-time teaching] is a waste of money and time. . . . They [the full-time teachers] are not well-trained enough to teach, not enough hospital experience.

The addition of new medical specialties can have all of the above-mentioned consequences simultaneously. It can mean the improvement of the hospital performances in patient care and education, the stimulation of the active and house staff, and result in the loss of authority and status for the attendings. *What determines acceptance or rejection is which of these consequences is most important to the physician—improvement of patient care or loss of authority, increased intellectual stimulation or loss of status.* When the work style is characterized by an emphasis on consultations and reading, then the physician values the former consequences as most important. Perhaps it is simpler to say that the emphasis on advice from others leads to more collectivistic values, but it does have far-reaching implications. It suggests that as the division of labor proceeds, new professional specialties become even more acceptable, and collective goals become even more important than individual ones. In the prologue we had suggested that a movement towards an emphasis on feedback and socialization was a movement towards an emphasis on the quality of client or customer service as a goal of the organization. Here we see some additional reasons as to why this is so. A physician who is concerned about socialization and not about his loss of authority and of status, is a doctor who is continuously learning. As he learns, he becomes more concerned with the quality of work he does. This in turn feeds back upon his work, making him more interested in continued learning. A never-ending cycle of self-improvement is started.

To believe that the emphasis on improved patient care and education is altruistic is to misperceive it. A physician's self-interests are benefited as well. He can gain increased prestige from a hospital that is known, at least within the medical profession, for the quality of its work. He also gains increased help. But again, what is interesting is that these benefits accrue to all. Some, those with particular work styles, find them to be more important than the disadvantages or costs.

With a panel study, one has additional opportunities for checking lines of reasoning or arguments. A series of questions evaluating the consequences of the medical-education program for the hospital and for the physicians as a group were added on the third wave at the end of the study. The active staff was able to specify whether each consequence was negative or positive: The question was:

> How has the presence of the full-time teachers affected the physicians attached to your service? Here is a list of possible consequences; tell me which ones have occurred, to the best of your knowledge, and whether the consequences were positive or negative.

This question was then repeated for the perception of consequences for the hospital, treating it as a unit of analysis.

The professional perception of consequences at the end of the period of change on balance was that increased specialization was negative. (See Table 6.5.) As might be expected, the rejectors were more likely to perceive the consequences as negative. What is more interesting is that one-fourth of the acceptors felt the same. In other words, *acceptors could favor the addition of specialists even though they perceived it as negative for themselves.* This again supports the idea that the division of labor can lead to greater emphasis on collective performances, even at personal expense. As might be expected, the acceptors who were medical specialists were more likely to state positive effect on balance.

The analysis of the perceived consequences for the hospital indicate a much greater polarization of opinion among the rejectors and the acceptors. (See Table 6.6.) The latter agreed that increased specialization helped the organization's functioning, while the rejectors were dubious. What is especially interesting is the differences regarding hospital control over physicians. All the crises and conflicts described in Chapter 5 lead to conflicts in opinions as to who had won and whether it was negative or positive.

Table 6.5 The Rejectors Received Negative Consequences for Their Authority and Status While the Acceptors Perceived Positive Consequences for Their Knowledge: Kind of Consequence

	Positive	None	Negative	(N)
1. Knowledge of physician				
Rejectors	—	75	25	(49)
Acceptors	53	38	9	(79)
2. Authority of physician				
Rejectors	4	39	57	(49)
Acceptors	13	50	37	(79)
3. Referrals of patients to the physician				
Rejectors	8	51	41	(49)
Acceptors	19	49	32	(79)
4. Prestige of physician				
Rejectors	—	51	49	(49)
Acceptors	16	47	37	(79)
5. Promotions of physician				
Rejectors	—	63	37	(49)
Acceptors	13	72	15	(79)
Net balance of consequences				
Rejectors	6	33	61	(49)
Acceptors	18	56	26	(79)

Table 6.6 The Rejectors Perceived Negative Consequences for the Hospital's Performances While the Acceptors Perceived Positive Consequences: Kind of Consequence

	Positive	None	Negative	(N)
1. Hospital's income				
Rejectors	4	39	57	(49)
Acceptors	20	53	27	(79)
2. Hospital's prestige				
Rejectors	19	50	31	(49)
Acceptors	86	6	8	(79)
3. Hospital's control over physicians				
Rejectors	49	14	37	(49)
Acceptors	43	34	23	(79)
4. Hospital's service to community				
Rejectors	6	63	31	(49)
Acceptors	67	23	10	(79)
Net balance of consequences				
Rejectors	24	24	52	(49)
Acceptors	76	15	9	(79)

THE CONTEXT OF WORK AND CONFLICT

The attending physicians, while having several basic differences in work styles, also work within specific departments. The characteristics of these departments can influence a physician's values as well, and, therefore, his resistance to change. It is clear from Chapter 5 that there were differential rates of implementation between departments with basically the same work style.

Why are there differences between these departments? Some of the characteristics of each of the clinical departments in Community Hospital are listed in Figure 6.2. As can be seen, the proportion of specialists within each department varies. If the nature of work represented the only explanation for resistance, pediatrics should have had more changes than the medical department, and yet this was not the case. One clear difference between departments indicated in Figure 6.2 are the differences in the number of program changes that had occurred in a ten-year period prior to the addition of new specialties (Hage and Aiken, 1967 and 1970).

Only the medical department had instituted many changes in their programs or services. The departments of pediatrics and ob-gyn had made some alterations; the surgical and surgical subspecialties had remained static. Medical, pediatric, and ob-gyn had all introduced residence training. Not only did this require a considerable amount of effort and a number of administrative changes, but the incoming residents provided a further impetus for changes, both administrative and technological. The ideas that they receive, especially about new treatments, were passed along to the physicians. In turn, this precipitated further alterations. The complaints of the pediatric residents reported in the previous chapter are an illustration.

The medical department had added a subspecialty in cardiology and instituted a program for teaching cardiac techniques to the private physicians who were interested. Most of the internists learned catherization and other diagnostic procedures. Grand rounds in cardiology were held every week and were well attended. The medical department attempted to institute a research program in cardiology and had obtained funds and personnel for cardiology fellowships. Although the program never resulted in many papers, it contrasted with the other clinical departments where research was seldom discussed.

Figure 6.2   Proportion of Acceptors Among Physicians Classified According to Department

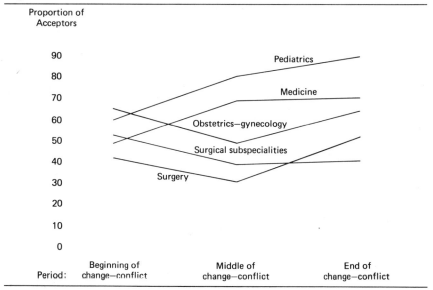

The attitudes of the physicians by clinical department, contained in Figure 6.2, support the connection between program change rate and acceptance of new specialties. There were no changes in the department of surgical subspecialties, yet this department shows the most resistance to assistant D.M.E.'s In experimental terms, this department can be considered our control group. The surgery department, even with the teaching ward crisis, has a higher rate of acceptance at the end of the period of change. These differences are much greater than they appear to be. As can be seen from Figure 6.2, the proportion of specialists is much lower in the department of surgery than in the surgical subspecialties. While the pediatrics department had twice as many specialists as medicine, its rate of acceptance was not as high as one would expect. If work patterns completely determined acceptance rates, the proportion in the department of medicine would be about one-half that of pediatrics. Because the medical department had a history of change during the decade prior to the hiring of Dr. Bacon, it was more prepared to accept various aspects of the Butler plan. For the same reason, ob-gyn could accept changes more readily than could surgery. This also explains why the surgical department could be, after a period of conflict, more accepting of the change plan in general and of the assistant D.M.E.'s in particular.

How can program change itself increase the likelihood of acceptance of change, especially radical changes, such as, the addition of assistant D.M.E.'s? One of the reasons why program change can become more acceptable is that as men become aware of the positive benefits, they are more willing to pay the price of progress. *The feedback of information about the consequences of these changes reduces fears about change.* (For another instance of this, see Colombotos, 1969.) Unfortunately, many of these positive benefits are slow to be recognized. The addition of new specialties means conflicts over the definition of the work style. Power and status struggles are usually the *first* consequences to emerge, as is clear from Chapter 5. Later, as other results become more visible, the costs involved do not appear to be as great as previously imagined. Toward the end of the second year of implementation, nearly a full quota of American-trained interns arrived, a rarity for a community hospital with training programs. While this consequence had been anticipated by some physicians, especially the medical specialists, the arrival of a full house staff made the new specialists much more desirable in the eyes of the professionals, except for the surgical subspecialists; this department did not receive any new house staff, and, therefore, showed no visible benefits.

Then, too, as time passed, the consequences of specialization for quality care and education became more apparent. In the third set of interviews, many more physicians stated that they thought there were positive benefits for the hospital than had been the case previously. Only the general practitioners on the surgical services did not change their perception of the consequences of the addition of assistant D.M.E.'s for patient care and medical education. The other physicians were more likely to perceive improvement in the functioning of the organization.

Other evidence to support the reasoning that change itself increases the acceptance of change was the alteration of tone of the interviews during the three waves. The hostility of the active staff appeared to decline during the second year. If, in the beginning, there were much concern about authority and status, in the end most of the objections were centered about the waste of money. Only the surgical subspe-cialists, who were the only department without clinical full-time teachers, still talked about consultations. The other physicians had learned through direct experience that their worst fears were not justified, and, thus, became more tolerant. The gradual recognition of positive consequences can have an ameliorative effect on resistance, but waiting for it requires patience, a quality which the new special-ists did not possess—perhaps precisely because they were innovators! *The feedback of information about the consequences of the change both for the functioning of the hospital, its impact on patient care, and the authority and status of the active staff, leads to attitude change.* Cybernetics and its ideas of steering across time forces us into a more dynamic perspective of how attitudes are formed and shaped and altered across time. While this idea is a very simple one, almost simplistic, it has been largely absent from many studies of attitude change. Likewise an absence of longitudinal studies makes it difficult to perceive this kind of feedback operating. And yet here as in the previous chapter we see information feedback working to regulate the organization. In the previous chapter we saw examples of how it dampened change; here we see it operating to bring about the necessary attitude changes that would make more change pos-sible. The irony is that both processes were occurring simultaneously.

CONCLUSIONS: DIFFERENTIAL ACCEPTANCE OF PROFESSIONAL CONTROL

We have drawn a portrait of two kinds of professional men. The one continues to learn because he reads and, in solving various client problems, he is quick to consult. What is especially striking is his emphasis on communication, both volume and quality. This profes-sional sees the need for continual socialization. Education is a life-time activity. Not unexpectedly, a person who accepts new specialties and their attempts to increase socialization and feedback can appre-ciate its necessity, and therefore accepts various mechanisms that will insure its exercise.

The professional who learns by experience and prefers to assume total responsibility cannot see the need for more control because he does not perceive that he makes errors. Likewise, his creed is practice makes perfect, and thus, the lesser need for new knowledge. Inevitably, he fights against the addition of specialists and socialization and feedback mechanisms. He sees them as unnecessary and as an infringement on his authority and status. What is thought provoking is that professionals are predisposed on the basis of their work towards one or the other perspectives.

Likewise, the environmental situation, in this instance the professional departments, affects the willingness of professionals to accept changes, including increased socialization. The more changes there have been, the more the professionals can accept, even changes they do not like, because they had received feedback of information and know as a consequence the changes were less than feared. Apparently, experience does lessen the magnitude of the resistance. If this were not so, professionals could not survive in a world that is changing ever more rapidly.

We must not lose sight of the fact that one kind of professional control mechanism, namely, the development of various kinds of rounds, was generally the most acceptable to all concerned. We might have anticipated that socialization is always a more readily appreciated control device than sanctions, especially with professionals. We have already suggested that no elite likes to discipline itself. Therefore, any proposal for increased professional control is likely to meet with more success if the accent is on communication and not on rewards and, especially, punishments. Readings and consultations are but special cases of this, as are grand rounds and teaching rounds. Thus, there is a fit between the kind of professional and the kind of professional control processes he is willing to accept. The process of specialization, or what Parsons (1966), Blau and Schoenherr (1971) have called structural differentiation, means that all professionals are becoming specialists and thus more and more like our first professional portrait, the image of cybernetic man.

VII

An Organic State of Stability

THE PERIOD OF CHANGE and the causes of conflict have both been analyzed. Throughout our analysis, we have found the concepts of feedback and socialization helpful in understanding how the change process came to an end at the same time that attitudes towards change were becoming more positive. The hospital had experienced a period of instability but equilibrium was beginning to emerge, as we noted at the end of Chapter 5. Now we report what this new state of equilibrium looked like.

First, however, we shall discuss in some detail how this new stability was achieved. Our theory of cybernetic control suggests that the period of instability was explained by the simultaneous appearance of a high score on complexity and on centralization. Under these circumstances, the organization can go to a new state of stability via several pathways, our concept of equifinality. The score on complexity could be lowered through the simple mechanism of the firing of the new medical specialists, especially the full-time teachers. This was, by the way, under active consideration by the administration, and the full-time teachers fully expected it. The pediatrics full-time teacher was, in fact, reduced from full-time to half-time after the crisis in that department. The other option was that the system of variables—that is, centralization, stratification, communications, and so on—itself could alter, an example of a moving equilibrium process. This had actually been occurring and was in fact one latent reason why the hospital administration did not fire the specialists. The altered structural situation, the changes in the distribution of power and of status, made this appear less necessary. Although again, the participants were largely unaware of these changes since they occurred day-by-day.

But there were more fundamental reasons as to why the administration did not fire the specialists. The emerging channels of horizontal communication and the increased volume of communication produced for a variety of reasons meant that the administration was now receiving feedback and being socialized. Without their realizing it, the administrators had become committed to quality patient care and had become convinced that this could only be achieved with the kind of medical-education program envisaged in the Butler plan. What they were not convinced of was whether they had the right people for the job. Just as the other groups in the hospital, the administration was part of this moving equilibrium process, and were swept along by it towards an organic state of stability. Now we must specify what this means.

SOCIAL STRUCTURE: HIGH COMPLEXITY AND DECENTRALIZATION OF POWER

The Degree of Complexity

It is obvious that Community Hospital became structurally more differentiated by the addition of four assistant D.M.E.'s in each of the major clinical departments and in the four medical subspecialties of hematology, endocrinology, cardiology, and infectious diseases. What is less obvious is that the division of labor became much more specialized in a number of areas. The house staff, or doctors in training as interns and residents, the active staff, and the laboratory staff were all affected.

The greatest changes in the division of labor occurred among the house staff. As the department of medical education was able to recruit more and more interns or doctors taking their practicum after medical school, the assistant D.M.E.'s decreased the number of residents (as can be noted in Table 7.1), that is, doctors studying a specialty of medicine and more particularly, the number of senior (third- and fourth-year) residents. The differentiation in work between the interns and the first- and second-year residents increased, so that there was a considerable change in activities as the house staff advanced through levels of training. Before the arrival of the full-time teachers, there was little or no variation between these years of house staff training. Correspondingly, the senior house staff began to assume more and more responsibility for the teaching and supervision of the junior house staff.

We have already noted in Chapter 5 that the definition of the responsibilities of the attending physicians altered as well, but it was not made clear that this varied by practice. Specialists were used for teaching rounds, while general practitioners were not, thus increasingly differentiated the work of the specialist and the generalist. The differential implementation of the Butler plan meant that this varied by department as well.

Table 7.1   The Increase in American-Trained House Staff Occurred First Among Medical Residents and Then Among the Interns[a]

House Staff[b]	Dr. Bacon's Arrival		Year Initiation		Implementation Years			
					First Year		Second Year	
	Total	American	Total	American	Total	American	Total	American
Medical residents	8	1	9	1	11	8	8	7
Pediatric residents	6	3	8	3	9	3	7	1
Ob-gyn residents	4	3	5	3	7	6	6	5
Interns	16	1	6	5	6	5	15	10
Total	34	8	28	12	33	22	36	23

[a] American-trained interns are considered to be better trained than interns from foreign medical schools. One of the major differences is that American-trained house staff is likely to have much more practical experience in various diagnostic tests.

[b] There was only one surgical resident in any year. The cardiac fellows have also been eliminated.

The medical subspecialists, especially those in the clinical laboratories, assumed administration of the laboratories. They trained specific laboratory personnel in specialized tests and procedures, and thus increased the degree of occupational specialization in this department of the hospital.

The increases in the division of labor by the addition of new specialists frequently meant the addition and not the subtraction of specific responsibilities for particular kinds of physicians and paramedical personnel. The specialists became involved in more teaching than previously. Since most sociologists tend to think of specialization as a narrowing, this finding has a great deal of interest (Caplow, 1954). If true for other professional occupations as well, then it means that greater and greater scope is demanded of the occupants of the new and old specialties as they achieve greater depth in a particular branch of knowledge. To put it in other terms, as one becomes a specialist, his job description becomes more complex, and not less so.

This may be one of the reasons that propel specialists in general to become more concerned about feedback and socialization. As their work becomes more complex, they perceive the necessity of having various measures of how well they are doing. Likewise, they feel the greater necessity for continued learning. As work becomes more complex, involving a variety of tasks, the professional can see the total process more clearly.

The Degree of Centralization

As a consequence of its many changes and conflicts, Community Hospital developed a network of power and authority. *The distribution of power became much more decentralized as a consequence of the addition of new medical specialties.* (See Figure 7.1.) The surgeons and the chief of staff did not lose a great deal of power; instead, they now had to share power with the administration and thus, the two chains of command, the basic coordination problem of community hospitals, was largely solved. The administration was equal in power to the executive committee. The house staff had as much power as the attending physicians. The department of medical edu-

Figure 7.1 Power and Communications Structure in Community Hospital.

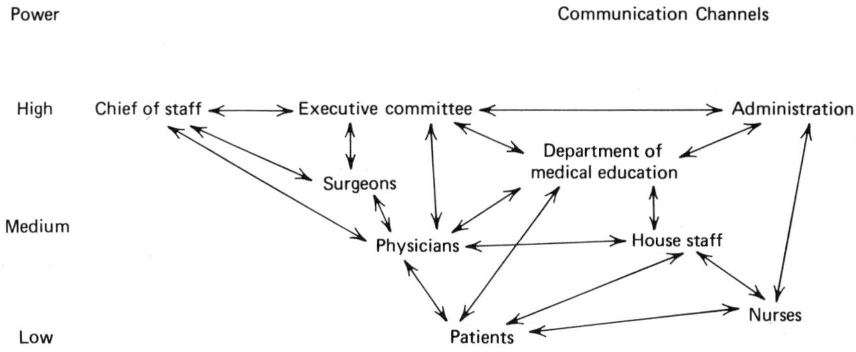

Power   Communication Channels

cation was on a par with the surgeons. This movement toward decentralization would appear to be an inevitable consequence of the addition of new specialists, especially specialists with long training, because they will demand some power for themselves in the operation of the organization, just as the assistant D.M.E.'s did. *What was unanticipated in the Butler plan was that the struggle of the new medical specialists and teachers for power would improve the relative position of other groups, especially that of the administration.*

The authority and influence of Dr. Bacon, as an individual and as Director of Medical Education, started rising with the arrival of the specialists. It rose steadily during the first year. Correspondingly, the power of the medical-education department rose steadily. The perception of the full-time teachers, however, was that they did not have enough power; Dr. Bacon continually lamented his lack of authority. Objectively, however, the department of medical education obtained many of its requests despite the opposition of specific groups. This is indeed the standard definition of power: Can one get what he wants despite opposition (Weber, 1947; also Mechanic, 1962)? By this meaning of the word "power," the department of medical education's star was rising, despite its many setbacks.

There were several factors that tended to increase the power of the department of medical education. First, the administration was growing more resistant to the executive committee's lack of interest in the hospital. Therefore, criticism of the ruling group of surgeons won a sympathetic ear with the nuns. Second, the many abuses of power by some of the physicians made them ripe for criticism. Their lack of control was becoming more and more obvious, in part, because of the changing patterns of communication, a point to be discussed below. Third, the new specialists were physicians themselves and therefore, could make suggestions about rules and regulations affecting doctors. Fourth, the new specialists appeared to have the better purposes; they had the constitution of the hospital on their side. Their interest in improving the quality of patient care and medical education was in sharp contrast to the requests of some attendings, who were concerned about the amount of money they made. The administrator once said: "I think the average doctor is only concerned about his pocketbook and doesn't care about the patient." All these factors increased the administration's support of the department of medical education despite its unpopularity with the executive committee.

Why should the full-time teachers perceive that they had no power, when, in fact, they did? A major reason is that they kept wanting to have as much power as a chief of service or professor of medicine in a university hospital. This was their reference for evaluating their own authority (Merton, 1957, Chapter 8). What the members of the department of medical education did not appreciate was that as Community Hospital itself became more decentralized, they themselves would not have complete control over the medical-education program. They had to share power with other groups, especially the physicians; this the assistant D.M.E.'s perceived as little or no power, even in matters regarding medical education, with each group setting checks on the other.

The most important alteration in the power structure was not the addition of the department of medical education but the altered balance of power between the executive committee and the administration. The former's power steadily diminished while the latter's increased. As conflicts developed between the full-time teachers and the physicians of the active staff, particularly the senior attendings, both of them deferred to the sister administrator to resolve the impasse. The consequence was an increase in her influence, and, thereby, the administration's power. This increase in her power meant that checks were now being placed on the power of both the chief of staff and the executive committee.

Perhaps the clearest and best indicator of the increased power of both the administration and the department of medical education was the conflict between Dr. Shore and the pediatricians described earlier. Although the pediatric attendings gave an ultimatum that either Dr. Shore leave or they would leave, they were forced to accept Dr. Shore's continued presence. The administration was, by far, the one that gained the most from this power test. Nonetheless, it had the consequence of making the department of medical education believe that it had no power.

These alterations in the power structure did not go unnoticed, and, as might be expected, the most vocal in opposition were the surgeons. One surgical subspecialist had this to say:

> If the administration of Community Hospital has in mind making the hospital a teaching university-affiliated institution, they should do so after making this intention known.

One general practitioner commented:

> I deplore the fact that the policy of the hospital has been geared to alienate the services as well as the opinion of the attending staff. I feel the administration is going over the head of regular channels which would provide means of policy determination by members of the attending staff. We are not being consulted on important matters that deal with education or training of house staff. . . . I would like to see closer rapport between the regular attending and the administration.

The alteration of the power distribution in Community Hospital also affected the house staff; their power steadily rose. The department of medical education brought many of the interns' and resident's requests to the administration and effectively pleaded for them. The assistant D.M.E.'s were concerned about obtaining a full complement of American-trained interns, and, therefore, supported many of the house staff's demands. The house staff's salaries and fringe benefits were increased and their housing improved. Perhaps the most significant change was the reduction in the number of patients assigned per intern and resident. Coverage was limited to 20 beds per intern because the full-time teachers felt that this would ensure the recruitment of a full quota of house-staff physicians. The executive committee opposed the change but it was overruled.

Another major reason for the realignment of power was the series of role, power, and status conflicts engendered by the addition of the assistant D.M.E.'s Each conflict between them and the active staff resulted in a number of extra organizational meetings in which each professional and managerial group had an opportunity to discuss its differences. At these meetings, the administration was usually placed in the position of having to make the decision, and, therefore, was tacitly given authority. Whenever two professional groups reached a stalemate, as the department of medical education and the active staff did on several occasions, the outside party gained considerable power as a consequence. In Community Hospital, the administration was the beneficiary.

In Community Hospital, *the power relationships moved closer to the authority structure as outlined by the constitution by the end of the implementation stage.* (See Figure 4.2.) Sociologists have noted the differences between the formal and informal authority structures. It would seem that when the informal power relationships are upset by the introduction of new social positions, especially if they have some power, the direction of alteration is toward the formal configuration. The formal authority structure represents the foundation. When conflicts occur, these positions or occupations with formal authority are most likely to profit.

PROCESSES OF COORDINATION AND CONTROL

The most striking changes in the pattern of control was the movement toward a network of communication and the proliferation of a number of mechanisms of professional control. (See Table 7.2.) Perhaps more importantly, control began to be exercised in some areas more than in others as a consequence of the new social structure.

Sanctions and Socialization

The institution of grand rounds and the attempts to increase attendance, especially in medicine, meant that there was much more education of both the house staff and the active staff, at least for those who attended. Since the house staff was required to attend, they were

Table 7.2   Mechanisms of Sanctions and Socialization: Physicians Affected

	House Staff	Active Staff
Mechanisms of Socialization		
Teaching ward service	Medical residents	Internists
Daily teaching rounds	All	All departments except surgical subspecialties
Weekly grand rounds	All	Medical, pediatrics, and ob-gyn departments
Subspecialty rounds	All	Mainly medical and pediatric departments
Lectures	All	Medical, pediatrics, ands ob-gyn departments
Morning report	Medical and ob-gyn residents	Medical and ob-gyn departments
Mechanisms of Sanction[a]		
Effective committees	None	None
Discharge for violations of regulations	None	None

[a] No attempts to change this except for this tumor board, but it provides a basis of comparison.

receiving stimulation from these conferences. Difficult patient cases were discussed, and, once a month, deaths were analyzed. Thus, there was a continued channel of communication for both feedback —what went wrong—and socialization—how it could be prevented.

The addition of full-time teachers resulted in a considerable increase in the direct socialization of the house staff and the indirect socialization of the active staff. Perhaps the most significant aspect of the education program for the house staff was its regularity. Lectures, rounds, journal clubs were scheduled and well attended.

The apprenticeship system of education for the house staff that had existed previously was replaced. The interns and residents, especially those on the medical services, were being exposed to a variety of physicians. In addition, the active staff was being socialized via the house staff and their recommendations for therapy. When a physician conducting teaching rounds discovered that some test or treatment appeared to be more appropriate, the house staff would make the recommendation, and, in the process, the private physician whose case it was would learn about patient care or some new development.

Perhaps the most significant change was increased supervision of both the active and house staffs. Through teaching and grand rounds, the patient was being provided with continual checks on the quality of his care. Patients admitted during evening hours were given immediate histories and physicals; there was a sense of urgency. Residents worked every third night, interns every other night, even though the size of the house staff had increased. The house staff was supervised by both the assistant D.M.E.'s and the medical subspecialists in the clinics and on the wards independently of teaching rounds, grand rounds, and morning reports. Most of the regulations dealing with the clinical laboratories were obeyed, and the techniques were supervised by the medical subspecialists.

Yet, many of the mechanisms for sanctioning the active staff still were not operative. The committees (tissue, records, and credential) were as ineffective as before. But since there were teaching rounds on most of the physicians' private patients, the effectiveness of the committees was no longer important. An alternative mechanism of professional control was now operating.

The full-time teachers gave many free consultations to the active staff in the hospital's corridors or on the telephone. The medical subspecialists were more frequently used for consultations than the assistant D.M.E.'s. The house staff referred active staff to the medical subspecialists as well. Since the house staff did the histories and physicals and followed the progress of the disease, they frequently made suggestions for particular tests or drugs.

These changes were mentioned by the physicians. One internist said:

> Residents teach me things because they have time to read articles and can offer good suggestions. Medicine changes all the time, and these boys can be of help.

A pediatrician supported the idea:

> It's stimulating to men who have private patients here. Every doctor needs stimulation now and then or they get into a rut.

A general practitioner in the ob-gyn department said:

> They [the house staff] seem to want to take over the case. If you don't give them the case, then on the next one, they don't give their full cooperation. They want a favor in return for every favor they do. . . .

If the resident says it isn't necessary to use forceps, he'll tell the nurse not to get them.

One senior attending in surgery commented:

> I'd like them [the house staff] to be more considerate of the attending staff. We're not stupid. We've been educated too. We naturally have had a lot of experience, especially on private cases. They should realize that the doctor who sends the patient in is responsible. They should have more respect for us.

Professional control was greater on medicine than in any of the other departments because there were more full-time teachers and they controlled the morning report. In ob-gyn, where the full-time teacher also took morning reports, his impact on patient care was greater. In pediatrics, the full-time teacher gave fewer suggestions because he did not control the morning report, nor did he participate in teaching rounds, so there was less opportunity to make them. But even here, the full-time teacher was asked by the house staff about specific patient problems. In surgery, there was no house staff to speak of—usually one or two interns—and the full-time teacher had much less of an impact on patient care.

Following Burns and Stalker (1961), we would call socialization a network of control because behavior is regulated via a chain of social relationships, from specialist to intern or resident to attending physician. Furthermore, it clearly did not involve discipline. There were no sanctions.

As we have defined sanctions, they include praise or blame, and the house staff was usually very careful not to give this kind of sanction. Since they were doctors in training they ostensibly did not have the authority or status to do so. How important the social approval of those who are lower in authority and status is to those who have higher rank is hard to say. Certainly the pediatric crisis was in part due to the pediatricians' feeling that their residents were critical of what they were doing. But it should be noted that their response was to eliminate or try to eliminate the full-time teacher, blaming him for their problems with the residents. In general, social approval does not seem to have played much of a factor in the other three departments. To be sure of this, one would have to have more sophisticated measures than were available at the time of this study.

What is certain is that the residents and interns were not criticizing the physicians. Likewise and for a wide variety of reasons, in grand rounds, criticism was not made or blame laid. Instead, everyone attempted to understand what had gone wrong. These differences may appear to be small but the difference between verbalizing criticism and not verbalizing it is enormous. The difficulties in pediatrics also indicate how important it is not to verbalize criticism when dealing with professionals.

Although this point is perhaps overstressed, it may be worth mentioning again that the key is the sheer volume of communication. As this increases—and here we are only discussing communication relative to work—its content is less and less likely to contain rewards and punishments and more and more to contain discussions of what is happening or feedback, and, the learning of new information, or socialization. As is well known, to increase the rate of rewards—whether praise, salary increases, or promotions—is to diminish its importance (Homans, 1961). An increase in the volume of communication does not mean a corresponding increase in the amount of praise but represents more and more information feedback and socialization.

Feedback and Standardization

Just as professional control became a matter of social network, primarily horizontal communication channels rather than vertical ones, so did coordination. Medical care was much more coordinated. But this is not the only place where greater coordination occurred. High feedback, as represented in higher volumes of communication, especially horizontal communication networks, developed between the professions, especially the two major hierarchies of authority, medical and administrative.

One unintended consequence of the Butler plan was that the hospital became more coordinated after the addition of the new specialists. Paradoxically, the increased structural differentiation led to higher feedback, and in turn, much better coordination between various departments, both professional and administrative, than had existed before (Landsberger, 1961). New pathways of communication were opened up which had an impact on the power structure

(McCleery, 1957). The key to all this was the department of medical education.

With the arrival of new specialists, Dr. Bacon created the department of medical education. Since each assistant D.M.E. and medical subspecialist was in a different section of the hospital, the weekly meetings of this department resulted in a pooling of information about the hospital, especially in matters pertaining to patient care and medical education. This was unexpected. The purpose of these meetings was to plan changes, thus they might be considered meetings leading to more conflict and instability. In fact, however, they helped to mitigate the fractionalization created by professional and administrative departments with power in the hands of a single group, the surgeons. In many instances, conflicts between departments were resolved by the new specialists without the knowledge of the chief of service, chief of staff, or the sister administrator. For example, questionable lab tests on a particular patient were passed directly to Dr. Fine, or one of the assistant D.M.E.'s might be recommended as a consultant. When the chief of department or a senior attending could not understand why another department had a particular problem or difficulty, the assistant D.M.E. would explain it. In this way, the barriers between departments were gradually broken down. At the same time, this meant increased power for the department of medical education.

One major consequence of the realignment of power was that new horizontal and vertical communication pathways were added. In the process, the administrators learned much more about the operation of their own hospital, especially about the behavior of the physicians. They started to ask questions and attempted to evaluate seriously the recommendations of various occupational groups within the hospital. Similarly, the active and house staff gained a better insight into the problems of the administration, and this encouraged a spirit of cooperation.

THE PRIMARY GOAL: QUALITY PATIENT CARE

Along with the changes in the power structure among the active staff, house staff, department of medical education, and administration, there was a reallocation of resources. The full-time teachers made many requests for space, equipment, and personnel. Because most of their requests were granted, other physicians lost some of their resources, and, implicitly, status in the process. Each new office provided for the full-time teachers was usually at the expense of the nurses. To pay for the increased costs of house staff, the hospital reduced the number of employees in many of the administrative departments. The administration assigned part of the animal rooms to the medical subspecialists despite the opposition of the thoracic surgeons. The purchase of the equipment for the research of the medical subspecialists resulted in a considerable expense for the hospital.

Prior to the arrival of the specialists, a large proportion of the hospital's funds were allocated to the department of cardiology. By the end of the two years of specialist activity, more hospital income was being allocated to medical education and patient care in areas other than cardiology. The number of salaried personnel in the department of cardiology was reduced and the hospital did not continue to purchase large amounts of cardiology equipment. Instead, the administration bought radioisotope equipment and laboratory equipment for infectious diseases, hematology, and endocrinology. They allocated some of their space and money to the department of medical education. The administration paid for the establishment of an intensive-care unit and the remodeling of some wards. The consequence was a more even distribution of resources among the various departments of the hospital.

Perhaps the largest reallocation of resources occurred within the house staff. The monthly pay of the interns had been increased from $145 per month to $250 per month. The residents' salaries were also increased. The hospital provided much more modern quarters in a new apartment building within several blocks of the hospital. The administration also paid for the patient care of some gynecological charity patients in order to increase the variety of teaching material available. In addition, on the medical service, 20 beds had been set aside for the purposes of providing a teaching-ward service.

The presence of the house staff and full-time teachers had resulted in an increase in the number of patient tests ordered per patient; there was a 25 percent increase in the three years. While it meant both a more intensive medical-education program and probably better patient care, it also meant increased costs.

The hospital also paid for a private physician to help in the emergency room and another to do histories and physicals on the surgical services on those patients not covered by the house staff. The administration reviewed the personnel in each department and eliminated a few positions in order to reduce costs to pay for these changes.

During the years prior to the initiation of the medical specialists, the purpose of self-maintenance had been the primary focus of the administration. *By the end of the change and conflict period, patient care and medical education assumed much greater priority.* The administration supported the full-time teachers in many instances even though they believed that the hospital was losing patients as a consequence. Although it is extremely difficult to document whether the hospital actually was losing patients as a result of the full-time teachers and the changes they introduced, the important point is that the administration felt that this was the case. In fact, the administration told Dr. Bacon this on more than one occasion; therefore, this social belief became real in its consequences. Despite this belief, the administration went ahead with specific changes.

In some instances, the administration approved changes which placed the objective of education above that of patient care. For example, they approved of the restriction of 20 beds per intern even though it meant some patients would not be covered. At the same time, the administration attempted to maintain patient coverage by hiring physicians to do histories. The priorities changed from maintenance, patient care, education, and research to patient care, education, maintenance, and research. The problem of weighing long-term versus short-term objectives remained. The administration learned that it was sometimes worthwhile to take a temporary loss in achievement of one objective by emphasizing another goal with the hope that, in the long run, more could be accomplished for the first objective. This was exactly the situation with the policy decision about the bed restriction for interns. The hope was that, in the long run, patient care would improve if education were given top priority. At the same time, the administration used several tactics to prevent the primary goal from suffering too much, again indicating its primary importance and attempts at balance. When the increase in American-trained interns occurred, the administration was happy with their gamble and continued the policy of bed restrictions despite many complaints from the surgeons, surgical subspecialists, and even the chief of staff. *This would suggest that, generally, multiple-objective organizations must, at times, overemphasize secondary goals at the expense of even the primary objective in order to prevent long-term losses for their primary goal.*

The emphasis on education during the period of change to the detriment of patient care would seem to have had many positive consequences in the long run for patient care. This also demonstrates how social purposes, to a certain degree, can be reinforcing. At the same time, the objectives of maintenance and patient service tend to be incompatible, as the above examples illustrate. Paradoxically, while some social goals are mutually reinforcing or mutually incompatible, an overemphasis on one goal for too long a period of time will result in the lack of realization of any goal, including the one being emphasized. It seems likely that if self-maintenance had always won in any goal conflict, eventually there would have been no house staff. Gradually many of the physicians would have left, resulting in a considerable loss of income (the lack of self-maintenance). Indeed, this took place in a community hospital with training programs, in Brooklyn, New York, in the 1960s.

The conflicts precipitated by the different attempts to exert professional control proposed by the department of medical education had forced the three major power and occupational groups—medical educators, senior attendings, and administrators—to have contact with each other (cf. Greenblatt, York, and Brown, 1955, for a study of emerging consensus, but as a consequence of planned conferences). In the many meetings created by the surgical teaching-ward crisis, especially the pediatric crisis toward the end of the period of change, these three groups achieved much more unanimity of objective. *Instead of each group pursuing its own specialized goals, there were now two common unifying collective objectives—patient care and medical education.* A paradox is that conflict made the major power groups realize that there were inherent differences in purposes, or latent conflicts over objectives. Once realized, the mechanisms of communication were established and these latent conflicts could be resolved. Out of this resolution emerged a concensus about organizational priorities.

CONCLUSIONS: THE STEADY STATE OF ORGANIC STABILITY

The increase in mechanisms of professional control presumably had a considerable impact on the quality of patient care. This impact was differential—greatest in medicine, less so in pediatrics and ob-gyn, little in surgery, and not at all in the surgical subspecialties. *The less impact in surgery indicates that the addition of a new professional specialty is not enough. Without students, continued socialization is blocked.* Without teaching rounds or morning reports with house staff, the amount of control is lessened, even though the teacher can arrange a series of lectures and provide free consultations, and, thus, to a limited extent, educate.

Since the clinical full-time teachers did not have much authority, they could not enforce attendance at teaching or grand rounds by the active staff; their effect was differential, even within specific departments, such as medicine. The full-time teachers most effectively reached those who sent patients to the hospital. The fewer the patients the physician sent to the hospital, the less effect the new specialists had on the physician since the number of opportunities for the passage of information either directly or indirectly, through the house staff, was decreased. At the same time, the increased knowledge should have had an impact on the doctor's patient care, both in the office and in the other hospitals to which he sent patients.

The lack of authority also meant that a number of changes which would have resulted in increased professional control were not made, such as regularly scheduled tumor board meetings, the establishment of a surgical teaching-ward service, or participation of attendings in teaching rounds and clinics. But could any professional specialists have been added without some restrictions on their power? We do not know the answer, but certainly the initial bargain resulted in the diminishing of the ultimate objective.

In summary, Community Hospital had evolved toward the organic model as tabulated in Chapter 2. The addition of the new specialties had precipitated increased specialization in other occupations of the hospital. Power was more decentralized, and many mechanisms of control via socialization had been added. Some of these resulted in more effectiveness, that is, better patient care, but only when there was house-staff coverage. *A network of communication resulted in better coordination of the disparate interests and the emergence of some consensus regarding organizational goals. This emerged because of the many conflicts over power and status, as well as the changes in the patterns of power and authority.* Thus, while much conflict and instability arose as the price of change, it would seem that there were some other beneficial consequences of the stormy evolution from a more mechanical social structure towards an organic steady state.

As we have suggested previously, the story of Community Hospital can best be seen as illustrative of the cybernetic theory of coordination and of control. The order of changes in the variables is clear even if the measures of these variables was not as precise as one would desire. It is striking that the arrival of specialists resulted in attempts to change the distribution of power. While the specialists were only interested in increasing their own power, the structural consequence was not the replacement of one elite by another but a decentralization of the power structure to include several groups.

Horizontal pathways of communication, created by the specialists, resulted in much better coordination, which, in turn, led to an emerging consensus. What is interesting is that these pathways were at first mainly at the lower echelons of the medical power structure. Likewise, the inevitable power, status, and role conflicts themselves also led to much more effort at establishing new communication pathways among the higher echelons as well. Again, this resulted in greater coordination by higher feedback via what Burns and Stalker (1961) would call a network of communication.

Parallel to the development of higher feedback for the purposes of coordination came the emergence of more feedback for the purposes of control. Indeed, it is somewhat difficult to separate the two levels of analysis. The various mechanisms of socialization have applicability to a wide variety of professional organizations which both educate and provide service for clients.

One of the more surprising findings is that the addition of new specialists meant more complex jobs for many of those who interacted with them. This occurred with the house staff, the active staff, and the laboratory staff. *In general, we might say that, as structural differentiation occurs, not only do organizations have more a complex division of labor, but many occupations become themselves more complex in the process.*

Therefore, an organic steady state is one in which there is high complexity, decentralization, high communication, and low sanctions. There is consensus about organizational priorities. The greater concern is over quality care, which parallels or mirrors the process control system. If the process of structural differentiation occurs slowly, then the organization, as reflected by the scores on the variables defining the system, can move towards the organic steady state with its increasing emphasis on feedback and socialization without difficulty.

The history of Community Hospital suggests that the maximum period of instability is when the struggle concerns the rights and responsibilities of the new professional specialties vis-à-vis other professional positions in the social structure. We might fruitfully describe this as a period when there is increased specialization without a corresponding decline in centralization; the result is heightened conflict or instability. To put it in other terms, mechanical and organic steady states are defined by the hypothesis that increasing specialization leads to decentralization of power. When there is *an exception* to the hypothesis, there is instability. Needless to say, the resolution of the problem can occur by the specialists leaving, as well as the decentralization of the power structure; both exist as possibilities.

Our theory of cybernetic control helps us understand how stability is achieved. In Community Hospital, when the pediatric crisis occurred—a period of intense conflict—the immediate organizational response was heightened communication rates, which, in turn, gradually led to a resolution of the conflict, or at least its diminishment, quite precisely what Ashby (1956, Chapter 12) means by cybernetic control. This is perhaps the best proof that conflict is one variable that almost everyone wants kept within certain limits; it is a homeostatic variable. Community Hospital illustrates how increases in the mechanisms of control and of coordination reduce conflict as well.

Another homeostatic variable would appear to be deviance. At least some physicians, namely, the new specialists, insisted upon conformity to certain rules—attendance at grand rounds being perhaps the most significant.

In contrast, the shift from a concern about quantity care to a concern about quality care is a change in standard. It refers to what is best seen as a moving-equilibrium problem. There is always some concern about quality. The key question is how much. As is suggested in this case study, specialists are more likely to be concerned, and, in turn, their proportion in the division of labor means a shifting emphasis in the quality of service.

Since this has been a single longitudinal study, although an approximation to an experiment, we cannot be certain that the same sequence of events will always occur. In general, comparative research has not focused on periods of instability. (A recent exception is Corwin, 1969.) The few case studies that report the addition of new specialists (mainly McCleery, 1957) indicate the same instability has occurred in other kinds of organizations that handle clients *when* professional specialization has taken place. A few personal reports of universities during the same process imply the same findings (see Hage and Aiken, 1970, Chapter 3). Community Hospital does not appear to be an isolated instance.

Although the addition of horizontal communications and an increase in communication volume reduced conflict, it cannot be said that Community Hospital was never in a state of instability. If the organization had been well coordinated and controlled, the conflict would not have occurred in the first place. What the history of Community Hospital demonstrates is that given instability, vigorous attempts will be made to return to a steady state. Otherwise, the organization would cease to exist as its various members left. Again, it is worth observing that this is only true for major group conflicts.

Another lesson to be learned concerns the critical organizational role of communication networks and the emphasis on horizontal pathways. In the end, high feedback proved to be most practical, given various professional norms, to say nothing of the various struggles for power.

Finally, our case study has rapidly accelerated the normal processes of evolution, or what is called moving equilibrium—the movement from a mechanical to an organic structure. While there was a period of anomic instability, this state as well as the mechanical and organic states are described by the same hypotheses. This is the vital connection between any theory and its casting in the terminology of cybernetics.

PART TWO

A TEST OF A CYBERNETIC THEORY
OF COORDINATION AND
CONTROL: A COMPARATIVE
STUDY OF ORGANIZATIONS
WITH VARIOUS STATES
OF STABILITY

VIII

A Research Design for Testing a Cybernetic Theory

ALTHOUGH A CASE STUDY can be insightful and even necessary to illustrate a theory, it does not provide an exacting test. The predicted associations among complexity, centralization, and communications may not hold in organizations other than that of Community Hospital. Since many of the reported findings were observed rather than measured by rigorous methods, the nagging doubt remains that another observer may have seen something else. Therefore, one objective is to develop measures that can be used in a variety of organizations. In this chapter, considerable attention is given to measures of general communication and horizontal communication volume. As part of this effort, some attention is also paid to the issue of how one would measure a communications network. This seems to be an important task because the word has been frequently employed but not operationalized in the context of organizations.

The findings reported in this part of the monograph are part of a much larger comparative study being conducted by Michael Aiken and myself (Aiken and Hage, 1966, 1968, and 1970; Hage and Aiken, 1967a and b, and 1970). We have been also helped by the insightful comments of our former research assistant, Cora Bagley Marrett.

THE METHODS OF RESEARCH

The data for testing the cybernetic theory was gathered in 16 social welfare and rehabilitation organizations located in a large midwestern metropolis in 1967. These agencies were all the larger welfare organizations that provided psychiatric and rehabilitation services, as defined by the directory of the Community Chest. There are three mental hospitals, three residential treatment homes, three rehabilitation centers, six case-work agencies, and a department of special education in the public schools. Ten of these organizations are private, six are publicly supported.

Each of these 16 organizations is different from Community Hospital, yet they are clearly within the health and welfare field. Many of them were tangentially involved in teaching, and some were attached to medical schools. Most typically, the training programs involved social workers. The mental hospitals had programs for nurses, residences in psychiatry, and, in some of the specialized rehabilitation occupations such as occupational therapy. The mental hospital was not the only kind of organization affiliated with a medical school. One of the sheltered workshops was affiliated with a school and carried on a very active research program as well as a wide variety of training programs. In summary, all these organizations provided client service, and many combined training programs as well. A few were actually affiliated with graduate schools of social work or medicine. Thus, the differences between these organizations, at least as being multipurposive and concerned with rehabilitation in the broadest sense, and Community Hospital are probably less than their similarities. Greater variety is likely to be found in business organizations, government bureaus, and research institutes.

Since there are so many organizations, not as much detail about each can be provided. Two of the three mental hospitals were very much like Community Hospital in terms of size, division of labor, and general ecological layout. All three were housed in a number of different buildings. Their staffs consisted not only of physicians—for the most part psychiatrists—but nurses, attendants, occupational therapists, social workers, dieticians, food handling, and house cleaning staffs. The size of the staffs ranged from about 250 in one mental hospital which treats many patients that can afford very high fees and which is affiliated with a medical school, to 600 or 700 in the country mental hospitals (there are two, one for acute mental illnesses and the other for chronic illnesses) which handle the poor and indigent and which have training programs but are more like community hospitals.

At the other extreme and quite dissimilar to Community Hospital are the six welfare agencies. For the most part, they have only a few occupations, and these are mostly variations on the social-work theme. Three are private, small, and do counseling. Three are public, large, and do mainly dispersing of funds, although one of the public agencies does do child placement.

The three rehabilitation agencies, which attempt to return either the physically or psychologically handicapped back to active participation in society, are more like the mental hospitals in that their staffs are larger, usually around 100, and complex, even more so than the mental hospitals. The residential treatment centers are smaller, usually below 50, and much less complex. However, the differences among the three rehabilitation agencies and among the three residential treatment centers are greater than this grouping implies. One rehabilitation center handles primarily the severely retarded and the deeply disturbed, another has focused on the rehabilitation of patients who suffered strokes, cardiacs, and forms of physical disability. This center is affiliated with a medical school. One treatment center specialized in very disturbed children, another in adolescent boys with problems, and so forth.

Some of the organizations have religious sponsorship, some county, and one, the department of special education, city sponsorship. But as stated above, they do share a common and more general focus, namely, rehabilitation, and the provision of primarily psychiatric and social rather than medical services per se. They are different from general hospitals, yet they are professional organizations whose staffs provide client service. The distinctive feature of the members of the staff is the application of skills acquired by extensive and intensive formal training. In summary, there is about as much variation in our sample as one can obtain in the health and welfare field, but not as much as we would have liked. Like so many research studies, we were restricted by the funding, which limited us to the field of rehabilitation.

Respondents within each organization were selected as follows:

1. All executive directors and department heads.
2. In departments of less than 10 members, one-half the staff was selected randomly.
3. In departments of 10 or more members, one-third the staff was selected randomly.

Nonsupervisory administrative and maintenance personnel were not interviewed. The procedures used in aggregating individual data in order to develop measures of organization structure have been described elsewhere (Aiken and Hage, 1966; Hage and Aiken, 1967a and b) and need not be repeated here.

Two different interview schedules were used. The executive director was asked a series of global items about various aspects of his organization; the staff was asked a series of questions about themselves. In this way, there was a considerable gain in the amount of data obtained without any loss of accuracy. For example, the executive director was asked about the size of the organization, the yearly budget, the number of organization-wide committees, and so on. Each of these items was then checked with a responsible office, such as the personnel manager or accountant. In the case of the staff, the aggregation procedures of computing first a positional and then an organizational mean resulted in the reduction of considerable error.

The cooperation with the study was exceptionally high. Only about three people out of over 500 respondents refused to be interviewed; one had a Ph.D. in psychology, and the others were middle-aged social workers who felt that sociology was a waste of time. The interviewing of the staff was done within the context of the organization by the Wisconsin Survey Laboratory. The executive directors were interviewed by Michael Aiken and myself. Since there was so much cooperation with the study, it was possible to complete the interviewing of the staff in about one month. Each organization, even the large ones, was done in the space of several days.

The various measurements of communication, formalization, and stratification are listed in Appendix A along with instructions on how indices can be constructed. In addition, the reader can learn more about these measures by reading Aiken and Hage (1966),

Hage and Aiken (1967a), and Price (1972). However, the measures for communications are new and require extended discussion.

The definition of organizational communications is verbal interactions about tasks, that is, those interactions that are most immediately involved in the achievement of organizational goals. We do not include written communications nor have we measured the content of these communications, although we make reference to their probable content. We phrased our questions so that respondents would exclude all purely expressive communications, such as, camaraderie among friends, or the exchange of gossip. Of course, this distinction may seem somewhat artificial since effective task communication usually involve some expressive elements like jokes or pleasantries. We only asked respondents not to report those communications that were completely expressive and which were in no way related to the accomplishment of some work objective.

We separated task communication into two major types. The first includes the more routine, usually planned, communication, such as staff or committee meetings; the second includes less routine, often unplanned, communication, such as informal, impromptu conferences between two staff members about a client's situation or the consultation between colleagues about a newly instituted organization activity. We refer to the former as *scheduled* and the latter as *unscheduled* communication.

Scheduled Communication

There are at least four kinds of scheduled communication in organizations: (1) meetings of the entire staff; (2) organization-wide committees; (3) departmental or unit meetings; and (4) treatment (or production) meetings. The first two, staff and committee meetings, are primarily *interdepartmental* communication, while the latter two, departmental and treatment meetings are primarily *intradepartmental* communication. To simplify presentation of the data, we have included only one kind from each category, clearly the most important ones: organization-wide committee meetings and internal departmental meetings. Staff meetings occur infrequently and are unlikely to be an important mechanism for achieving coordination and control. Similarly, treatment meetings are more affected by the nature of the technology being employed, and, therefore, less applicable to all of our organizations. They are also harder to classify as either inter- or intra-departmental.

Interdepartmental committee meetings are particularly critical since they are vitally linked to the achievement of organizational coordination and represent one major mechanism for horizontal communication. Intradepartmental communication is more important for social control within the various departments of an organization and represents an important form of vertical communication. These forms of communication are similar in that they are likely to maximize the possibilities of information feedback.

The staff meetings usually involve the reporting of decisions taken and agreements reached. Production or treatment meetings, in the case of our 16 welfare organizations, are more difficult to classify. For those organizations which have them, and there are only a few, they represent a critical mechanism.

Information about scheduled communications was obtained by asking each respondent the following question:

> Now we would like to find out something about the committees and staff meetings. Please list all staff committees or meetings of which you are a member.

For each committee or meeting reported, the following two questions were then asked:

> How many times per month does the committee meet?
> On the average, how many hours per month do you spend in meetings of this committee?

To aid in the classification of each response, a list of all the permanent committees and departments of the organization was obtained from the head of each organization and compared with the answers of respondents. In this way, we were able to classify responses into the four-fold classification of staff, organization-wide committee, departmental, and treatment (or production) meetings.

For each type of scheduled communication, three measures were then constructed:

1. The *proportion* of all staff members who participate in any meeting of a given kind each month.
2. The average *number* of organizational meetings of a given kind attended by each staff member each month, that is, a rate.
3. The average number of *hours* spent in meetings of a given kind by each staff member each month, again a rate.

The addition of the number of hours per member was, naturally, an attempt to be aware of the possibility that some organizations might have infrequent, but lengthy meetings. When analyzing the data, we discovered that this qualification was usually unnecessary. Relationships between frequency and average duration per member and our structural properties showed the same patterns. In order to simplify the presentation of data, we only report the first two measures, proportion involved and number of meetings, attended.

Thus, four measures of scheduled communication are included in this study, two measures of organization-wide committees—number of meetings attended and proportion attending such meetings—and two comparable measures for departmental meetings.

As can be seen from Table 8.1, there is considerable variation among the organizations in this study in communication rates. For example, the average number of organization-wide committee meetings attended per member ranges from 0 to 1.9. There is some variation by kind of organization. The rehabilitation organizations are highest, followed by the mental hospitals and the special education department. Social casework and homes for the emotionally disturbed have the fewest committee meetings. The same is true for the proportion of staff members participating in such meetings; it varies from a high of 60 percent in a private social casework organization to none in a public social casework organization. Again, the rehabilitation organizations and mental hospitals have the highest scores, while social casework agencies, homes for the emotionally disturbed, and a special education department have the lowest proportion of their staff participating in such meetings.

The measure of the average number of departmental meetings attended per month per staff member reflects the intensity of the flow of communication within the various departments of an organization. The measure of proportion involved in departmental staff meetings

Table 8.1	Means and Ranges of the Scheduled and Unscheduled			
	Rehabilitation Centers		Social Casework Agencies	
	Means	Ranges	Means	Ranges
Scheduled Communication (Monthly)				
A. Organization-wide committee meetings				
1. Average number attended	1.44	.96– 1.91	.70	.00– 1.67
2. Proportion of staff involved	.42	.34– .52	.30	.00– .60
B. Departmental meetings				
1. Average number attended	1.39	1.07– 1.64	1.09	.18– 4.00
2. Proportion of staff involved	.43	.24– .72	.38	.06– .80
Unscheduled Communication (Weekly)				
C. Department/division heads				
1. With the executive level	11.04	8.80–13.00	4.22	1.00–10.80
2. Among themselves	15.77	10.00–25.00	.00	.00– .00
3. With their supervisors	10.91	7.00–16.00	3.03	.00–11.25
4. With their workers	8.33	3.00–14.33	12.47	4.25–47.20
5. With other dept./div. heads	6.39	2.29– 9.80	2.08	.00– 6.20
6. With other supervisors	4.99	1.25–11.43	.73	.00– 4.00
7. With other workers	5.75	.60–12.86	2.37	.00–13.00
D. Supervisors				
1. With the executive level	2.64	.10– 4.33	.54	.14– 1.00
2. With their dept./div. heads	6.27	4.67– 8.64	3.93	.00–10.80
3. Among themselves	7.27	3.56– 9.83	2.44	.00– 5.80
4. With their workers	15.57	12.00–22.22	11.15	.25–25.71
5. With other dept./div. heads	2.82	.00– 8.25	.20	.00– .50
6. With other supervisors	4.36	.50– 8.83	18.48	.00–90.00
7. With other workers	9.13	6.33–11.00	1.51	.00– 4.33
E. Workers				
1. With the executive level	2.23	.09– 3.50	.28	.02– .64
2. With their dept./div. heads	6.53	.32–18.57	1.98	.54– 7.00
3. With their supervisors	11.69	5.59–21.00	2.69	.00– 8.80
4. Among themselves	10.55	2.25–17.79	7.81	1.33–15.91
5. With other dept./div. heads	4.10	.00– 8.86	.44	.00– 1.00
6. With other supervisors	4.53	1.21– 9.25	.13	.00– .40
7. With other workers	9.67	4.41–13.50	1.50	.06– 5.10

Communication by Type of Organization[b]

Residential Treatment		Mental Hospitals		Total[a]	
Means	Ranges	Means	Ranges	Means	Ranges
.68	.40– 1.07	1.26	1.15– 1.33	.95	.00– 1.91
.35	.25– .41	.42	.41– .44	.38	.00– .60
3.63	.33– 2.58	2.14	1.21– 2.70	1.78	.18– 4.00
.33	.13– .58	.50	.39– .56	.39	.06– .80
12.33	8.33–16.67	5.74	2.06–10.33	1.01	1.00–16.67
1.33	.00– 4.00	9.94	8.33–10.75	5.07	.00–25.00
4.08	.00–12.00	9.26	2.50–14.29	5.55	.00–16.00
49.77	33.00–65.00	13.93	10.25–14.47	19.42	3.00–65.00
2.83	.00– 8.50	8.50	4.47–16.11	4.71	.00–16.11
.00	.00– .00	2.42	.67– 4.35	1.76	.00–11.43
20.39	15.67–29.50	5.73	2.19– 8.67	7.07	.00–29.50
3.44	.00– 8.33	2.09	1.82– 2.61	1.78	.00– 8.33
1.77	.00– 4.33	4.06	3.36– 6.71	3.76	.00–10.80
4.00	.00–10.00	6.28	.62– 9.43	4.11	.00–10.00
15.33	.00–42.33	25.92	8.14–61.30	15.18	.00–61.30
1.55	.00– 4.00	2.15	1.33– 2.86	1.50	.00– 8.25
.00	.00– .00	1.00	.29– 1.73	8.02	.00–90.00
1.44	.00– 4.33	6.94	2.43–10.00	3.99	.00–11.00
1.84	.43– 4.10	1.16	.27– 2.86	1.17	.09– 4.10
4.85	2.43– 8.00	2.86	1.46– 3.14	3.74	.32–18.57
1.85	2.43– 2.33	3.18	.00– 7.50	5.57	.00–21.00
12.55	8.11–20.33	7.58	4.79–11.40	9.18	1.33–20.33
4.11	.57– 8.20	2.21	.50– 5.57	2.16	.00– 8.86
.43	.00– 1.29	.93	.08– 2.14	1.18	.00– 9.25
7.14	5.93– 8.00	17.05	6.71–34.00	7.13	.06–34.00

[a] Includes the department of special education

[b] Unloged rates

reflects the degree to which members of various departments have access to the flow of information within their respective departments. As shown in Table 8.1, there is considerable variability in both the average number of departmental meetings attended per staff member each month and the proportion of staff members attending departmental meetings.

Unscheduled Communication

Information about more spontaneous and informal communication was obtained by asking each respondent the following questions:

> In every position it is sometimes necessary in fulfilling one's job to confer with other people. How many times in a typical week do you confer with people here in the organization other than at committee meetings?
> What are the names of these people?
> What are their job titles?
> How many times in a typical week do you confer with each of these persons?

The word confer was carefully chosen after a pretest indicated that the words "to seek advice" was too threatening to professionals, at least the ones in our pretest. (Pretests were always conducted in a different city so that there would be no contamination of the study sample.) The word confer would seem to cover a broader form of task communication than advice, and, therefore, perhaps is a better measure of communication flow in the organization.

Two types of information were obtained from these questions. First, the *number* of different persons in the organization with whom communication occurred and, second, the *frequency* of these contacts. To simplify the presentation of the data, we only include the frequency, which is a measure of the *intensity* of information flow among members of the organization. In this analysis, we are concerned with the volume and direction of communication, not the variety of individuals involved. In any case, analysis of data indicated few differences in the direction and magnitude of the findings with these alternative approaches.

These few simple questions proved to be an embarassment of riches. Committees and departmental meetings are easy to classify. The locating of every individual in the organization by status and department requires infinite patience in coding the elaborate lists of the staff. As a consequence, the author did much of the coding himself with the aid of two experienced research assistants. For the problem was to classify each contact not only by the respondents' department and authority level but also each of his confers by their department and authority level. Needless to say this required a considerable amount of time in the larger organizations.

In a previous article (Hage, Aiken, and Marrett, 1971), we reported the results of an analysis of the data for the more simple notion of six pathways of unscheduled communication. In this monograph, I made a more elaborate level—specific classification on a suggestion from Michael Aiken, as follows. *First,* pathways of unscheduled communication are categorized as being within a department and/or division and among departments and/or divisions. In other words, either the respondent conferred with someone in his own department or in a different one. Everyone of the 16 organizations had at least two departments; the average was about four. *Second,* pathways are categorized by level as follows: executive level, including executive assistant; the divisional and departmental level, including assistants; the supervisory level, including several intermediate levels; and the worker level. The few aids were included with the workers. The divisional and departmental levels were collapsed together because only the larger organizations had this additional level. Likewise, a department, to be called a department, had to have at least three subordinates. This means that some staff positions, such as public-relations director, are categorized not as department heads but as supervisors because they had only one subordinate. *Third,* both the respondent and his conferee are classified, defining what can be called the level specific pathway. What this means is that a department head conferring with a worker in his own department is different from a worker conferring with his department head. The first is vertical downward communication, the second is vertical upward communication. Probably, although less assuredly, the content of the message is different as well. Certainly, the sociological significance is vastly different, at least as outlined in our theory of coordination and control, because as any disciple of exchange theory will admit (Homans, 1961), the person who confers loses at least a little status in the process. Thus, for the boss to confer with the subordinate means symbolically less status between them. Conversely, the boss gains in status when his subordinate asks questions of him. Regardless of this interpretation, as is evident in the next chapter, the distinction between up and down is an important one.

One reason for combining the various levels (department with division, several intermediate supervisors as one, and aides with workers) is to standardize the configuration of the organizational chart as much as possible. Thus, all 16 health and welfare organizations have basically the same organizational chart. This procedure has wide applicability since most organizations, except for very large ones, vary between seven and four levels (Blau and Schoenherr, 1971; Kaufman and Seidman, 1970). Our procedure makes these all equivalent, at least for the number of levels. Likewise, by saying that all respondents have two departments, their own and all others, we have again standardized our organizations vis-à-vis another critical aspect, namely, the number of departments.

There are other advantages to collapsing the department and division levels as well as the intermediate supervisory levels. The higher echelons have fewer individuals, and, therefore, the rates at this level can potentially be much more a function of personality and individual variation than organizational structure. Thus, the increase in the number of individuals included in the middle two levels reduces measurement error given our averaging procedures.

From a theoretical viewpoint, the four-level, two-department organization appears to make a great deal of sense. The executive, the department head, the supervisor, and the worker appear to be the main categories in any hierarchy of authority. Together, they allow us to make not only the familiar horizontal and vertical distinction (Landsberger, 1961) but to expand upon it in the following ways: (1) horizontal, (2) criss-cross, (3) vertical down, and (4) vertical up.

The first is represented by department heads, supervisors, or workers talking with their colleagues in other departments. The second is represented by department heads, supervisors, or workers conferring with a level other than their own in other departments. The third is each of these levels conferring with their subordinates within the same department, and the last is the converse.

The Six Major Pathways for a Department Head

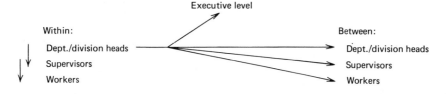

The Six Major Pathways for a Supervisor

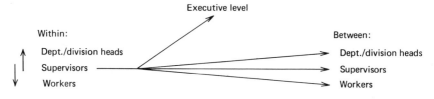

The Six Major Pathways for a Worker

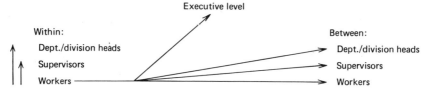

Figure 8.1   The pathways of unscheduled communication.

There are 21 pathways, even with the combination of division and department heads as a single level. However, some of these are of less interest than others. (See Figure 8.1.) Certainly, the supervisors' conferences among themselves is less important because it is neither cross-level or cross-department. Also, communication within a social position tends to be less stable because of the smaller numbers of individuals, except for the worker position within departments.

In order to determine whether a communication was intradepartmental or interdepartmental, we obtained a complete membership list of each department of each organization. The level within a department was determined by asking a series of questions at the outset of each interview about a respondent's job title, his major activity, names and titles of persons in the organization to whom he reported. Since we had included most supervisors in our study, we were able to construct an "operative" organizational chart for each organization, which proved to be more useful than the formal organizational chart, which, if one existed, was outdated or inaccurate, or both. We were able, with a great deal of care, to classify each unscheduled communication mentioned in one of the 21 pathways. In this work, I was much aided by Cora Bagley Marrett who constructed organizational charts for the more complicated organizations.

Beyond this, one additional piece of data was generated: the average rate of unscheduled communication. As becomes clear in Chapters 10 and 11, this is, in some respects, the most useful bit of information because the key impact is first on volume of unscheduled communication, which this measures.

As can be seen in Table 8.1, the differences within each kind of organization are enormous, much greater than with scheduled communications. We see the range on conferences with the executive level (line C1) by the department/division level varying between once per week to 17 times per week. Supervisors conferring with their workers (line D4) can vary between 0 to 61 times per week. This high score occurs in the mental hospitals where ward nurses spend a lot of time conferring with subordinates and thus act as a major upward communication link with the psychiatrist. Likewise, the extreme in the residential treatment centers is an organization that attempts to maintain a complete therapeutic milieu.

Although there are great differences in the ranges for particular pathways, what is of more interest is the difference in the means between pathways. Thus, on the average, we see division and department heads conferring more with their own workers than with their supervisors, with much of this occurring in residential treatment centers. Likewise, supervisors, on the average, confer more with their workers than with anyone else, and this is characteristic of mental hospitals.

Given some of these extremes, skewness tests were performed on each of the 21 pathways of unscheduled communication. Most of the distributions are indeed skewed, and as a consequence, the variables were transformed logarithmically. Some consideration was also given to the idea of reducing some of the more extreme scores as well, but this might mean moving too far from the actual distribution. It might be noted that almost all pathways have a skewness of less than 1.0

once a transformation is made. Logarithmic transformation has a theoretical basis, namely, that communication rates may grow exponentially as the division of labor grows arithmetically. In Chapter 2 we had suggested that as the number of positions grows, the number of their interrelationships can grow geometrically, thus one would expect some power function to be a more accurate description of the distribution. Statistically logarithmic transformation is appropriate, given the desire to use regression techniques and avoid unduly inflating correlations with extreme scores (Wonnacott and Wonnacott, 1970).

SOME METHODOLOGICAL PROBLEMS

Despite the care taken and the great variety of communication measures used, there are limitations to what was done. The first is that not all forms of communication were measured. What has been excluded are various measures of written communication, such as memos. It is doubtful that this is a critical channel since it takes much more time to write a line than to say the same number of words. Thus, our hunch is that this addition would not add much to the scores. We also suspect that written communications grow in the same proportion as verbal ones, if university departments of sociology are any indication of the relationship between written and verbal communication. Also the study of Community Hospital indicates that physicians rely much more on verbal than written communication channels.

Although feedback has been tapped by communication rates, both scheduled and unscheduled, it is also true that feedback as such has not been measured directly. Our inference is that as information flows increase in volume, whether during meetings or in individual conferences, more and more reports about difficulties will be made and appropriate adjustments will occur. In other words, high communication volumes means a high monitoring of the treatment and managerial processes in each kind of organization. But this phenomenon has not been measured.

For this reason, a great deal of stress is placed on the idea of direction as well as volume. The notion of feedback implies integrating the parts of the organization. Therefore, any horizontal or criss-cross pattern becomes the major focus of analysis. Concretely, this means organization-wide committee meetings should be more important than departmental ones, and unscheduled communication between departments more crucial than within departments.

Much of the same reasoning applies to socialization. We are assuming that all communication contains elements of socialization, but again, volume and direction make a great deal of difference in understanding how much socialization occurs. We have not measured it, as was done, at least implicitly, in the study of Community Hospital. Our inference on a probabilistic basis is that a greater amount of socialization occurs, and more effectively at that, when there are higher volumes of communication, especially of a horizontal nature. Learning is much more likely to occur between equals.

IX

The Nature of Unscheduled Communication Networks

ONE OF THE MORE INTERESTING findings in the study of Community Hospital was the emergence of a network of communication links as a consequence of the addition of a number of specialists and the conflicts they generated. Here we are referring to the flow of unscheduled communication, and not the creation of an elaborate committee system. The creation of new committees is a simple and easy way of directing communication flows between the many parts of an organization. What is usually implied in the phrase "a network of communication" is the spontaneous emergence of horizontal linkages, especially between various departments. Although the phrase network of communication readily evokes an image, its measurement poses some difficulties. There are more distinctions than the black of hierarchical communication pathways and the white of network ones. Networks vary in the number of pathways as well as in direction. We have already noted the usefulness of the distinctions among horizontal, criss-cross, vertical up, and vertical down pathways. We need to explore their interrelations as well.

In the previous part, we observed, at least roughly, how communication pathways grew across time. Now we need to ask with more precise measures whether there is more than one way to evolve. We suggested in Chapter 3 that one helpful concept in cybernetic thinking was that of equifinality, that is, the idea that organizations can evolve towards the same new equilibrium point in more than one way. Also important is the precise way in which a communication network is built up. With 21 pathways, there are a large number of possible sequences. Presumably some of these are more important to add first, others second, and so on, especially from the viewpoint of what makes an effective communications network for high feedback and socialization.

Another critical issue is what pathways are associated together. We can well imagine that pathways are not added randomly or sequentially, but activated in clusters. We want to identify the linkages in each of these clusters as much as we can to draw some conclusions regarding an ideal communications arrangement.

The analysis is straight-forward. The volume of communication in one level-specific pathway is correlated with the volume in another. (It should be remembered that these are for the most part logarithmic transformations.) For example, if the department head confers frequently with his supervisors, do they, in turn, confer frequently with their workers? (For our purposes, statistical significance levels provide a simple way of defining when a relationship is important or can be said to exist: the correlation must be above .50, which is slightly above the 10 percent level with 14 degrees of freedom; it has the advantage of being a number that is easy to remember for the present analysis.) If they are associated, then we have some insight into the appropriate communications job description for our supervisors.

For the moment, we are leaving aside the issue of how structure determines communication flow. We shall return to this problem and our main concern in the next two chapters. Here, our task is simply to understand which organizational pathways are most active, given a particular volume of unscheduled communication, and, then, summarize this as several kinds of feedback.

THE UNSCHEDULED COMMUNICATION RATE AND THE MOST ACTIVE PATHWAYS

Our first task is to understand what pathways are most strongly affected by changes in the average total rate of unscheduled communication. We can easily imagine two different situations. As feedback via unscheduled communications increases, it grows uniformly in all directions or pathways. Much of our argument, however, about the nature of feedback and of socialization would suggest that this is not the case. As we have already observed in Community Hospital, horizontal communication links are much more likely to be involved in the context of coordination and of control. *We would, therefore, expect communication rates to grow proportionally faster among departments than within, horizontally rather than vertically.*

Perhaps an analogy can make this clear. Suppose we suddenly opened the floodgates of a dam and let loose a large volume of water. We are now interested in predicting if more water runs in tributary A than in tributary B. We are in effect correlating the measured water flow in 21 tributaries with the total spill-off of the dam. This is the average communication rate per member. From this, we can infer that some pathways become activated when there is a moderate volume of unscheduled communication and others when there is a higher volume. More specifically, the prediction is that as the volume of water increases, more and more will flow into the horizontal tributaries.

Another reason for being concerned about the differential impacts of the volume of unscheduled communication on various pathways is practical. If an organization is having some feedback problems—a lack of information flow, or communication difficulties—it may be a consequence of some missing links in the communication network. While empirical findings do not necessarily represent the ideal, they can sometimes provide some glimpse of what it might be. In other words, the best way of building a network of communication for an organic steady state can be inferred from this kind of analysis.

If we release a large volume of water, which tributaries carry the biggest share? The answer is provided in Table 9.1. We might expect that the most active link would be professionals at the worker level conferring with their colleagues in the same department because there are the greatest number of readily available personnel. This is not the case. Given a high rate of unscheduled communication, the pathway most strongly associated is a horizontal one, namely, professional workers conferring with workers not in their own department but with their colleagues in other departments (E7, $r = .84$). This would seem to be the precise meaning of horizontal communication;

Table 9.1   The Correlation Between Average Unscheduled Communication Rates and the Rates Within Specific Pathways

	Pearsonian Correlation-Coefficient of Average Communication Rate per Member in an Organization[a]
C. Department and division heads[b]	
1. With the executive level	.40
2. Among themselves	.58*
3. With their supervisors	.54*
4. With their workers	.08
5. With other dept./division heads	.56*
6. With other supervisors	.44
7. With other workers	.45
D. Supervisors	
1. With the executive level	.42
2. With their dept./division heads	.32
3. Among themselves	.62*
4. With their workers	.56*
5. With other dept./division heads	.56*
6. With other supervisors	−.02
7. With other workers	.70*
E. Workers	
1. With the executive level	.65*
2. With their dept./division heads	.46
3. With their supervisor	.63*
4. Among themselves	.37
5. With other dept./division heads	.38
6. With other supervisors	.66*
7. With other workers	.84*

[a] It is inappropriate to use statistical tests when two variables are based on some of the same information; the same can be said for correlations as well. However, it is instructive to see what pathways are most strongly associated with *changes* in the volume of unscheduled communication, and for this reason an asterick is placed after those with a correlation higher than .50.

[b] For ease of interpretation we are keeping the same letter and number designations as used in Table 8.1.

it is occurring at the lowest level in the organization, the bottom of the status and authority hierarchy. This is the extreme antithesis of a hierarchical communication pattern.

But one might reason that even though rates per member or respondent are computed, that since there are so many individuals at the bottom, this still reflects a structural opportunity rather than a more interesting observation about organizational life. As we shall see later, however, the proportion of lower participants actually is *negatively* associated with the average rate; it depresses rather than facilitates communication volume.

Regardless, the horizontal pattern emerges elsewhere, where the objection of sheer numbers is less easily raised. Equally important is the volume of communication between department heads (C5, $r=.56$) of different departments. Here, we see again horizontal communication, this time at the top of the authority and status pyramid.

One might then assume that the same pattern would hold for the supervisors, that is, that they would confer frequently with their counterparts in different departments. This communication link should also carry a good share of information flow given a high volume of communication. But just the reverse is true. The more communication between supervisors of different departments, the *less* the rate per member. In fact, this is the only channel with a negative association, which is substantively significant even if the correlation is not statistically significant.

Whom do the supervisors confer with? An inspection of Table 9.1 indicates what we have called the criss-cross pattern: Supervisors confer with workers in other departments (D7, $r=.70$) and with other department heads (D5, $r=.56$). *This is a more efficient way of knitting together the organization, because the supervisors are the middle echelon, given four basic levels. Thus, with horizontal flow between different department heads and between professional workers, all parts are united effectively by the middle echelon conferring actively with the top and the bottom echelons in the other departments.* A simple horizontal pattern between supervisors of different departments would not create as strong an organizational structure. One can visualize this as the hypothenuses of two triangles. Supervisors to workers in other departments and workers to other departments represents one triangle, while supervisors to department heads of other departments and department heads to their counterparts represents another.

The other legs of these communication triangles are furnished by the downward flow of communication of department heads to their own supervisors (C3, $r=.54$) and supervisors with their own workers (D4, $r=56$). This pattern is also reinforced by department heads and supervisors conferring actively with their assistants (C2, $r = .58$ and D3, $r = .62$, respectively). *Since our question asked whom the respondent conferred with, the direction of supervisor conferring with his workers is clearly different in meaning from a professional conferring with his supervisor.* We would suspect the content is different as well. Regardless, *it is likely that as the volume of communication increases, the content changes, or more probably, there is less emphasis on instructions and interpretations of rules—understanding the program—and more on finding out information needed to do an effective job—the meaning of feedback and socialization.*

In the example of Community Hospital, we noted that some physicians, and this was especially true of the medical specialists, had what was called a consultative work style. We can imagine in this comparative study of organizations that as unscheduled communication increases, more and more of the professionals are developing the same pattern, consulting relative to their work. This is even true for the supervisors and department heads, who consult their subordinates and at the same time obtain a more detailed understanding of what is happening in the organization.

If we combine the criss-cross and horizontal patterns, the two kinds of unscheduled communication between departments, we have the definition of a communication network. What is essential to our whole line of reasoning is that these patterns develop precisely as the volume of unscheduled communication increases. To return to our analogy, as more water is released from the dam, it does not add to the flow in the vertical tributaries, but, for the most part, activates the pathways connecting departments. *Different tributaries or linkages in the communication network are added; none are subtracted.* Communication rates, at least at certain levels or volumes, result in actual feedback and socialization. Both the horizontal and criss-cross patterns appear to have this function.

How should one construct a communication network, given a high volume of communication? The answer, at least as suggested in Table 9.1 is the double triangle—part horizontal and part criss-cross, with the key linkage being the supervisor. In other words, the intermediate supervisors help link the organization together for coordination by feedback. The criss-cross or triangular communication of the supervisors with the horizontal flows at the top and bottom knit together the organization into a relatively strong communication structure. The analogy with the triangle, which is the strongest geometrical form, is an intriguing one. There is little advantage in having all 21 pathways equally burdened with communication. The eight or nine links of the two triangles would appear to be the essential ones for defining a feedback and socialization network of communication.

It should follow that some of the pathways which are correlated with a high volume of unscheduled communication are, on logical grounds, less essential. Workers conferring with the executive level (E1, $r = .65$) does not seem to be a necessary linkage in an organic network. As we shall see below, it is much more likely associated with a different set of communication pathways.

The double triangle or the combination of a horizontal with a criss-cross pattern is not the only viable way of constructing an unscheduled communication network, but it appears to be an appropriate one for an organization that wants high feedback and high socialization as the mechanisms of coordination and control. Other possibilities will be explored later as we attempt to see which pathways tend to be correlated with each other.

INTERRELATIONSHIPS OF COMMUNICATION PATHWAYS: THE ROLE-SET PROBLEM

The previous analysis concentrated on the question of how the sheer volume of unscheduled communication affects the choice of unscheduled pathways. We have inferred that certain highly active pathways are likely to be linked in the same network. Our inference is best ascertained by intercorrelating the intensity of communication in a particular pathway with each of the 20 others. Does the communication rate between department and division heads of different departments correlate with the communication rate between department heads and supervisors in other departments, and so forth. Knowing which pathways tend to be associated—and causality is hard to infer —again gives a prescriptive guideline in advising organizations about coordination difficulties.

This analysis is akin to defining the role-sets for particular positions (Merton, 1957, Chapter 9). Figure 9.1 contains the definition in quite general terms of three role-sets: for the department head, for the supervisor, and for the worker. A role-set is nothing more than all the role relationships that the occupants interact with in the course of their work. In Figure 9.1 we have drawn all major role relationships. In practice they are not all articulated. What is of interest is to know how many of these are activated at the same time. Again, we have a problem of separating out the frequent relationship from the relatively infrequent one. More importantly, we want to determine if certain role-relationships tend to occur together. By correlating the intensity of communication of one pathway, for example, workers conferring with their supervisors, vis-à-vis the other possible pathways, we can then define operationally the role-set of the professional worker, at least for those organizational situations when he must, for whatever reasons, confer frequently with his supervisor. We can also define the role-set of the other two major participants, namely the supervisor and the department head. For readers with a practical concern as how best to construct an organization with high feedback and high socialization, this is an important issue. We need to observe not only the specific mechanisms of feedback and socialization, as we did in Community Hospital, but also the necessary pathways of unscheduled communication, the general role-sets.

The ways in which particular pathways are linked together tell us a little about the ways in which organizations operate. Although no causality can be argued, some inferences about particular combinations can be suggested. We shall examine the four most important network patterns: horizontal, criss-cross, vertical down, and vertical up.

The Horizontal Networks

Figures 9.1 and 9.2 are two graphs indicating which channels are associated with, first, changes in the rate between department and division heads, and, second, changes in the rate between workers of different departments. In the first figure, we see part of the triangular pattern that we have already noted. Workers confer with their colleagues (.60) in other departments and so do their own supervisors (.56). At this point, it might be worth reiterating that these workers are, by and large, professionals. As a consequence, one expects much

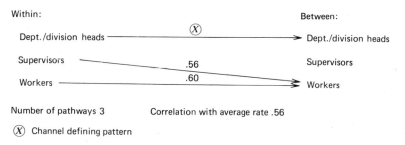

Figure 9.1 Pathways of unscheduled communications associated with communication rates between department heads.

more freedom of movement and the opportunity to ask for advice from individuals located in different parts of the organization. Likewise, on the department head and divisional level, there is considerable internal conferring. In general, there are only a few linkages that vary in a like manner with variations in the flow of unscheduled communication between heads of different departments and/or divisions.

This pattern of findings suggests that horizontal conferring between departments may vary independently of what is occurring in a number of other pathways or linkages. We might infer that the content of unscheduled communication at the departmental and divisional level may be different from what is discussed in many of the other pathways. It does seem to be associated, however, with another horizontal flow between departments, namely, the rate of unscheduled communication between professional workers. It might be worth repeating that a significant size correlation in this instance means that changes in the frequency of interaction between department heads are associated with changes in the unscheduled communication rates in some other pathways. Figure 9.1 indicates that only three other linkages are so associated. Perhaps we should examine the role-set of the workers vis-à-vis workers in other departments, another horizontal linkage.

The contrast of the next pattern is striking. What we see portrayed in Figure 9.2 is the organic network. Two-thirds of our pathways are activated, that is, 12 of the 18 are associated with variations in the flow of unscheduled communication between workers in dif-

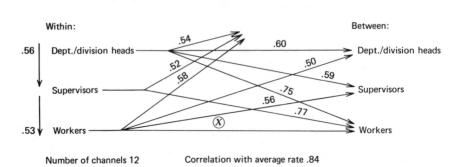

Figure 9.2   Pathways of unscheduled communications associated with communication rates between workers.

ferent departments and/or divisions. The twin triangles are clearly delineated. The department heads confer with their counterparts (.60), with supervisors in other departments (.59), and with their own supervisors (.56). Supervisors confer with workers in other departments (.77), with their assistants (.69), and with their own workers (.53). What also emerges is the strong upward but interdepartmental flow of information feedback. Workers confer with supervisors in other departments (.56), with the heads of other departments (.50), and with the executive level (.58). The supervisors (.52) and the department heads (.54) confer with the executive level. Since we did not ask the executive directors the same question, we do not have the possibility for a downward flow to occur. Presumedly, the executive level would reciprocate with the departmental level and perhaps also the supervisory one.

One way to decipher this network is to ask what pathways or links in the unscheduled communication network do not appear to be involved. Workers do not confer with their supervisors, nor do supervisors confer with their department heads. In other words, what is missing is the hierarchical communication pattern within departments, what we have labeled vertical up. That professional workers confer with all levels in other departments and with the executive level in at least this sample of professional organizations only reinforces our understanding of the significance of the absence of workers conferring with their supervisors. This is additional evidence that as volume of unscheduled communication increases, it is disproportionately added to horizontal, criss-cross, and vertical down linkages. *There is always a need for some upward flow within departments,* even in the most programmed of organizations. This is the first requirement. Once this need is met, then additional increases in communication are employed for other needs, namely, for feedback from all parts of an organization. *Workers, who in our sample are, for the most part professionals or semiprofessionals, consult and feel free to do so with a wide variety of other individuals, especially those in other departments, and as they do so, they are, of course, being socialized.* This is how a professional work style of consulting and an organization with a high volume of unscheduled communication fit together.

Since so many links are associated with the flow of communication between professional workers of various departments, we can conclude that this is one of the main tributaries. Once this pathway is opened, a large number of others will be opened. One major reason is that professionals who work with the clients are key to any treatment process. Their coordination and control, therefore, becomes the critical level for the major production process. When this production process is coordinated by feedback, there must be a number of pathways or links for feedback or mutual adjustment, to use James Thompson's (1967) term. One of the more interesting empirical observations is that this is most likely to occur when the workers confer with other workers rather than when department heads confer with other departments heads.

Perhaps not all these pathways are necessary. One wonders if workers conferring with the executive level is desirable. Here, we may have another ideal type of communication pattern being confounded with the double-triangle pattern because we are inferring a process from cross-sectional data.

The critical elements in the organic network, besides the double triangle, are the interdepartment flows of communication and the openness of the executive level to members of *all* levels. Again, this presumably reflects the nature of our health and welfare organizations. It also goes to the heart of what is meant by an organic network. A worker is most likely to confer with those in other departments irrespective of their authority or status.

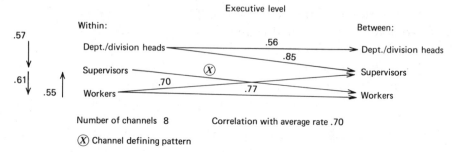

Figure 9.3 Pathways of unscheduled communications associated with communications of supervisors with workers in other departments.

The Criss-Cross Networks

A key figure in the double triangle is the supervisor. It is worth examining what pathways are associated with his being involved with other departments at a different status level. This will give us a check on our interpretation of the above clusters, or role-sets. We should find the same linkages. When we look at the pathway between supervisors and workers in other departments, an active channel in both of the previous graphs, we find essentially the same double-triangle pattern. (See Figure 9.3.) Although there are only 8 links associated together, and some links are different, it is still an organic network.

When supervisors confer with the heads of other departments a different pattern emerges. As can be observed in Figure 9.4, we have fewer pathways, and most of them involve either the executive or

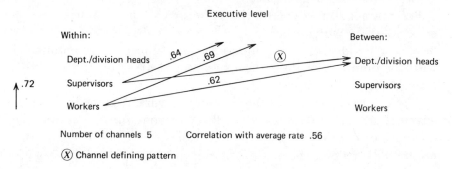

Figure 9.4 Pathways of unscheduled communications associated with communications of supervisors with heads of other departments.

departmental level. There is no downward or horizontal flow, two of the distinguishing characteristics of the organic network. This suggests that here we have a different communication pattern. Perhaps what is most striking is the absence of the link between professional workers of different departments. This provides some basis for the interpretation made of Figure 9.2, that upward flows from worker to the executive level may not be a part of the double-triangle pattern even though they appear associated. Again, it seems reasonable to assume that workers conferring with executives has a different meaning than conferring with their counterparts in other departments. As we suggest later, there are also different structural causes as well.

The juxtaposition of these two figures indicates that supervisors conferring with heads of other departments is not the obverse of their conferring with workers in other departments. The direction of the communication, that is, up or down status levels, implies a difference in content. This can be appreciated better if we now explore the networks associated with vertical flows, first downward and then upward.

Vertical Downward Networks

When supervisors confer with their own workers, there are six other channels in the same network. Workers will confer with their supervisors (.61) and with workers in other departments (5.3). Supervisors confer with workers in other departments (.61), with their assistants (.73), and with their own department heads (.62). Department heads confer with their supervisors (.67) as well. This is nothing more than one of the two triangles. When department heads confer with their supervisors, six other links are associated. These are strong downward flows and a criss-cross pattern. Supervisors confer with their own workers (.67), with workers in other departments (.62), with their assistants (.91), and with their department heads (.83). Finally, workers confer also with supervisors in other departments (.62) and with other workers (.56).

Clearly, then, the definition of an organic network is really the combination of three basic kinds of unscheduled communication: horizontal, criss-cross, and vertical down. This leaves vertical up as the one remaining pattern to be explored.

Vertical Upward Networks

The pattern of workers conferring frequently with their supervisors does not have the same significance as supervisors meeting frequently with their department/divisional head level, as a comparison of Figures 9.5 and 9.6 makes apparent. In the former situation, we see the emergence of a criss-cross pattern at the bottom of the authority and status hierarchy. In the latter, we observe a heavy downward flow. This suggests that the content of communication in these two patterns may be quite different.

The pattern emerging in Figure 9.6 would appear to be another viable unscheduled communication arrangement, what Burns and Stalker (1961) would call the hierarchical arrangement. It is clear that an organization does not need more than these few links within each department. This is the appropriate pattern for an organization which has largely programmed its managerial and production process and uses sanctions to enforce the standards of behavior. If one can infer the level of total unscheduled communication by the strength of the association, we see that these pathways are not that related to increases in unscheduled communication. We have already suggested that is because every organization must first build these vertical links. *What is particularly interesting is the job description of the supervisor in the hierarchical versus the network of unscheduled communication. In both instances, they confer with department heads and professionals but in the first pattern it is within, and in the second it is without.* If there are communication problems at the super-

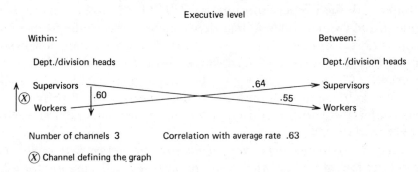

Figure 9.5 Communication pathways associated with communications from workers to their supervisors.

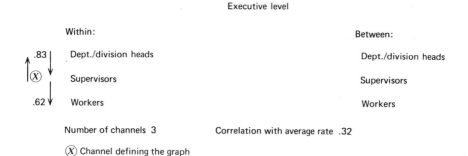

Figure 9.6 Communication pathways associated with communications from supervisors to their own department heads.

visory level it may be because of the violation of this ideal typical arrangement.

The pattern of Figure 9.5 is essentially the one described by Dalton (1950) and the one analyzed by Victor Thompson (1961), who noted that horizontal communication can undercut the traditional authority structure. Since the correlation with the average communication rate is .63, that is, less than the pattern of Figure 9.2, it is interesting to speculate that it occurs in time prior to the emergence of a complete organic network. Here, one assumes that the size of the correlation between a particular pathway and the average rate is a *rough* approximation of the order in which pathways become activated. The history of Community Hospital suggests this kind of sequence as well. If our assumption is correct—and there are dangers in inferring temporal sequence with cross-sectional data—then it provides some clues as to what might be other kinds of networks than the hierarchical one of Figure 9.6 and the organic one of Figures 9.2 and 9.3, a problem discussed below.

Other Possibilities

We have not explored all the unscheduled communication pathways, nor do we need to. Each of the links that is intralevel, for example, supervisors conferring with their assistants and vice versa, have too

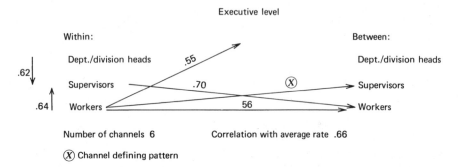

Figure 9.7 Pathways of unscheduled communications associated with communications of workers with supervisors in other departments.

few individuals to represent stable patterns. In addition, they are generally associated with the horizontal, criss-cross, and vertical downward pattern of the organic network. This leaves only a few of our 21 channels unaccounted for.

One of these is professional workers conferring with supervisors in other departments. Again, this link is associated with moderate rates of unscheduled communication $(r=.66)$ and is very much like Figure 9.4. This pattern might be called the upward flow of communication (see Figure 9.7.) When there are variations in the frequency of communication of workers with supervisors in other departments, then the following pathways are also activated: workers conferring with their own supervisors $(r=.64)$, workers with the executive level $(r=.55)$, workers with workers in other departments $(r=.56)$, and department heads with their supervisors $(r=62)$, supervisors among themselves $(r=56)$, and supervisors with other workers $(r=70)$. Given the several horizontal flows—both workers and supervisors with workers in other departments—and given that the correlation of this pattern with average communication rate is between that of Figures 9.4 and 9.3, we again have the implication of the evolution of an upward flow towards a truer network pattern of information flow.

Another pattern we have not considered is the pathway between department heads and supervisors in other departments. When the correlations are examined, what emerges is a slight variation of

Figure 9.1. In other words, a horizontal and a vertical downward pattern of unscheduled communication.

INTERRELATIONSHIPS BETWEEN UNSCHEDULED AND SCHEDULED COMMUNICATION

So far we have been discussing only unscheduled communication. Even though the imagery of a communication network is more appropriate for this channel, one can construct a network of committees that would knit an organization together. Indeed, a large number of coordination problems are more effectively handled within committee meetings involving individuals from different parts of the organization. There is some suspicion that unscheduled communication speaks more to the issue of professional control by socialization than coordination, while committees have the opposite content. This is particularly true for what might be called the executive committee. Just as in Community Hospital, most of our 16 organizations have a committee composed of the executive level and all department heads, the inner circle, to use James Thompson's (1967) term for it. Unlike the executive committee of the physicians, none of the positions are elected and the committee meets more frequently. Furthermore, it is an organization-wide committee in our comparative sample rather than a professional one as it is in most community hospitals, and, thus, it is more concerned with coordination of the organization per se.

One objective of having an elaborate committee and departmental set of meetings is to facilitate an efficient flow of feedback. Thus, there is the distinct possibility that organizations with widespread participation in committees that meet often would have less need for unscheduled communication. We could speculate that the two channels are alternative mechanisms and therefore negatively associated. We need to explore this possibility again for practical reasons in giving counsel to organizations on how they might construct their organizations. Table 9.2 reports the correlations between these two channels.

Several quick summary observations can be made about Table 9.2. If committee and/or department meetings were a substitute for un-

Table 9.2   The Correlation Between Unscheduled and Scheduled Communication Rates

	Committees		Department Meetings	
	Average Frequency of Meetings	Proportion in Meetings	Average Frequency of Meetings	Proportion in Meetings
C. Department and division heads				
1. With the executive level	.16	− .19	.09	− .17
2. Among themselves	.47[a]	.41	.28	.25
3. With their supervisors	.40	.33	.03	.06
4. With their workers	− .22	− .46[a]	.00	− .39
5. With other dept./division heads	.33	.32	.35	.23
6. With other supervisors	70[c]	.29	.06	.09
7. With other workers	.13	− .01	.21	− .03
D. Supervisors				
1. With the executive level	.25	.43	.26	.19
2. With their dept./division heads	.35	.20	− .11	− .03
3. Among themselves	.48[a]	.32	.06	.01
4. With their workers	.55[b]	.25	− .15	− .26
5. With other dept./division heads	.00	.27	.13	.26
6. With other supervisors	.66[b]	.56[b]	.59[b]	.50[a]
7. With other workers	.65[b]	.45[a]	.05	.18
E. Workers				
1. With the executive level	.15	.24	.25	.19
2. With their dept./division heads	− .23	− .03	.15	.11
3. With their supervisors	.37	.06	− .16	− .04
4. Among themselves	− .05	− .57[b]	− .16	− .56[b]
5. With other dept./division heads	.09	.20	.21	.11
6. With other supervisors	.36	.28	.19	.37
7. With other workers	.43	.19	.24	.08
F. Average unscheduled communication rates	.27	.03	.10	.00

[a] P < .10.
[b] P < .05.
[c] P < .01.

scheduled communication rates, then we would expect to see a large number of negative correlations in this table. This is not the case. If anything, the reverse is true. An active flow of scheduled communication tends to be associated with an active flow of unscheduled communication. Although the correlations are small for the most part, they are in the positive direction. This association is especially true for the first column in the table, the average attendance in committee meetings. In particular, it is interesting to note that active committee meetings do not preclude workers conferring frequently with other workers (D7, $r=.42$), department heads conferring with other supervisors (C5, $r=.75$), supervisors with other workers (C7, $r=.65$), supervisors with other supervisors (C6, $r=.76$), or other channels in a downflow, such as department heads with their own supervisors (C3, $r=.40$), or supervisors with their workers (D4, $r=.58$).

At the same time, an active participation in committees does seem to lessen relatively the flow between department heads (C5, $r=.33$), as one might expect. The upper echelons are the individuals most likely to be involved in these meetings and thus there is less need for unscheduled communication.

Department meetings appear to be almost totally unrelated, or certainly less than committee meetings, to the various level-specific pathways of unscheduled communication. This is perhaps the most surprising. One would assume that this kind of meeting is more likely to replace the spontaneous seeking out of individuals. We do see that rates are depressed in some cases. Supervisors talk less to their workers (D4, $r=-.11$) and workers among themselves (E4, $r=-.16$). Given the general pattern of positive correlations, these negative relationships are at least substantively significant. But these associations are not large enough to be statistically meaningful. Again, we find, if anything, more positive than negative correlations, although very small ones.

Increases in unscheduled communication activate the horizontal and criss-cross flows between departments and not within them. This means that departmental meetings are substituted for vertical flows both up and down and not between departments. This makes the generally positive association between unscheduled communication rates and frequent participation in committees all the more substantively significant. *An active committee system is associated, in part at least, with an organic network of unscheduled communication.*

THE MECHANICAL AND THE ORGANIC NETWORKS

In general, both channels of communication increase together more or less. They are not substitutes for each other. Each channel may specialize in a particular content, scheduled communication is concerned more with the content of feedback and unscheduled more with socialization. We would assume that organization-wide committees are more concerned with managerial coordination. Unscheduled communication rates between department and/or division heads should also have this content. Thus, at the departmental/divisional level the parallel growth is not as strong as it is at some other levels. Supervisors are likely to be involved with both managerial and production coordination and are perhaps one of the key links, like the full-time teachers in Community Hospital, in socialization. As a consequence, the strongest associations occur between scheduled and unscheduled communication channels at this level in the hierarchy. In contrast, the professional workers are more concerned with production coordination and socialization, communication content not likely to be found in organization-wide committee meetings. They are part of the content of the department meetings, and this kind of scheduled feedback mechanism is more likely to be a substitute for unscheduled communication. Again, a necessary word of caution. We did not measure content, in part because we felt there are some great reliability problems. But if we can make some inferences about content, then the different patterns of findings become one general story about communication processes whether involved with programming or with feedback. We have used the same inferences in interpreting the results, but it is still important to recognize that an inference is all that one can make about communication content in a comparative study of organizations.

In analyzing our communication networks, we should repeat the various restrictions which this particular sample of 16 organizations imposes on our own interpretations. The sample does not represent as wide a diversity of organizations as one would like. The range of communication rates is also restricted. Most of the organizations are professional ones, and, therefore are likely to rely upon high feedback and socialization, the organic model of Burns and Stalker (1961). Only the public welfare departments, staffed by nonprofessionals and concerned with dispersing financial aid rather than counseling or therapy, are close to what a mechanical organization might be like. But again, as in our analysis of Community Hospital, we can speak of relative degrees of organicity or of the evolution from a hierarchical arrangement to a network of communications.

Community Hospital can be conceptualized as a speeded-up description of this moving equilibrium process. As part of this process, we observed a movement from a hierarchical arrangement to a network of coordination and control via increases in both scheduled and unscheduled communication. The comparative data, although collected at one time, can be interpreted as approximately some evolutionary process from low to high unscheduled and scheduled communication rates. Suppose we assume that the correlation of a particular pattern with the average rate is a very rough approximation to the order in which pathways are developed or activated. If we do this, we can delineate at least four coordination and control types, that is, two variations on the mechanical and organic themes, the hierarchical and network patterns. We can also suggest that these represent states moving in equilibrium.

The first state is not well represented in our data. It is depicted in Figure 9.8 as a simple upward flow of conferring from bottom to top. Figure 9.6 comes close to this pattern, having some downflows as well. One only needs three links—in terms of our simplified organization chart—to unite the structure together. As long as there is an upward flow of information within each department there is total knowledge about the organization, at least at the executive level. However, this means much less volume of unscheduled communication. Correspondingly, there are few organizational committees or department meetings, or the department meetings are used as a substitute for the unscheduled communication flow. As Burns and Stalker suggest, when subordinates confer with superiors, they probably receive instructions. *The key point is that in this pattern of communication, there is not much actual feedback or socialization.* Other studies (Blau and Scott, 1962) have indicated that lower-level subordinates will actually withhold information in order to protect themselves. Again, it is important to recognize that there is not an absence of other communication links. We are speaking about a relative emphasis on particular pathways.

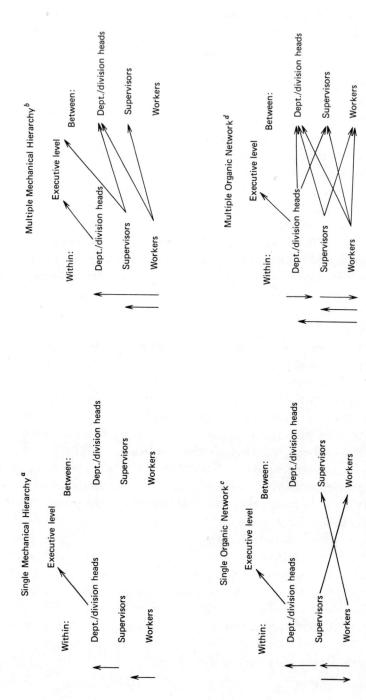

Figure 9.8 States in the evolution of feedback and socialization. (a) See Figure 9.6. (b) See Figure 9.4. (c) See Figures 9.5 and 9.7 (d) See Figures 9.2 and 9.3.

184

Two intermediate states in the emergence of a complete organic network, our idea of equifinality, appear to be represented in our data. One we can call the multiple mechanical hierarchies, as seen in Figure 9.4. Its distinctive feature is that instead of conferring with only one's immediate superior, one can ask almost anyone in the organization for advice. Most importantly, one can ask one's superiors in other departments. Thus, the name multiple hierarchies. But it is still a mechanical form in spirit because of the heavy emphasis on conferring with superiors. We would expect a relative absence of committee and department meetings in this structure. Burns and Stalker argue that an emphasis on vertical communication flow is characteristic of mechanical models. We are suggesting that these hierarchies can be more or less open. One can imagine many stages of openness, with more and more vertical channels of upward communication being established as authority and status differences diminish. *Thus, given fewer differences in rank but little diversity—a particular combination of our premises in our theory of coordination and control—we expect the multiple mechanical hierarchical system of coordination and control.*

In contrast, the opposite combination of forces—a great deal of diversity but great differences in rank—should produce the single organic network. This is depicted in the lower left-hand corner of Figure 9.8. The name is perhaps not the best that one can imagine, but it does call attention to two important characteristics. The word organic means a greater emphasis on downward flows as opposed to upward and the emergence of a criss-cross pattern. The word single calls attention to the fact that there is only one of the two triangles. In this pattern, we would expect a number of organization-wide committees, perhaps a viable substitute for the second triangle.

What is striking about this pattern is its similarity to the changes which occurred in Community Hospital. The department of medical education resulted in coordination at the bottom and not the top. It also parallels Dalton's early analysis of staff and line conflict (1950). Here, he observed that the managerial specialists, lower in the echelon, established horizontal pathways which tended to undermine the authority of the superiors. The single organic network would appear to be exactly this. One would expect, in time, that rank differences would be diminished and that a multiple or true organic network— the double-triangle structure—would emerge.

What additional assurances are there that these two patterns are indeed intermediate states in some moving-equilibrium process, and more importantly, that one is a variation on the mechanical model and the other is a variation on the organic? One piece of supporting evidence is provided by examining which pathways are associated with each of these patterns or their defining characteristic at a lower level of statistical significance, thus relaxing our criteria somewhat. If we now accept all correlations about .40 as being important, the second triangle begins to emerge—department heads conferring with their supervisors, who do likewise, and supervisors who confer with other department heads in the single organic network.

The relaxation of the standard with the multiple mechanical hierarchical arrangement does not produce the same effect. More upward vertical links are added between supervisors and their department heads and also with other department heads. One horizontal pathway is added—department heads conferring with their counterparts, the beginning of a movement towards an organic form. But this occurs at the top and not at the bottom of the status pyramid. The proliferation of more upward vertical links rather than horizontal leads to the interpretation that this is more a variation on a mechanical hierarchy than an organic network.

As the volume of unscheduled communication steadily increases, the full-blown organic network emerges. The criss-cross pattern is supplemented by horizontal networks and the preponderance of downward flows. Here, presumably, both factors—great diversity and few differences in rank—are operating to produce an organization with a high volume of scheduled and unscheduled communication. This is represented in our data by Figures 9.2 and 9.3. We might speculate that Figures 9.5, 9.7, and 9.3 are the precise intermediate steps before Figure 9.2, because they can be ordered·by the size of their correlation with the total volume of unscheduled communications.

Another important point is the number of links which tend to be active. In the mechanical network, we suggested that three linkages are enough. The two intermediate stages have six, the organic has 10 or more. This is far short of the full 21, but then it does not mean that there is not some information flow in all 21 pathways. We are discussing only the most critical ones under a certain set of conditions. All three networks we have observed in the data have the basic upward flow of the mechanical hierarchy. It is not as important in the organic network. Likewise, the hierarchical arrangement has some criss-cross and horizontal flows. Again, this is less important in the overall definition of this pattern of coordination and control.

CONCLUSIONS: THE EVOLUTION OF FEEDBACK AND SOCIALIZATION

Our analysis, by simplifying the larger number of level-specific channels into a few meaningful hierarchies and networks, provides a framework for future work. Each pattern has a relationship to our theory of coordination and control. The multiple mechanical hierarchies presumably exist when there are few rank differences and little diversity, or low centralization and low complexity. This might occur in a small organization where everyone is professional, well-trained, and of the same profession. Examples are elite social-work agencies and residential treatment centers. The single organic network exists when there are great differences in rank and great diversity, or high centralization and high complexity. This form does not remain for long. It creates conflict until the differences in rank are diminished, although the speed of change in Community Hospital was part of the problem there. The mental hospitals, in part because of their very large size, might be considered typical of this pattern. There are strong pressures towards a more complete organic form, multiple triangles of unscheduled communication supplemented with an active committee structure. If our proposed theory of cybernetic control is correct, then we can expect that the two intermediate states, the multiple hierarchical and the single organic, are temporary on the road to a complete communication network, what we have called the double triangle pattern. Both can have certain tendencies towards instability, depending upon the speed of change and the kind of changes that occur.

Parallel to the development of single and multiple networks is the proliferation of committees and their activation on a widespread basis. Although committee meetings somewhat diminish unscheduled communication on the departmental and divisional levels, they do not affect the lower echelons.

This underlines the importance of studying committee and department meetings separately. These findings also give increased confidence that the two forms of scheduled communication have different content. The department meetings are more likely to contain instructions and discussions about interpretations of rules; the committee meetings are more likely to be concerned with coordinating the organization by feedback.

Similarly, one can reasonably infer that the content of unscheduled communication varies depending upon the particular pathways involved. The more emphasis on vertical upward flows of conferring—and here the wording of our questions is critical—the more likely the content involves receiving instruction. Horizontal and downward flows between departments are more likely to represent true feedback and socialization. Obviously, feedback occurs in both extremes. But these extremes vary, at least in the volume of information feedback. This is the distinctive feature of the organic network. It contains *heavy* flows of information feedback.

Our findings suggest that the growth of information feedback can occur in several ways. One chain of events is as follows. For a variety of reasons, there are few rank differences. As a consequence, professionals feel free to consult with whom they choose. As this occurs more and more, active upward links are established. Gradually, perhaps as a consequence of other factors, such as the addition of new specialties, horizontal links between departments are created as well. With this, we have the emergence of a full-grown organic network, where feedback occurs from all parts of the organization. This is probably the peaceful path of evolution, one very different from that depicted in Community Hospital.

The later scenario is that changes first occur in the complexity of the organization's division of labor, which, in turn, leads to the single organic network. This pattern is unstable because it produces conflicts. It must evolve toward the diminishing of centralization and stratification, the multiple or two-triangle network of feedback. There are at least two conceivable evolutionary directions between the hierarchical arrangement and the network arrangement, between the mechanical steady state and the organic one. One is probably less likely to produce conflict than the other. Of the two, the pattern as represented in Community Hospital is probably more typical. This does not mean the same intensity of conflict, because Community Hospital accelerated the normal process of structural differentiation, but it still means some conflict, as Victor Thompson (1961a and b) has suggested.

If our line of reasoning is correct, and it must be verified in other studies, then we have some prescriptive advice for organizational elites. There is a clearly preferred way of adding linkages and creating committees with changes in centralization, stratification, or complexity. The role-set of the supervisor appears to be a very important element in creating an effective communication structure, whether for a programmed organization or one with high feedback and socialization.

X

Testing a Theory of Coordination and Control

THE COMMUNITY HOSPITAL ILLUSTRATED the emergence of a new form of coordination and control via the development of a communication network. But we want to test the cybernetic theory comparatively, in organizations that are somewhat different. More specifically our concern is whether complexity, formalization, centralization, and stratification are related to the volume of scheduled and unscheduled communication, especially of a horizontal direction as hypothesized.

Premises
1. All organizations require coordination and control.
2. There are two basic mechanisms for achieving coordination and control: Programming with sanctions and high feedback with socialization.
3. The greater the diversity of organizational structure, the greater the emphasis on high feedback with socialization.
4. The greater the differences of rank in the organizational structure, the greater the emphasis on programming with sanctions.

Derived Hypotheses.
A. The greater the degree of complexity, the higher the rate of communication.
B. The greater the degree of complexity, the higher the rate of horizontal communication.

C. The greater the degree of formalization, the lower the rate of communication.

D. The greater the degree of formalization, the lower the rate of horizontal communication.

E. The greater the degree of centralization, the higher the rate of rewards.

F. The greater the degree of centralization, the higher the rate of punishments.

G. The greater the degree of stratification, the higher the rate of rewards.

H. The greater the degree of stratification, the higher the rate of punishments.

The definitions for each of these concepts was provided in Chapter 1. Complexity was defined as the diversity of occupations; formalization, as the absence of diversity in work; centralization, as the differences in rank of power; and stratification, as the differences in rank of rewards. Each concept is a special case of the more abstract concepts used in the premises. In this sense, we can say that the hypotheses are derived from the premises. (For a more extended discussion of derivation, see Hage, 1972.)

A frequently ignored problem in testing a theory is the determination of the correct or valid measures for each variable deduced from the premises or assumptions (Hage, 1972). As we examine alternative indices for the theoretical concepts, we are more likely to learn the best measures for a variable. Furthermore, we lessen the chance of disproving a theory erroneously. Oddly enough, theories have died too soon because they were tested with the wrong measures, not because they were bad theories. In the present state of development in the sociology of organizations, there are a variety of indices and indicators for major structural concepts (Price, 1972) of complexity, formalization, and centralization. (Stratification has not played a prominent role as yet in organizational research.) To have multiple measures is not to say that each is equally valuable in testing the cybernetic theory of coordination and control.

The thrust of the theory of coordination and control is that, as organizations become more complex and decentralized, whether the elite wants to or not, they are forced to rely more and more upon increased communication rates, both scheduled and unscheduled, especially those between departments.

As the various hypotheses are examined, alternative measures for each concept are tested as well. In the present state of organizational knowledge (Price, 1972), there is agreement about the importance of variables, such as complexity, centralization, and formalization, but there is less agreement about the best measures of these variables. Therefore, we must consider several measures for each variable. The second objective is to discover the best operationalizations of particular concepts.

DIVERSITY, FEEDBACK, AND SOCIALIZATION

Complexity and Communication

Three measures of organizational complexity are considered: the number of occupational specialties, the degree of professional activity, and the number of departments. The first is the number of specific occupational activities carried out by the various respondents in each organization. (See Appendix A for a discussion of these measures.) The second reflects the degree to which organizational members are active in professional organizations (i.e., the degree to which they belong to professional societies, attend professional meetings, and present papers or hold office in such organizations). The third is self-explanatory.

The first derived hypothesis is that the intensity of both scheduled and unscheduled communication will vary directly with the degree of complexity. The second hypothesis is that such communication is most likely to be in a horizontal direction.

As shown in lines A1 and F of Table 10.1, the more diversified the occupational structure of an organization, the greater the involvement in organization-wide committees ($r = .66$) and the higher the intensity of total unscheduled communication ($r = .51$). The relationship between the diversity of the occupational structure and the frequency of attending departmental meetings is in the predicted direction, but quite weak ($r = .20$), as shown in line B1. The second measure of complexity, the degree to which the staff is professionally active, has no strong relationships with any of the measures of intensity of communication, although each is in the predicted direction; in the case of the intensity of overall unscheduled communication, the relationship is quite high as shown in line F ($r = .42$).

Table 10.1 Pearsonian Correlation Coefficients Between Indicators of Complexity and Measures of Scheduled and Unscheduled Communication Among 16 Health and Welfare Organizations

	Number of Occupational Specialties	Professional Activity	Number of Departments
Scheduled communication			
A. Organization-Wide committee meetings			
1. Average number attended per month	.66[a]	.32	.48[b]
2. Proportion of staff involved	.31	.20	.14
B. Departmental meetings			
1. Average number attended per month	.20	.25	.00
2. Proportion of staff involved	.13	.30	.07
Unscheduled communication			
C. Dept./division heads			
1. With the executive level	.42	−.08	−.06
2. Among themselves	.79[c]	.52[b]	.44
3. With their supervisors	.36	.08	.26
4. With their workers	−.09	−.04	−.15
5. With other dept./division heads	.46[b]	.12	.31
6. With other supervisors	.76[c]	.33	.62[a]
7. With other workers	.32	.00	−.10
D. Supervisors			
1. With the executive level	.37	.23	.02
2. With their dept./division heads	.25	.15	.31
3. Among themselves	.43	.05	.27
4. With their workers	.44	.16	.25
5. With other dept./division heads	.15	.47[b]	.02
6. With other supervisors	.12	.05	.00
7. With other workers	.77[c]	.37	.47[b]
E. Workers			
1. With the executive level	.40	.28	−.11
2. With their dept./division heads	−.18	.13	−.37
3. With their supervisors	.44	.39	.15
4. Among themselves	.28	−.16	.17
5. With other dept./division heads	.15	.03	−.14
6. With other supervisors	.55[b]	.37	.12
7. With other workers	.66[c]	.33	.33
F. Average Rate	.51[b]	.42	.28

[a] $P < .01$.
[b] $P < .10$.
[c] $P < .05$.

The number of departments, a common measure in the organizational literature for complexity or structural differentiation (Blau, 1970; Hall, Haas, and Johnson, 1967b; Price, 1972), like professional activity, has the same pattern of findings, but in general, it appears to be a weaker measure, at least as far as one can judge by the size of a correlation in a cross-sectional analysis.

Our first hypotheses is supported for both scheduled and unscheduled communication. As for our second hypothesis, there is little relationship between our measures of departmental meetings and our measures of complexity, which indicates that it is horizontal organization-wide committee meetings and not vertical departmental meetings that are affected by complexity. A better test of the direction of communication is seen in examining the flow of unscheduled communication. We discover that criss-cross links tend to be positively affected by the number of occupational specialties. Thus, department and division heads confer among themselves (C2, $r=.79$) and with their colleagues in other departments (C5, $r=.46$), but also with supervisors in other departments (C6, $r=.76$). Supervisors also confer among themselves (D3, $r=.43$) and with workers in other departments (D7, $r=.77$). Workers confer with supervisors (E6, $r=.55$) and workers in other departments (E7, $r=.66$). In other words, we have the basic two triangle pattern of the organic network. This is further seen in that supervisors confer with their own workers (D4, $r=.44$) and the latter do likewise (E3, $r=.44$), though the magnitude of the association is more modest.

For unscheduled communication rates, the impact of professional activity is much less. Supervisors are more likely to confer with other department heads (E5, $r=.47$). Most of the links in the double-triangle pattern are weaker or nonexistent.

In most instances, the number of departments reflects the same pattern as the number of occupational specialties. The size of the correlation, however, is usually diminished. This indicates that the number of occupational specialties may indeed be the best measure for the degree of complexity or structural differentiation. There are good theoretical reasons as to why the number of departments may not be the best measure of complexity. Diverse occupations are sometimes combined into teams within the same department. Under these circumstances, the number of departments and the variety of occupational specialties will not be highly correlated, thereby reducing or obscuring the real amount of organizational complexity, assuming that the number of different specialties is most important. Theoretically, it can be argued that organizational struggles for power, rewards, and rights are more likely to center around occupational than departmental groups. Certainly, the problems of coordination appear to be greater among occupational groups, each with their own perspectives and terminologies, and values and beliefs, than departments per se, unless the latter are organized around occupational groups as they were in Community Hospital.

For many of the same reasons, professional activity is not the best measure either. It taps how professionalized each occupational group is rather than the number of groups. Diversity is more directly measured by the variety of occupational specialties. Professional activity can be best seen as a qualification to our measure of the number of occupational specialties; each one might be weighed by the degree of professional activity.

Formalization and Communication

The measures of formalization included here are, first, the degree to which respondents reported that a complete job description for their job exists, and, secondly, the degree of job specificity. (See Appendix A for a discussion of these indices.) The latter measure included a number of additional items reflecting the programming of jobs, such as the existence of specific procedures for various contingencies, written records of job performance, and well-defined communication channels. The derived hypothesis is that the greater the degree of formalization, the lower the rate of communication, and second, the interactions that exist are likely to be upward communication within the chain of command.

In general, we find that the correlations between formalization and measures of scheduled and unscheduled communication are not as strong as those between complexity and communication rates. The existence of job descriptions tends to be negatively associated with the average frequency of participation in organization committees ($r = -.30$), as shown in lines A1 and A2 of Table 10.2. The existence of job descriptions has no relationship with the measure for departmental meetings, however. Job specificity also has weak negative

Table 10.2 Pearsonian Correlation Coefficients Between Indicators of Formalization and Measures of Scheduled and Unscheduled Communication Among 16 Health and Welfare Organizations

	Presence of Job Descriptions	Index of Job Specificity
Scheduled communications		
A. Organization-Wide committee meetings		
1. Average number attended per month	−.30	−.31
2. Proportion of staff involved	−.40	−.29
B. Departmental meetings		
1. Average number attended per month	−.09	−.57[a]
2. Proportion of staff involved	−.06	−.30
Unscheduled communications		
C. Dept./division heads		
1. With the executive level	−.17	−.02
2. Among themselves	−.09	.10
3. With their supervisors	−.29	.20
4. With their workers	−.16	−.15
5. With other dept./division heads	−.06	.04
6. With other supervisors	.06	−.10
7. With other workers	−.32	−.30
D. Supervisors		
1. With the executive level	−.30	−.10
2. With their dept./division heads	.03	.42
3. Among themselves	−.42	.00
4. With their workers	−.58[a]	−.05
5. With other dept./division heads	−.32	.12
6. With other supervisors	−.11	−.53[b]
7. With other workers	−.42	−.11
E. Workers		
1. With the executive level	−.40	−.26
2. With their dept./division heads	−.30	−.11
3. With their supervisors	−.35	.03
4. Among themselves	.16	.12
5. With other dept./division heads	−.16	−.01
6. With other supervisors	−.19	−.06
7. With other workers	−.47[b]	−.16
F. Average Rate	−.50[b]	−.12

[a] $P < .05$.
[b] $P < .10$.

relationships with these same measures. On the other hand, job specificity is highly related to the frequency of attendance at departmental meetings, meaning that the greater the degree to which jobs are programmed (as reflected by this measure), the fewer departmental meetings. The greater the degree to which there are job descriptions in an organization, the fewer the overall unscheduled interactions there are ($r - -.50$), although the relationship between job specificity and this measure of communication is quite small.

The relationships of the measures of formalization and intensity of organizational communication, both scheduled and unscheduled, suggest that the reduction in diversity or the increase in predictability has the effect of reducing the need for coordination and socialization via the communication rate. This is not to suggest that there is no information flow in such organizations, but rather that the need for a high volume of communication is less in such organizations than in those in which coordination and control is based primarily on feedback and socialization.

An examination of the unscheduled communication pathways indicates that, as one would expect, there is almost the exact opposite picture of what emerged with complexity. We find supervisors not conferring among themselves (D3, $r = -.42$), or with their workers (D4, $r = -.58$), or with other workers (D7, $r = -.42$). Likewise, workers do not confer with other workers (E7, $r = -.47$). While the association is weak (E6, $r = -.19$), workers also do not confer with supervisors in other departments when there are job descriptions. In other words, one of the key triangles, the one at the bottom, appears unnecessary, given formalization. This strengthens our interpretation that formalization is tapping only some aspects of organizational diversity.

In general, our index of job specificity indicates somewhat the same pattern of findings, but the correlations tend to be weaker, with some interesting exceptions. We find department heads conferring with their supervisors somewhat (C3, $r = .20$), but more importantly supervisors checking with their department heads (D2, $r = .42$). We see workers talking to their colleagues in the same department but not with those in other departments. Although the correlations are not statistically significant, they assume substantive interest because most of the correlations are negative. *These few positive associations reflect a basic theme in the previous chapter, namely that a general decline in the volume of unscheduled communication most affects the horizontal and criss-cross links.* It does not mean their absence, but a much greater reliance upon vertical up communication. We can reasonably expect that the content of these interactions is about the interpretations of rules and procedures.

We have explored several other measures of formalization (Aiken and Hage, 1968; Hage and Aiken, 1969), finding that different measures appear to work in different instances, which suggests that much remains to be done in the improvement of the measurement of this variable. A measure of the presence of a rules manual and of the amount of job codification behave in much the same manner as the index of job specificity. They suggest the same pattern of findings, but the associations are usually weaker and there are exceptions in particular instances. One reason these measures may contain a great deal of error is that the indicators are quite crude, employing a modification of a Likert-type scale. The measures for complexity have a much wider range, allowing for a greater discrimination than presence or absence of job descriptions, rules manuals, or even the various indicators in the several indices of formalization. While the latter have multiple items, their range in these 16 organizations is quite small relative to the degree of complexity and centralization.

RANK DIFFERENCES, FEEDBACK AND SOCIALIZATION

Centralization and Communication

Two different measures of centralization of organizational power are included here. The first is the index of participation in decision-making. It reflects the degree to which organizational members report participating in decisions about the hiring of personnel, the promotion of personnel, the adoption of new organization policies, and the adoption of new programs or services, or what we have called strategic decisions. The second measure of decision-making, which is concerned with the control over work, is the index of hierarchy of authority. Our hypothesis is that the first is positively related to the intensity of organizational communication, the second is negatively related to the communication variables.

Only one of our measures of centralization, the degree of participation in agency-wide decisions, was found to have strong relationships with the frequency of communication. There is a strong positive relationship between the degree of participation in organization-wide decisions and the frequency of attending both committee meetings (A1, $r=.60$) and departmental meetings (B1, $r=.45$). The relationship between participation in organization-wide communication and the frequency of unscheduled interactions is in the predicted direction (F, $r=.36$), but not strongly. The measure of control over work decisions is negatively related to the frequency of attending departmental meetings, as predicted (B1, $r=-.39$), but there is no relationship between this measure and the frequency of attending committee meetings (A1, $r=.10$) and the frequency of unscheduled communication (F, $r=.00$). Thus, participation in decisions about wider organizational issues, not work autonomy, is most highly related to the intensity of both scheduled and unscheduled communication.

Table 10.3 suggests the following patterns of findings. In general, there is much more vertical communication, especially across two status levels, when there is widespread participation in organization-wide decisions. We see both supervisors (D1, $r=.53$) and workers (E1, $r=.46$) conferring with the executive level. Supervisors and workers also confer with each other (D4, $r=.55$, and E3, $r=.46$, respectively). Supervisors confer with other department heads (D5, $r=.50$). Although the associations are weak, department heads confer, regardless of status level, with those in other departments, as do the supervisors. Only the workers seem less likely to have this pattern of communication behavior. All these findings indicate that decentralization lowers authority and status barriers. It appears to affect upward and downward communication more than the horizontal or crisscross patterns.

In the previous chapter we suggested that, from an evolutionary perspective, organizations might have fewer status barriers before they developed greater diversity. If this is so, Table 10.3 suggests that the multiple hierarchical pattern of unscheduled communication does occur. There is also much greater reliance on another vertical communication mechanism, namely departmental meetings. The contrast with the impact of complexity in scheduled and unscheduled communication is striking.

The hierarchy of authority should represent an opposite pattern

Table 10.3   Pearsonian Correlation Coefficients Between Indicators of Centrali-zation and Measures of Scheduled and Unscheduled Communication Among 16 Health and Welfare Organizations

	Index of Participation in Decision-Making	Index of Hierarchy of Authority
Scheduled communication		
A. Organization-Wide committee meetings		
1. Average number attended per month	.60[a]	.10
2. Proportion of staff involved	.61[a]	.03
B. Departmental meetings		
1. Average number attended per month	.45[b]	−.39
2. Proportion of staff involved	.37	.09
Unscheduled communication		
C. Dept./division heads		
1. With the executive level	−.06	.06
2. Among themselves	.36	.08
3. With their supervisors	.17	.17
4. With their workers	−.20	−.07
5. With other dept./division heads	.39	−.20
6. With other supervisors	.33	−.01
7. With other workers	.25	−.18
D. Supervisors		
1. With the executive level	.53[b]	−.00
2. With their dept./division heads	.10	.20
3. Among themselves	.26	.07
4. With their workers	.55[b]	.23
5. With other dept./division heads	.50[b]	.32
6. With other supervisors	.39	−.22
7. With other workers	.41	.06
E. Workers		
1. With the executive level	.46[b]	.02
2. With their dept./division heads	.11	.06
3. With their supervisors	.46[b]	.52[b]
4. With themselves	−.14	−.13
5. With other dept./division heads	.19	.07
6. With other supervisors	.17	.17
7. With other workers	.43	−.06
F. Average Rate	.36	.00

[a] $P < .10$.
[b] $P < .05$.

from the index of participation; a series of negative signs as opposed to positive ones. However, this is not the case. The associations are quite weak and appear to be inconsistent. Thus, this might not be the best measure for centralization. Elsewhere (Hage and Aiken, 1967b), we have shown this is true for a number of other structural variables, and we suggest some of the reasons for it.

Stratification and Communication

Although we have attempted to make our organizations identical in terms of the number of authority and status levels, the organizations do vary considerably in the proportion of members at particular levels. This proportion can be considered a rough measure of the degree of stratification in the organization. The greater the proportion of staff members in nonsupervisory positions, the more likely there will be great status differences between levels. We expect that the greater the degree of stratification, the lower the volume of communication, especially communication in a horizontal direction. An income ratio measure is the ideal for measuring the extent of stratification in an organization. Thus we are assuming that organizations with a large number of individuals at the bottom will have greater differences in rewards at each level of the status hierarchy. In any case, even if this assumption is unwarranted, where few people are at the top of the status pyramid, the position of a department or division head has more prestige.

Table 10.4 supports this assumption. The more the distribution of people among status levels reflects a peaked organizational structure—that is, a large proportion of staff at the bottom of the pyramid —the less the amount of upward communication. This is true for each category of upward communication included here. There is also less participation in committee meetings and fewer people involved in committees in organizations with this organizational characteristic. The same is true for the proportion involved in departmental meetings, although in each of these cases the correlations are not strong.

The volume of all unscheduled communication is also negatively related to this measure of stratification (F, $r = -.42$). We see that

Table 10.4 Pearsonian Correlation Coefficients Between an Indicator of Stratification and Measures of Scheduled and Unscheduled Communications Among 16 Health and Welfare Organizations

	Proportion of Nonsupervisors
Scheduled communication	
A. Organization-Wide committee meetings	
1. Average number attended per month	—.31
2. Proportion of staff involved	—.39
B. Departmental meetings	
1. Average number attended per month	—.06
2. Proportion of staff involved	—.42
Unscheduled communication	
C. Dept./division heads	
1. With the executive level	.26
2. Among themselves	—.53[a]
3. With their supervisors	—.19
4. With their workers	.32
5. With other dept./division heads	—.30
6. With other supervisors	—.38
7. With other workers	.12
D. Supervisors	
1. With the executive level	—.28
2. With their dept./division heads	—.08
3. Among themselves	—.11
4. With other workers	—.17
5. With other dept./division heads	—.66[b]
6. With other supervisors	—.15
7. With other workers	—.50[a]
E. Workers	
1. With the executive level	—.37
2. With their dept./division heads	—.36
3. With their supervisors	—.58[b]
4. Among themselves	.28
5. With other dept./division heads	—.22
6. With other supervisors	—.52
7. With other workers	—.27
F. Average Rate	—.42

[a] $P < .10$.
[b] $P < .05$.

there is little horizontal communication between workers of different departments (E7, $r = -.27$) ; yet, this is, on the basis of the numbers of individuals involved, the most likely place for it to occur. Workers even more strongly tend not to confer with their supervisors (E3, $r = -.58$) or with supervisors in other departments (E6, $r = -.52$), again indicating the status barrier.

Supervisors do not confer with department heads of other departments (D5, $r = -.66$), or with workers of other departments (D7, $r = -.50$). Status is a two-edged sword. It inhibits interaction on the part of both superior and subordinates, which is one reason it depresses volume. The inhibition is strongest with those of status in other departments. For example, we see less effect of this rough measure of stratification on the relationship between supervisors and their department heads (D2, $r = -.08$) and their workers (D4, $r = -.17$). Both are negative correlations but very small ones.

The only exceptions to the general decline in communication volume are that department heads do confer with their own workers (C4, $r = .32$) and workers in other departments (C7, $r = .12$). This is an anomalous finding which is hard to explain. That workers confer among themselves (E4, $r = .28$) makes a great deal of sense. Given the inhibition of status, one checks on the meaning of a rule with someone at the same status level in the same department. Again, none of these correlations is statistically significant, but since their sign is positive, they are of interest.

Several other measures of stratification were found to be weakly related, although in the predicted direction. These indices, which are a result of a factor analysis of a stratification scale developed in the hospital research by Seeman and Evans (1961) in their hospital research, are called affective orientation and social distance. Again, we have found that they are also weaker, that is, they have smaller size correlations with a number of other variables (see Hage and Aiken, 1969).

DIVERSITY, RANK DIFFERENCES, FEEDBACK, AND SOCIALIZATION

Although our theory of coordination and control treats diversity of structure and rank differences as separate factors affecting the choice

Table 10.5 Pearsonian Intercorrelations of Complexity, Formalization, Centralization, and Stratification Among 16 Health and Welfare Organizations.*

Organic Variables	Diversity				Rank Differences	
	High Complexity		Low Formalization		Low Centralization	Low Stratification
	1.	2.	1.	2.		
High complexity						
1. Number of occupational specialties	—					
2. Professional activity	.58	—				
Low Formalization						
1. Job description	.15	.16	—			
2. Job specificity	.02	.15	.52	—		
Low centralization	.40	.48	.59	.44	—	
Low stratification	.44	.72	.17	−.14	.45	—

* All signs have been changed to test how much the variables are interrelated as hypothesized in Hage (1965) and as depicted in the states of stability and instability of Chapter 2. Also see Aiken and Hage (1971).

of coordination mechanisms, in fact they are not separate. Organizations that have some diversity in their structure also tend to have fewer differences in rank (Hage, 1965). We have already seen this implicitely in the description of stability and instability states and in the study of Community Hospital. Table 10.5 shows the variables or structural coordinates of an organic system. Comparatively speaking, for these 16 health and welfare organizations, we find that if they are complex, they are also low in formalization, centralization, and stratification. The formalization measures, that is, the lack of job descriptions and job specificity, tend to have the weakest set of intercorrelations. They are related only to low centralization as measured by participation in decision-making. The other three variables, high complexity, low centralization, and low stratification are highly interrelated, with correlations of .40 or above. That the correlations are *not* perfect, that is, 1.00, indicates, to a certain extent, that differences in rank diversity can vary somewhat independently. They are two very general forces affecting the selection coordination and control mechanisms, as we have suggested in Chapter 4. In terms of our hypotheses, complexity can increase before centralization decreases; the reverse is equally likely. We have already seen this in the study

of Community Hospital. In our analysis of unscheduled communication networks, we noted situations where these variables can vary
independently as part of an evolutionary moving-equilibrium process. Thus one explanation for our less than perfect correlations is that
there are *several* intermediate states, our concept of equifinality again,
between the equilibrium points we have labeled mechanical and
organic stability. We can imagine that our cross-sectional data represents, even in this somewhat restricted universe of organizations,
both intermediate states, thus preventing the correlations from being
perfect. It should be noted that they are sizable, however.

Turning to the prediction of the precise combination of unscheduled communication and rewards and punishments, although we
have not measured rewards and punishments, we can ask whether the
combination of structural variables increases the correlation with
communication rates, especially those in a horizontal direction. There
are two separate ways this might be explored. One can estimate the
separate effects or influences of complexity as measured by the number of occupational specialties, for example, holding constant the
effects of centralization or stratification. One can estimate the combined effects of the two factors. The first problem is handled by partial correlational analysis, the second is amenable to analysis by modern multiple-regression techniques.

A word of caution is necessary regarding the use of multiple-regression techniques with the present study. Since there are only 16
organizations, one very rapidly loses degrees of freedom as additional
variables are added to the analysis. Thus, it requires much higher
correlations to be significant. At the same time, one quickly is
squeezed at the upper limits by measurement error, that is, it is
rather difficult to get much above a multiple r of .8 because even
small amounts of measurement error in the two variables will set this
as an upper limit. As a consequence, the multiple-regression analysis
reported in the next three tables should be regarded as only explora-
tory, a way of understanding better how the variable system affects
the reliance upon feedback socialization via communication rates
and especially in horizontal linkages.

The first issue of the impact of diversity independent of rank differences is explored in Table 10.6. The partials of complexity, as
measured by number of occupational specialties, are reported with,

Table 10.6 Partial Correlations of Complexity With Measures of Scheduled and Unscheduled Communication Holding Constant Centralization and Stratification.

	Centralization (Participation)	Stratification (Proportion of Workers)
Scheduled communication		
A. Organization-Wide committee meetings		
1. Average number attended per month	.58[a]	.62[a]
2. Proportion of staff involved	.10	.17
B. Departmental meetings		
1. Average number attended per month	.02	.19
2. Proportion of staff involved	−.02	−.07
Unscheduled communication		
C. Dept./division heads		
1. With the executive level	.49[b]	.62[a]
2. Among themselves	.75[c]	.73[c]
3. With their supervisors	.32	.32
4. With their workers	−.02	.06
5. With other dept./division heads	.36	.38
6. With other supervisors	.73[c]	.72[c]
7. With other workers	.25	.42
D. Supervisors		
1. With the executive level	.20	.28
2. With their dept./division heads	.23	.24
3. Among themselves	.37	.42
4. With their workers	.29	.41
5. With other dept./division heads	−.06	−.20
6. With other supervisors	−.04	.06
7. With other workers	.73[c]	.71[c]
E. Workers		
1. With the executive level	.26	.28
2. With their dept./division heads	−.25	.41
3. With their supervisors	.31	.25
4. Among themselves	.37	.46[b]
5. With other dept./division heads	.09	.07
6. With other supervisors	.54[a]	.42
7. With other workers	.60[a]	.63[a]
F. Average communication rate	.43	.40

[a] $P < .05$.
[b] $P < .10$.
[c] $P < .01$.

first, centralization and, then, stratification held constant. In each instance, only the strongest indicator is used. Complexity by itself affects the volume of scheduled communication represented in line A1 ($r_p = .58$ and $r_p = .62$); to a lesser extent, it also affects the volume of unscheduled communication (F, $r_p = .43$ and $r_p = .40$). Beyond this, particular pathways of unscheduled communication are activated, given a proliferation of occupational specialties. There is a criss-cross pattern in that department heads confer with supervisors in other departments (C6, $r_p = .73$ and $r_p = .72$), supervisors confer with workers in other departments (D7, $r_p = .73$ and $r_p = .71$), and workers confer with supervisors in other departments (E6, $r_p = .54$ and $r_p = .42$). There is one major horizontal pathway activated, workers with their counterparts E7, $r_p = .60$ and $r_p = .63$). In other words, we see basically the single organic network.

Holding constant the two variables tapping differences in rank is analogous to looking at an organization with increases in its division of labor without corresponding changes in other aspects of its structure, the situation in Community Hospital. Especially striking is the absence of supervisors conferring with other department heads. The partials are actually negative, and the small correlation for the pathway between department and division heads (C5, $r_p = .36$ and $r_p = .38$). *This provides support for our speculation in Chapter 9 that the single organic network was created by a change in the division of labor.* Again, partial correlation analysis is not a complete equivalent, but it can be suggestive of what might happen in a true experimental situation where only one variable is manipulated at a time. Since we actually did observe this situation in another study, we can have much more confidence in our interpretation.

There are several other points worth mentioning. The same pattern emerges regardless of whether one holds constant centralization or stratification. There are one or two differences, but in general the partials are, given the sample size of 16, remarkably similar. This provides some increased confidence that we are seeing the impact of a more complex division of labor independently of at least differences in rank. Ideally, one would like to compute second- or even third-order partials, but the small number of organizations precludes a more sophisticated analysis.

Table 10.7 reverses the procedure. One can examine the effect of

Table 10.7 Partial Correlations of Centralization and Stratification With Measures of Scheduled and Unscheduled Communications Holding Constant Complexity.

	Decentralization (Participation)	Stratification (Proportion of Workers)
Scheduled communication		
A. Organization-Wide committee meetings		
1. Average number attended per month	.50[a]	−.03
2. Proportion of staff involved	.56[b]	−.30
B. Departmental meetings		
1. Average number attended per month	.42	.03
2. Proportion of staff involved	.35	−.41
Unscheduled communication		
C. Dept./division heads		
1. With the executive level	−.28	.54[a]
2. Among themselves	.09	−.34
3. With their supervisors	.03	−.03
4. With their workers	−.17	.31
5. With other dept./division heads	.26	−.12
6. With other supervisors	.04	−.07
7. With other workers	.15	.30
D. Supervisors		
1. With the executive level	.45[a]	−.15
2. With their dept./division heads	.01	.04
3. Among themselves	.11	.09
4. With their workers	.46[a]	.03
5. With other dept./division heads	.49[a]	−.67[c]
6. With other supervisors	.38	−.11
7. With other workers	.18	−.29
E. Workers		
1. With the executive level	.36	−.24
2. With their dept./division heads	.21	−.50[b]
3. With their supervisors	.35	−.48[b]
4. With themselves	−.29	.46[c]
5. With other dept./division heads	.14	−.17
6. With other supervisors	.07	−.37
7. With other workers	.24	.03
F. Average communication rate	.21	−.25

[b] $P < .10.$
[b] $P < .05.$
[c] $P < .01.$

centralization and of stratification, holding constant complexity. Given low centralization, we see that there is an active committee structure, presumably to faciliate the decision-making implied by decentralization. There is a small tendency toward more department meetings and a higher volume of unscheduled communication (F, $r_p = 21$). The more striking effects are seen in particular pathways. Supervisors confer more with their workers and with department heads in other departments (D4, $r_p = .46$ and D5, $r_p = .49$) and with the executive level (D1, $r_p = .45$). But this is the limit of its independent effects. We see with this variable some movement toward the multiple mechanical network where vertical pathways between departments are activated. This is not an exact duplicate of the pattern suggested in the previous chapter. There is some tendency for workers to confer upwards, both internally and externally, with their departments, but all the partials are quite small, between .20 and .30.

Stratification, our other variable tapping status differences, has some of the same patterns. There are some differences. Stratification appears to inhibit upward flows of the supervisors to the executive level and especially other department heads (D5, $r_p = -.67$), and workers are inhibited from conferring with their supervisors and department heads (E3, $r_p = -.48$ and E2, $r_p = -.50$). Indeed, we see much conferring among themselves (E7, $r_p = .46$) as a structural and probably psychological necessity. There are some inconsistencies. We find some tendency for department heads to confer downward, which seems inexplicable (see lines C4 and C7). Also stratification, as we have measured it, and it must be remembered this is a crude approximation to what one would like, has little affect on the volume of scheduled or unscheduled communications.

If we could compute the combined effects of centralization and stratification holding constant complexity, we would see some aspects of the multiple mechanical network. There are suggestions of other factors affecting the variations on the mechanical and organic networks. As we have already indicated, size is probably one of them. Also, holding constant complexity does not exactly replicate the situation of a small welfare agency with a single occupational specialty, a special set of circumstances.

We could also explore the same variables, holding constant formalization. There seems to be no advantage in doing this, however, espe-

Table 10.8 Multiple Regressions of Various Two-Variable Combinations of Structure With Measures of Scheduled and Unscheduled Communication

	Complexity[a] Decentral- ization[b]	Complexity Formal- ization[c]	Complexity Stratifi- cation[d]	Decentral- ization Stratification
Scheduled communication				
A. Organization-Wide committee meetings				
1. Average number attend per month	.76[e]	.69[f]	.66[f]	.61
2. Proportion of staff involved	.61[f]	.47	.42	.62[f]
B. Departmental meetings				
1. Average number attended per month	.45	.21	.20	.48
2. Proportion of staff involved	.37	.13	.43	.47
Unscheduled communication				
C. Dept./division heads				
1. With the executive level	.49	.43	.65[f]	.26
2. Among themselves	.79[e]	.79[e]	.81[g]	.55[h]
3. With their supervisors	.36	.44	.37	.21
4. With their workers	.20	.20	.32	.32
5. With other dept./division heads	.51	.46	.47	.41
6. With other supervisors	.76[e]	.77[e]	.76[e]	.41
7. With other workers	.35	.42	.43	.36
D. Supervisors				
1. With the executive level				
2. With their	.56[h]	.45	.39	.54
dept./division heads	.25	.25	.25	.11

cially as our measures of it appear to be weaker. It might be more fruitful to try to improve our prediction by combining two variables in a multiple-regression analysis. An inspection of Table 10.8 indicates that complexity is so strongly related to other aspects of the social structure that in combination with each of the other variables, again only taking the strongest measure, there is only a slight improvement in the variance explained in scheduled and unscheduled communications. Complexity, in combination with decentralization or a lack of stratification, produces a high volume of scheduled and unscheduled communications, and we see essentially the multiple organic network; the two triangles emerge. Some links in this are not strong, however, at least in their statistical significance. The

Table 10.8   (*Cont.*)

	Complexity[a] Decentral- ization[b]	Complexity Formal- ization[c]	Complexity Stratifi- cation[d]	Decentral- ization Stratification
3. Among themselves	.44	.56[h]	.43	.26
4. With their workers	.60[h]	.68[f]	.44	.56[h]
5. With other dept./division heads	.51	.34	.68[f]	.70[f]
6. With other supervisors	.40	.15	.16	.40
7. With other workers	.78[e]	.83[g]	.79[e]	.54
E. Workers				
1. With the executive level	.51	.52	.45	.49
2. With their dept./division heads	.27	.38	.53	.37
3. With their supervisors	.54	.52	.61[f]	.62[f]
4. Among themselves	.39	.34	.52	.28
5. With other dept./division heads	.21	.20	.23	.24
6. With other supervisors	.56[h]	.56[h]	.63[f]	.53
7. With other workers	.69[f]	.76[h]	.66[f]	.44
F. Average communication rate	.54	.67[f]	.55[h]	.46

[a] The index is the number of occupational specialties.
[b] The index is the participation in organization-wide decisions.
[c] The index is job descriptions.
[d] The index is the proportion of workers.
[e] $P < .01$.
[f] $P < .05$
[g] $P < .001$
[h] $P < .10$

department heads conferring with other department heads (C5, $r_m =$ .51 and .47) and supervisors with other department heads (D5, $r_m = .51$) for the variable of centralization, while almost at the 10 percent level, are still below it. Even weaker is the link between supervisors and department heads within the same department (C3, $r_m = .36$ and .37; D2, $r_m = .25$ and .25). Thus, the bottom triangle is the stronger of the two. The tendency for all levels to confer openly with the executive level is present, although there are differences in the effect of decentralization combined with complexity and stratification combined with the same variable.

Table 10.8 also explores complexity in combination with formalization and decentralization in combination with stratification. An inspection makes clear the essential similarity of results regardless of which two variables are combined. *This demonstrates, perhaps more than anything else, that we do have a system of variables which are operating together, an organic system.* It is not only an assumption necessary to employ an analytical method, it is also a statement of fact about these 16 professional organizations.

CONCLUSIONS: COMMUNICATION AS FEEDBACK

These findings suggest the following story about the patterns of communications within organizations. As organizational structure becomes more diversified and, in particular, as specialization increases, the volume of communication increases because of the necessity of coordinating the diverse occupational specialists. The major direction of this increased flow of information is horizontal, especially cross-departmental, at the same authority and status levels. Committee meetings represent a greater emphasis on horizontal information flows than do department meetings because the former involve other departments. There is also an increased horizontal flow of unscheduled task communication. Conversely, insofar as organizational leaders attempt to coordinate the organization via programming, the necessity for information flow declines. The communication that exists is likely to be concerned with interpretation of regulations. Concomitantly, as power is dispersed in the organization, not only does the volume of communication increase, but the flow of communication across departments is also increased. Organization-wide committees and department meetings, which are both scheduled communication channels, are likely to be increased as well. As organizations have more and more of a sharp status pyramid, upward communication tends to be considerably inhibited just as it is when the power is concentrated in the hands of a small elite.

Alternative indices have been explored for each variable. Insofar as one can judge from a consideration of their face validity and the pattern of correlations, occupational specialties is the best measure of complexity, participation in organization-wide decisions is the best measure of centralization, and job descriptions is the best measure of formalization. Our measure for stratification, again on the basis of face validity, is not ideal, even though its pattern of correlations is generally consistent. Future research can explore other measures of these variables.

In evaluating the theory of coordination and of control, we cannot examine not only the size of correlations, the consistency of findings, and the utility of various indicators, but the validity of inference from our measures of communication—volume, direction, kinds, and the patterning of networks—that this represents feedback and socialization. Not all communication is of this kind. Consistently, organization-wide committees and the categories of unscheduled communication between departments—measures which themselves are associated—were most sensitive to the hypothesized scores on the structural variables. We suspect the reason is that these kinds of interaction are most likely to reflect attempts to provide feedback and socialization. Likewise the importance of our study of Community Hospital, although in a different context, increases because it provides other evidence that this is a reasonable inference. In contrast, upward communication or interaction with one's superiors within the same department is less likely to involve such content. They are the forms found in the more programmed organization. Unfortunately, we have no way of precisely determining if this is the case. Future research should explore the content of communication relative to coordination and control to ascertain if certain pathways, kinds, and networks represent an emphasis on feedback and socialization as opposed to instructions, orders, and discussions about the meaning of rules and rewards and punishments—the kinds of communication associated with a mechanical steady state.

It is worth repeating that all organizations have feedback and socialization. Here we are concerned with its volume, suggesting that organizations vary considerably along this dimension. Not all communication repeats information feedback, but the active organizational-wide committees and the between-departmental links are more likely to have this content. As volume increases, so does the possibility that the content is information feedback and socialization.

XI

Testing Alternative Theories
About Coordination and Control

ONE CAN IMAGINE A NUMBER of variables other than complexity, formalization, centralization, and stratification which influence the selection between the two basic coordination mechanisms. Technology, size, and ecology represent competing possibilities for a theory of coordination and control. Examples of work in the first two theoretical traditions are in the theories of Perrow (1967) and of Blau (1970). Since various variables within these theoretical orientations are imporatnt predictors, at least for some organization variables, they need to be tested vis-à-vis the direction and volume of scheduled and unscheduled communications rates to ascertain if they are superior in their capacity to predict. Although the number of possible variables within these traditions is infinite, there are at least three that should be explored, especially since they have frequently appeared in discussion of organizational communication. These are organizational size, "ecological spread," and routine technology.

The three theories might be called contextual theories, after the name given to variables by the Aston group of organizational researchers (see Pugh et al., 1963, 1968, 1969a). The name refers to the intermediate link between the environment and the organization. Size presumably shapes the organization; it is also a consequence of various environmental factors (Blau and Schoenherr, 1971). Likewise, technology is a link between the knowledge in the environment and the structure and function of an organization (Lawrence and Lorsch, 1967). This is in sharp contrast to the structural theory tested in Chapter 10. Although implicit in the theory is the notion that diversity and differences in rank are affected by other factors, such as a turbulent environment (Terreberry, 1968) or a stable one (Hage and Aiken, 1970), there is still the possibility of some direct effects. For example, size may increase complexity, but does it have an independent and direct effect on the volume of communication?

Besides exploring contextual theories, we also want to test the thesis of Lefton and Rosengren (1966) about the characteristics of the client affecting the structure and process of organizations. This theory is not as frequently employed as the above three, but it is a thesis that has some strong empirical support in the work of Pugh et al. (1969a). They found the variety of technologies, which they called operational variability, to be an important predictor of structure. The exploration of our measures of client variety and involvement are reported in the second section of this chapter.

Finally, we need to study whether social integration is affected in the same way as coordination and control. In addition to the literature on coordination and control, there is another one almost as large on whether workers are socially integrated (Blauner, 1964; Fullan, 1970). This goes to the heart of the distinction between task and expressive communication and integration. Again, to understand the limits of our theory of coordination and control, we need to see if it can include social integration.

CONTEXTUAL THEORIES OF COORDINATION AND CONTROL

Organizational Size and Communication

We would expect size to increase the volume of communication because of the coordination problems involved in controlling more individuals (Blau, 1970). By size we mean the number of individuals who work to achieve the goals of the organization. However simple this definition is, the exact measurement is somewhat more complicated. In our organizations, we specifically excluded the members of various boards because usually the boards only meet once a month for several hours. Full-time workers were counted as one member each, part-time workers as one-half a member. Volunteers were counted as one-tenth of a member. Since size has been hypothesized by Blau to be a cause of greater structural differentiation, or increased complexity, one might wonder if the increased size of the organization would not lead to greater communication rates among people. Certainly, the rank order or organizational size (which is used because of our skewed distribution) is somewhat correlated with number of occupational specialties $(r=.33)$ and number of departments $(r=.60)$, although somewhat less with professional activity $(r=.39)$—the three measures of complexity. This raises the question of whether it is size, not complexity, that leads to the proliferation of communication pathways and an increased information flow within them.

The relationship between organization size and each of the measures of scheduled and unscheduled communication is reported in Table 11.1. *Despite the correlation between size and number of occupational specialties, there is only one correlation between size and communication which is statistically significant but substantively not interesting—department heads conferring among themselves (C2, r=55).* Even the number of occupations has a stronger association $(r=.79)$. The measure of professional activity also has a higher zero order correlation. Of course, this is no means for not entertaining the idea that there may be some long-term process relating changes in size to changes in complexity and in communication. This would require an extensive panel study to determine. All that can be said with this cross-sectional data is that our measures of complexity are more *directly* associated with our communication measures than is size. There is a good theoretical reason for this. Organizations can grow by adding different kinds of jobs (Starbuck, 1965) as well as adding people. Our data suggest that it is the former kind of growth that is most likely to lead to greater reliance on interaction.

What is interesting, however, about the relationship between size (simply a rank ordering and therefore a conservative measure) and the frequency of all unscheduled communication is that the latter is a rate, that is, an average per member. In other words, size is in the computation controlled, yet it still has some association with this measure.

Table 11.1 Pearsonian Correlation Coefficients Between Size, Ecological Spread, and Routine Technology and Measures of Scheduled and Unscheduled Communication Among 16 Health and Welfare Organizations

	Organization Size (Rank Order)	Ecological Spread	Routine Technology
Scheduled communication			
A. Organization-Wide committee meetings			
1. Average number attended per month	.31	.50^a	− .72^b
2. Proportion of staff involved	.21	.41	− .53^a
B. Departmental meetings			
1. Average number attended per month	.20	.62^c	− .36
2. Proportion of staff involved	.11	.23	− .20
Unscheduled communication			
C. Dept./division heads			
1. With the executive level	− .16	.41	− .07
2. Among themselves	.55^c	.53	.05
3. With their supervisors	.35	.23	− .17
4. With their workers	− .02	.32	.10
5. With other dept./division heads	.38	.24	.05
6. With other supervisors	.35	.21	− .29
7. With other workers	.13	.50^c	− .21
D. Supervisors			
1. With the executive level	.25	.47	− .19
2. With their dept./divisional heads	.32	− .07	− .12
3. Among themselves	.26	.30	− .31
4. With their workers	.21	.18	− .54^c
5. With other dept./division heads	.27	.08	.06
6. With other supervisors	− .12	.20	− .57^c
7. With other workers	.30	.29	− .25
E. Workers			
1. With the executive level	− .16	.30	− .11
2. With their dept./division heads	− .11	.01	.23
3. With their supervisors	− .19	− .14	− .27
4. Among themselves	− .12	.05	.18
5. With other dept./division heads	.15	.34	− .01
6. With other supervisors	− .03	.16	− .01
7. With other workers	.39	.50^a	− .17
F. Average rate	.18	.19	− .02

^{a} P < .10.
^{b} P < .05.
^{c} P < .01.

Ecological Spread and Communication

Still a different factor that can affect communication rates is the sheer physical arrangement of the organization. Several studies in the ecology of organizations and homes have suggested this (Rosengren and De Vault, 1963; Festinger, 1950). While the general relationship between ecology and interaction is well appreciated, it has been much more difficult to find variables to describe ecological arrangements so that general hypotheses can be tested. We have attempted to create one variable, a crude trichotomy which we have labeled ecological spread. In our visits to the 16 organizations, we noticed that some were located on a single floor, others were located on several floors, others occupied a whole building, still others were scattered over a larger area. Physical opportunities for communication are decreased, although the need for interaction may be greater. Indeed, ecological spread could be the countervailing trend that would reduce the impact of size on interaction rates of organizational members. The more an organization is scattered in various buildings, the fewer opportunities the members have to interact.

Table 11.1 indicates that this is *not* true for the 16 organizations. *Indeed, there is a greater average intensity of both committee and department meetings (r = .50 and .62 respectively) as the physical plant is more widely dispersed.* Even the average unscheduled communication rate is positively correlated with ecological spread ($r = .19$). What is perhaps most interesting is that the frequency of interactions within departments are decreased while those between departments are increased. In other words, the spread of the organization in physical space apparently creates its own coordination difficulties, leading to attempts, as reflected in heightened communication volume, to bring together the scattered segments of the organization. Thus, contrary to the usual line of reasoning, namely that physical distance creates communication barriers, it seems to lead to higher interaction rates within these 16 organizations.

As one might expect, ecological spread is correlated with many of our structural variables. The correlation coefficient is .57 with the number of occupational specialties, .42 with participation in decision-making, and −.32 with the presence of job descriptions. It is not correlated with the measure of stratification ($r = .02$). This then raises the question of whether the correlations between our structural variables and communication measures would disappear when controlling for ecological spread.

The major impact in the level-specific unscheduled communication pathways is with workers conferring with their colleagues in other departments (E7, $r=.50$), an important link in the organic network, and with department heads conferring with workers in other departments C7, $r=.50$). In the former instance, complexity has a stronger impact, and in the latter, it does not. Also, a comparison of Tables 10.1 and 11.1 makes clear that the patterns of association for these two variables are not completely the same.

This leads to the conclusion that ecological spread independently has some minor effects on communication rates, but the structural effects are stronger. A partial correlational analysis indicates that in most instances, the structural variables are unaffected by ecological spread. Thus, while it represents a force, it is not as strong as the structural variables we have examined. One can also imagine that ecological spread is a physical manifestation of the social structure. One sees it not as an alternative explanation but as parallel to the structural variable. This comes about quite simply because different occupations usually desire to have their own separate location or organizational home. Thus the proliferation of occupations usually means the need for more physical space. One could also make a technological argument as well. Attached to each occupation is a set of tools and equipment—the radio isotope of the endocrinologist, for example, or the printing press of the rehabilitation trainer. These require physical space, frequently different shaped rooms, and thus there is a tendency to have several buildings when there are very disparate occupations. It is also worth noting that our variable ecological spread is a very crude one and much more needs to be done before any definite conclusions can be drawn about the importance of this tradition.

Routine Technology and Communication

Of our three contextual explanations for the choice of feedback as a mechanism of coordination and control, the technological explanation is the best thought out and articulated, as represented in the work of Perrow (1967) and James Thompson (1967). Perrow argues that programming should be mechanism, given a routine technology. Certainly, this variable is strongly related to our various measures of centralization and formalization (Hage and Aiken, 1969), if not complexity. Materials technology refers to the tools or physical artifacts used in a production process. In a broader sense, technology refers to the skills as well as tools and might be called knowledge technology (see Hickson et al., 1969, for a discussion of these concepts). Perrow appears to be more concerned with the latter than the former. Routine technology means that routine or predictable skills and/or tools are used to work on raw material, whether a physical or a social object. In the case of these rehabilitation agencies, the untreated client is conceived of as the raw material. A nonroutine technology would mean that each client was treated as a special case. Routine technology implies the opposite. The measures used for this measure (Hage and Aiken, 1969) largely tap how often something new or unusual occurs in work.

Routine technology is weakly related to most of our measures of communication as can be seen in Table 11.1, except for the volume of communication of scheduled communication, and several channels of unscheduled communication—supervisors conferring with workers (D4, r= −.54) and with other supervisors (D6, r= −.57). Thus, there is much support for the idea that routine technology leads to a choice of programming as a mechanism for coordinating and controlling the behavior of individuals. In this instance, routine technology strongly affects the average attendance at organization-wide committees (A1, r=.72) and weakly affects the average attendance at department meetings (B1, r=.36). What is striking is that it has no effect on the (F, r= −.02) average rate.

Does this mean that our theory is incorrect, at least for the volume of scheduled communication? Routine technology has a stronger impact than even our measures of formalization. Routine technology or its converse can be seen as another aspect of diversity. It represents diversity in the variety of work and may, in fact, be less of a technological measure than a structural one.

Routine technology increases centralization and formalization (it appears to have no impact on our measure of stratification) and thus the choice of programming. This means a lesser need for communication, especially those that reflect a content of feedback.

CLIENT SCOPE AND VARIABILITY

Each of the previous variables—size, ecological spread, and routine technology in the basis input, throughput, and output production process which is part of cybernetic thinking—can be conceived of as inputs that may shape the structure of the organization, although not necessarily determining directly the coordination and control mechanism. The variables of client scope and variability are somewhat harder to classify. In one sense, they are inputs as well—the clients are the raw materials processed by the agencies. Rehabilitation is a value-added process, a work flow. Thus, the amount of time a client spends in an organization (scope) and the number of client distinctions made (variety) can be seen as a technological or knowledge input. These two variables can also be conceived of as goal variables. In fact, some similar ideas are labeled charter, by Pugh and his associates (1969a) because they reflect a policy decision about the organization's objectives and what means will be taken to achieve them. Thus, the problem of knowing how to conceptualize the two measures of client scope and client variety.

From my own perspective, the two variables represent measures of what is known rather than a policy or a goal. It is the larger environment that generally develops the various techniques and skills which translate into a client being handled in a certain way, that is, confined to a mental hospital for the entire day, working in a sheltered workshop during the day or attending school, or having an hour-long conference with a social worker. Likewise, the growth of research leads to the recognition of many more kinds of clients, variations on the theme of physical or psychological handicaps. The question is whether it is policy to add these new distinctions as they are delineated. Only future research can determine whether this interpretation is correct.

Regardless of the interpretation of the meaning of the variables, an examination of Table 11.2 reveals that they have some impact, especially on certain pathways of unscheduled communications. The

Table 11.2 Pearsonian Correlation Coefficients Between Client Size and Client Variability and Measures of Unscheduled and Scheduled Communication Among 16 Health and Welfare Organizations

	Client Scope	Client Variety
Scheduled communication		
A. Organization-Wide committee meetings		
1. Average number attended per month	.15	.39
2. Proportion of staff involved	.13	.39
B. Departmental meetings		
1. Average number attended per month	.30	.10
2. Proportion of staff involved	.10	.37
Unscheduled communication		
C. Dept./division heads		
1. With the executive level	.34	.02
2. Among themselves	.47[b]	.46
3. With their supervisors	.29	.34
4. With their workers	.52[b]	−.36
5. With other dept./division heads	.19	.18
6. With other supervisors	.04	.39
7. With other workers	.61[b]	.00
D. Supervisors		
1. With the executive level	.53[a]	.42
2. With their dept./division heads	−.02	.25
3. Among themselves	.32	.31
4. With their workers	.25	.13
5. With other dept./division heads	.59[a]	.42
6. With other supervisors	−.26	.49[a]
7. With other workers	.28	.49[a]
E. Workers		
1. With the executive level	.41	.57[a]
2. With their dept./division heads	.45	.35
3. With their supervisors	.15	.59[a]
4. Among themselves	.06	−.10
5. With other dept./division heads	.48	.47
6. With other supervisors	.19	.74[c]
7. With other workers	.70[c]	.17
F. Average communication rate	.53[a]	.29

[a] P < .10.
[b] P < .05.
[c] P < .01.

222

variety of clients and the amount of time they spend in the organization in general does not significantly affect the volume of communication, except in one instance. The more time clients spend in the organization, the higher the overall volume of unscheduled communications (F, $r = .53$). Presumably, much of this deals with the problems of treating clients and perhaps also problems of their control.

The scope of client involvement appears to affect the breakdown of status differences because the pathways crossing more than one level are all affected. Thus, department heads confer more with their own workers (C4, $r = .52$) and with workers in other departments (C7, $r = .61$). Supervisors confer more with the executive level (D1, $r = .53$) and with department heads in other departments (D5, $r = .59$). Workers confer more with their department heads (E2, $r = .45$). Note the contrast with their own supervisors and with department heads in other departments (E5, $r = .48$). Only one horizontal link is activated, between workers (E7, $r = .70$). However, we do not see the emergence of the familiar triangle associated with complexity in particular.

Therefore, the client scope does seem to lead to the development of the multiple mechanical hierarchical pattern, discussed in Chapter 9. As clients spend more time in the organization, they present many more problems and difficulties that result in much upward communication, both within and between departments. Since scope only appears to affect unscheduled communication, we again have some evidence that it is important to measure each channel independently.

The contrast with the variety of clients is of interest. Workers confer more than their supervisors (E3, $r = .59$) and with the executive tive level (E1, $r = .57$) and with supervisors in other departments (E6, $r = .73$). Supervisors confer more with workers in other departments (D7, $r = .49$) and with their counterparts (D6, $r = .49$). In other words, we see a pattern more like the single organic network. *The variety of clients presumably creates a number of coordination and control problems which manifest themselves in the emergence of a triangle of unscheduled communication at the bottom of the authority and status pyramid.*

Do these findings cast some doubts on the theory of coordination and control? The impact of complexity, as measured by the number of occupational specialities, is seen in Table 11.3, first with scope held

Table 11.3 Partial Correlations of Complexity Controlling for Client Scope and Client Variability With Measures of Scheduled and Unscheduled Communication Among 16 Health and Welfare Organizations

	Client Scope	Client Variability
Scheduled communication		
A. Organization-Wide committee meetings		
1. Average number attended per month	.66[a]	.60[b]
2. Proportion of staff involved	.29	.19
B. Departmental meetings		
1. Average number attended per month	.09	.17
2. Proportion of staff involved	.10	−.02
Unscheduled communication		
C. Dept./division heads		
1. With the executive level	.34	.45[c]
2. Among themselves	.75[a]	.74[a]
3. With their supervisors	.29	.27
4. With their workers	−.36	.06
5. With other dept./division heads	.43	.43
6. With other supervisors	.81[a]	.72[c]
7. With other workers	.13	.35
D. Supervisors		
1. With the executive level	.22	.24
2. With their dept./division heads	.28	.17
3. Among themselves	.35	.35
4. With their workers	.38	.42
5. With other dept./division heads	−.09	−.02
6. With other supervisors	.24	−.09
7. With other workers	.75[a]	.72[a]
E. Workers		
1. With the executive level	.29	.23
2. With their dept./division heads	−.42	−.37
3. With their supervisors	.41	.27
4. Among themselves	.28	.35
5. With other dept./division heads	−.03	−.04
6. With other supervisors	.53[b]	.43
7. With other workers	.61[b]	.66[b]
F. Average communication rate	.40	.45

[a] $P < .01$.
[b] $P < .05$.
[c] $P < .10$.

constant and second with variability clients held constant. As can be seen, the essential pattern largely remains of an active committee structure with horizontal and criss-cross downward flows. Department heads confer frequently with supervisors in other departments (r_p = .81 and .72) regardless of the two client input variables. Supervisors do so with workers in other departments (r_p = .75 and r_p = .72). Workers confer with their colleagues in other departments (r_p = .61 and r_p = .66), again regardless of which variable is held constant. Somewhat affected is the horizontal relationship between department heads (r_p = .43 in both instances), and workers with supervisors in other departments (r_p = .53 and r_p = .43). Strongly influenced is the link of supervisors with other department heads (r_p = .09 and r_p = −.02).

Both client scope and variability appear to be a plausible alternative explanation for the emergence of unscheduled communication links. This is perhaps the sharpest difference in pattern that emerges when one compares Table 11.3 with Table 11.2. *Actually, they may be seen as reaffirming the critical importance of our premise that diversity affects the choice of feedback and socialization as a mechanism of coordination.* The amount of time spent by the client and the variety of clients are other aspects of diversity. However, they are not measures of organizational structure. They may be seen as causes of a diverse structure. Interestingly enough, their zero order correlations with the degree of complexity are slightly higher than the zero order correlation of size. The original insight of Lefton and Rosengren (1966) was exactly this, that both the longitude and latitude, so to speak, of client involvement would direct an organization towards a more complex social structure. The research of the Aston group (Pugh et al., 1969a), although on business firms in Birmingham, England, also shows about the same strength association between variety of operations and degree of specialization in the labor force. In other words, like size, routine technology, and ecological spread, these variables can be seen as forces that shape and affect the structure. Most of them do not have an impact directly on communication, scheduled or unscheduled.

The fact that client scope and variety does influence some patterns of unscheduled communication again argues for the necessity of studying both kinds of communication. Presumably, in part, this may reflect the differences in content. One can easily see how certain communication pathways of unscheduled communication, especially those at the bottom of the authority and status hierarchy, may reflect a concern with treatment per se rather than the issues of coordination and control, more strictly defined as the control of professionals rather than the control of clients. But it would require a very detailed and subtle research design to determine the kinds of content carried in the various channels. At best, we can only speculate about this.

SOCIAL INTEGRATION

Our remaining task in this chapter is to ask if our theory of coordination and control can explain the phenomenon of social integration. One can well imagine that organizations with high diversity and few differences in rank will have a large amount of feedback and of socialization as well as social integration. By this we mean that members will visit the homes of their colleagues after working hours for the purposes of friendship. This could occur via two different mechanisms. First, complexity, centralization, formalization, and stratification could create the conditions for friendship. Second, the sheer volume of communication, the interacting of different personalities, could lead to the development of friendship.

This second alternative is explored in Table 11.4. (See Appendix A for the measures of social integration.) In general, there is little relationship. In other words, sheer increases in volume per se do not matter nor does the particular level-specific pathway.

There are three kinds of social integration explored, the organizational integration, the community of workers, and the neighborhood community. A high proportion of unscheduled communications between departments affects the first two, but, as one might expect, not the third. In part, being socially integrated with fellow professionals is a substitute for being integrated in one's neighborhood. Occupation rather than residence becomes the social bond (Nisbet, 1970). (The correlation of average social visits with fellow workers and with neighbors on a weekly basis is $r = .09$, that is, there is no association.) This is further proof that the gesellschaft society in the vision of Toennies (Marwell and Hage, 1970) is a misrepresentation, at least for professional organizations.

Table 11.4 Pearsonian Correlation Coefficients Between Measures of Social Integration and Measures of Scheduled and Unscheduled Communication Among 16 Health and Welfare Organizations: Average Frequency of Visits

	With Fellow Workers	With Other Workers	With Neighbors
Scheduled communication			
A. Organization-Wide committee meetings			
1. Average number attended per month	.08	.24	.24
2. Proportion of staff involved	−.10	.13	.26
B. Departmental meetings			
1. Average number attended per month	.28	.12	.37
2. Proportion of staff involved	.29	.04	.35
Unscheduled communication			
C. Dept./division heads			
1. With the executive level	.31	−.52[a]	−.11
2. Among themselves	.05	.09	.29
3. With their supervisors	−.29	−.35	−.15
4. With their workers	.01	−.01	−.17
5. With other dept./division heads	.18	.26	.53[a]
6. With other supervisors	.36	.38	.32
7. With other workers	.39	.01	−.03
D. Supervisors			
1. With the executive level	−.07	.14	.11
2. With their dept./division heads	−.16	−.34	−.07
3. Among themselves	−.11	−.13	−.11
4. With their workers	−.19	.05	−.24
5. With other dept./division heads	−.14	.06	−.02
6. With other snupervisors	−.12	.10	.51
7. With other workers	.13	.11	.29
E. Workers			
1. With the executive level	.16	.10	.23
2. With their dept./division heads	−.30	−.16	.26
3. With hteir supervisors	.09	−.06	.01
4. Among themselves	.37	.21	.12
5. With other dept./division heads	−.16	−.08	.14
6. With other supervisors	.15	−.34	.26
7. With other workers	.32	.07	.14
F. Average communication rate	.16	.05	.14

[a] $P < .05$

A word of caution in interpreting these findings is necessary. We have correlated averages for organizations. This does not mean that an individual who interacts frequently with colleagues in other departments is necessarily going to have many friends among them. We are suggesting a more subtle relationship. The organic organization produces a climate that facilitates the development of work-related friendship. This climate is created by the diversity of occupations, which, in turn, means a greater variety of personalities (Lawrence and Lorsch, 1967a and b). The lessening of authority and of status means greater access to this variety. There are other factors on the individual level that affect the development of work-related friendships.

If one explores the first alternative, namely the direct impact of various structural variables, such as complexity, centralization, formalization, and stratification, on the average frequency of friendship visit with fellow workers, it is clear that there is no impact. Only the number of occupational specialties has some modest impact ($r = .37$). This means again that the key factor may be the diversity of individuals, thus, the importance of complexity and the proportion of unscheduled communications between departments. *But beyond these minor influences, the theory of coordination and control does not handle the problem of social integration.* Presumably, there are other variables that are more decisive in explaining patterns of integration.

CONCLUSIONS: TOWARD AN EXPANDED CYBERNETIC THEORY OF COORDINATION AND CONTROL

The testing of alternative theories has clearly indicated some strengths and weaknesses in our cybernetic theory of coordination and of control. Both size and ecological spread do not appear to be important contenders. Routine technology is a critical factor in explaining scheduled communication and client scope and client variability appear to be important for certain kinds of unscheduled communication. Finally, the theory, as presently constituted, is not very effective in explaining social integration.

However, to say that a particular variable does not have a direct

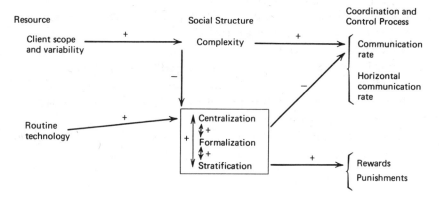

Figure 11.1   An expanded path diagram of the cybernetic theory of coordination and control.

impact on our measures of feedback is not to say that it has no indirect influence. Unfortunately, the small number of organizations prevents us from performing a path analysis. We have too many variables and too few organizations. But we can at least propose a probable path model. This helps expend a theory of coordination and control towards a more systematic analysis of resource inputs, structure variables, and the processes of coordination and control.

The proposed model is contained in Figure 11.1. The technological inputs of client scope and client variability, or the diversity of inputs and their complexity, in turn, affects the complexity of the division of labor. Not unexpectedly, variety in one area triggers variety in another. This, in turn, affects the communication rate, expanding its volume and, as we have already noted, extending its channels of unscheduled communication and activating organization-wide committee meetings.

In contrast, routine technology leads to centralization and formalization, which, in turn, inhibit the need for high communication volume because of the status differences that are generated. Centralization and formalization, in turn, are associated with stratification. Together, the three variables represent a mechanical model of organization. One cause of this structural model is the routine technology (Perrow, 1967; Burns and Stalker, 1961; Hage and Aiken, 1969). The competing thesis or trajectory of effects is the client scope and variability leading to an organic model with its network of scheduled and unscheduled communications.

Naturally, organizations are buffeted by countervailing forces at the same time. New clients are "discovered" just as greater routinization of technology occurs. The images of an organization oscillating from year to year within the overall trend towards an organic structure because of the process of structural differentiation is probably more accurate. Certainly, expansions of knowledge in the larger environment leads to more variability in clients because of fine discrimination and more routinization of the technology for treating the clients Lawrence and Lorsch, 1967b). While the former has perhaps the stranger effect, this is only true in the long run of organizational evolution.

Several variables have not been included. Size has been excluded because its patterns of effects are not yet completely understood. On a priori grounds, size would appear to lead to greater complexity (Blau, 1970; Blau and Schoenherr, 1971), although this is still being debated in the literature (Hall, Haas, and Johnson, 1967b). It would also appear to lead to greater centralization if there is some truth in Michel's iron law of oligarchy (Michel, 1949; see also Blau and Schoenherr, 1971, Figure 5.5). These contrary indirect influences may explain why size does not have that much direct influence on communication rates. Its indirect effects tend to cancel each other.

Although Figure 11.1 cannot be tested with the data we have collected, it has emerged from a pattern of findings, and thus represents hypotheses for future research; the figure does provide a framework for thinking about organizations systemically. The system of the organization has been broken into several critical parts: resource or input variables, structural variables, and process variables (Azuni and Hage, 1972; Chapter 7). The causal chain is assumed to move from left to right. The inputs shape the structure, which, in turn, affects the development of information feedback within the organization. The identified variables, while hardly an exhaustive list of coordinates, represent a start towards describing the system.

EPILOGUE

MAKING THE
SPECIFIC CYBERNETIC THEORY
MORE GENERAL

XII

The Cybernetic Theory:
Implications and Extensions

THE RICHNESS OF A PARADIGM is always much greater than one man's vision. This present example is no exception. Much of our effort has been to indicate how cybernetic thinking with its emphasis on feedback of information can unite the structural-functional, conflict, social· control, and task integration literatures into a broader perspective. The same theory can handle states of stability and instability, periods of consensus and conflict, and different pathways of evolution from one steady state to another. Some mention of other kinds of ideas buried in a cybernetic perspective should be made in our concluding chapter.

One very important theme in the Butler plan and a key implication of feedback information is its consequences for quality control. Today much is being written about how evaluation might be built into the control process. There is a widespread concern about quality control. Yet, many of the proposed attempts to effect evaluation may well prevent quality from emerging since they are concerned about evaluating outputs and not process. The proposals also tend to be unrealistic because they attempt to evaluate professionals who are frequently in a position to block the evaluative efforts. Thus some attention should be paid to the general implications of the Butler plan for creating quality control systems in professional organizations.

Buckley (1967) has correctly called attention to the idea of a moving equilibrium of open systems as an essential insight of modern systems thinking. Since I have been primarily concerned with a homeostatic regulatory process which unites several seemingly disparate literatures, not much attention has been paid to the idea of a moving equilibrium and its place in organizational analysis. It represents one way in which the present theory needs to be extended and expanded.

IMPLICATIONS FOR A QUALITY CONTROL PROCESS

The Butler Plan was concerned with trying to improve the quality of patient care. There have been many discussions about the quality of education. Demonstrations in front of public welfare agencies have indicated that they have problems as well. Nader's Raiders have called into question the extent and interest in quality control in large business organizations, such as General Motors. The problem of quality, whether in services or products, has become increasingly important to the client and the customer. If feedback is operating—and it would be hard for organizational elites to remain oblivious to these danger signals—then we can infer that the heads of organizations are becoming more concerned with obtaining quality control of their products and services.

Cybernetic control over quality is very different from control over quantity. If one takes a very simple example, college education, we might be concerned with the quantity of students handled, especially relative to a certain input of investment and faculty. To keep track of how many students there are, the dean or administration would institute reports on how many students graduate each year, the total number classified by field. If enrollments dropped, then some corrective action would be taken. This kind of checking on outputs could even occur on a classroom basis. If student enrollment in a particular course went too low, the course might be discontinued. These are examples of cybernetic control where information feedback results in some action. However, they are illustrations of where the concern is for only the quantity of student or graduates being produced. This is a concern with control by output monitoring, and while there is feedback, it is of a small amount.

When there is an emphasis on the quality of education being produced, there is a need for much greater volumes of feedback. The entire process of education must be monitored at each step of the way. This is frequently accomplished by reducing class sizes so that each faculty member can interact with his students, by having tutors review student progress, and other mechanisms of review. When there is a difficulty found in the educational production process, some corrective action is taken. This is quality control. Its distinctive characteristics are much higher volumes of feedback because feedback must be accomplished at each stage in the process if it is really to be quality control. One reason why quality control—and this is especially true of human systems—requires feedback at many points in the production process is that its standards or measures are much more elusive. Therefore, greater attempts must be made to ascertain how things are progressing.

There is an intermediate point along the continuum of quantity to quality control. This is where some attempts are made to measure quality at the output stage. For example, we might measure how many of our graduates got jobs or graduate degrees. But note that while this information can result in corrective action, it is less quick and also likely to be less subtle. Real control over the quality of the product can be ascertained only checking at every step in the process and making adjustments when errors or mistakes are discovered.

The difference between quality and quantity control is very easy to understand when we discuss machine or man-machine systems. Counting the number of cars produced per hour is the extreme quantity control system. Performing various tests on cars once they are produced, such as checking to see if the motor runs or if the paint peels or if the fabric is finished, is the mixture between quantity and quality control. Finally, continuously checking on the car as it is produced, at each step on the assembly line, represents the best in quality control.

Obviously, quality control is expensive if for no other reason that high feedback is itself time-consuming. To pay tutors to monitor students or to pay quality control men to check the cars means more manpower per student and per car. Indeed, this is one of the major differences between the low- and high-cost car. It is equally true for the low- and high-cost college education.

It might be noted that many of the techniques developed for monitoring the quality of the automobile—sampling a certain number, special tests for various parts of the car—have not been really applied in man-man systems of coordination and control. This can represent a future line of development for many organizations which provide services rather than products.

Perhaps the clearest example of quality in college education is to be found in graduate education. Here, the process of producing a professional is highly monitored. There is much reliance on apprenticeship training with all of its implications for high feedback, there are yearly reviews relative to progress by way of, for example, scholarship grants.

Coordination and control have different consequences for the extent and subtlety of control. To sanction either by firing or by salary raises is not as finely tuned a mechanism of control over human behavior. Indeed, this is one of the major problems of reinforcement techniques. They work well in getting the desired conformity relative to highly specific standards or detailed programs. They are excellent for extinguishing or encouraging certain explicit patterns of behavior. Programmed learning gets students to memorize languages, spelling, and facts, but it does not seem effective for developing curiosity or creativity. Perhaps in the future reinforcement techniques will be successfully expanded to these more generalized and diffuse standards. For the moment, *socialization without sanctions* appears more effective. Admittedly, rewarding conformity is more effective than punishing deviance. But still more effective, at least in certain situations and with certain kinds of people, is socialization without any sanctions. Beyond the issue of identifying the problems for which the alternative mechanisms are most appropriate is the issue of identifying the people with whom the alternative mechanisms work best.

The most distinctive aspect of socialization as a mechanism of control is that it provides much more control over the behavior of the individual. This is hard to visualize unless one recognizes the importance of continued learning for the advanced professional, such as the physician in a hospital, the professor in a graduate school or the lawyer in a highly competent law firm. Here, the issue is not so much correcting nonconformity as being sure that the professionals are kept abreast of current developments. We need to be less concerned about their knowledge and more concerned about their excellence. The problem with the control over professional behavior is one of quality, as we have noted, and this is, for obvious reasons, a problem of a much more total kind of control.

Therefore, both quality and quantity control are examples of regulation in the cybernetic sense of the term. We are arguing that quality control is control over process, which requires high volumes of feedback with socialization. Quantity control system is control over output, which does not require much feedback. Coordination is achieved through standardization or programming, and correctives occur with the manipulation of sanctions. Quality control is an expensive regulation system, quantity control is not. Each have their place in organizations.

As organizations become more concerned with quality control, it seems that they will have to adopt some proposals like the Butler Plan. The essential ingredients are the addition of teachers who monitor various stages of the production process and make suggestions to students who, in turn, pass on the information to practicing professionals. This implies the need for teachers inside service organizations or the addition of internship programs in organizations other than hospitals. We already see this program in government. Why not have interns in businesses as well?

Another simple illustration of how the establishment of feedback in the production process can be made is in our graduate training programming in the University of Wisconsin. We have established several classes which are team-taught for students working toward their masters degrees, and which are supervised by other professors. Thus even in the teaching and research process itself, one can add mechanisms of socialization by which faculty members are educated by the students they supervise. Team teaching is itself one very helpful corrective and an interesting mechanism of continued socialization, assuming the team members keep changing.

Proposals to evaluate output are not likely to be very helpful even though they are themselves examples of increasing feedback. It is more necessary to increase the socialization of the professions involved in the throughput or production process. Analogies from the Butler plan are helpful for those who are concerned about quality. It would also appear to be a plan that has some chance of being acceptable, although its introduction will generate conflict.

NEEDED EXTENSIONS TO THE THEORY

As we noted in the prologue, the present theory of cybernetic control is primarily concerned with the problem of coordination and control vis-à-vis conflict and deviance, or a homeostatic regulation process. We have observed regulation over moving-equilibrium processes. Although increased feedback and socialization have obvious consequences for these as well, the theory needs extension to handle this problem more effectively.

Extending the Regulatory Processes

Conflict and deviance are not the only variables which are monitored in organizations, nor is the coordination and control process the only kind of system regulation. The other two processes—adjustment and adaptiveness—are perhaps the most interesting, especially for those concerned with organizational systems moving across time. Adjustment and adaptiveness are less concerned with the problem of homeostatic control and more with a moving-equilibrium control. The adjustment process concerns the monitoring of organizational outputs and their increase or maintenance in the light of changing circumstances; the adaptive process concerns the monitoring of organizational performances. The distinction may appear somewhat arbitrary, yet it flows from the fact that the variables that control outputs, such as the volume of production, appear to be primarily inputs, whereas the variables that regulate performances are the structural variables.

Perhaps some examples are in order. If automobile orders decline, typically the manufacturers lay off workers and thus reduce their costs. Here, output, the profit margin, is maintained by cutting back on the inputs, that is, staff and salaries. This is a common adjustment technique. In universities, when student enrollment declines, we see a freeze on hiring and a reduction in staff through attrition.

A very different kind of environmental problem is created by competition. Suppose a competitor brings out a new product or service. Here we see an organization competing by offering new products or services. This creates a changing environment, in which the organization increases its rate of program innovation (Hage and Aiken, 1970: Chapter 3). But to do this, it must alter its structure.

The three processes of regulation—what we can call coordination and control, adjustment, and adaptiveness—are diagrammed in Figure 12.1. Indicated are the different parts of the system that are involved as the variables that are monitored and the variables that alter as a result of information feedback. Thus, increases in communication or coercion presumably affect the rates of conflict or consensus and the rates of deviance or conformity. Adjustment relates output with input variables. If the production output becomes too high, workers are laid off and investment declines. In other words, the inputs are adjusted accordingly. Adaptiveness is a more complex process of regulation. It involves changes in the social structure to produce changes in priorities. Community Hospital is an illustration

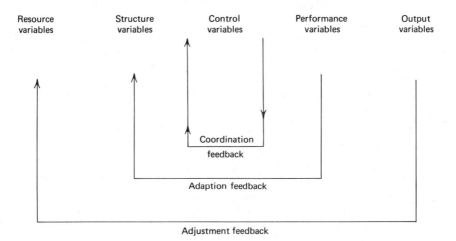

Figure 12.1 The basic regulatory processes: coordination and control, adjustment, and adaptiveness.

of this. The changing emphasis on medical education and quality of care can be seen as an adaptive process associated with structural differentiation, that is, the addition of medical specialists led to increasing emphasis on the performance of quality care.

Whereas control and coordination is presumedly an internal problem, adjustment and adaptiveness are critical in a changing environment. It will be remembered that our definition of environment was those variables that affect inputs, outputs, or performances in the production process of the organization. Fluctuations in demand affect the outputs, requiring adjustments in the volume of inputs. Competition can also affect outputs and performances, and thus it is an extremely critical interorganizational process. For both regulatory processes, high internal feedback is an important precondition. Communications thus acquire a central role. The higher the volume of communication and the closer it approximates the multiple organic network, the more likely there is to be a detection of problems in the production of outputs or in priorities in certain performances. Thus, scheduled and unscheduled communications are not only mechanisms for coordination but they are the best mechanisms for quick responses when the environment suddenly causes a decline in particular outputs—cars that won't sell, or courses that students do not want. Here, it might be noted that a programmed organization can handle the adjustment process because it does receive reports on the volume of production. We are only suggesting that its response tends to be much slower. For the adaptive process, the programmed organization is at a loss because to adapt to the need for changing priorities, the elites must give up their program for action.

These ideas lead to a whole series of questions. How fast do organizations respond to changes in the environment which affect their outputs or performances? What structural characteristics affect the amount of information about what is happening internally and externally? What predicts whether the organization selects the right solution? We can imagine that organizational elites may change the wrong variable with disastrous consequences. An excellent example of this is the history of DuPont (Chandler, 1962), which increased centralization when the correct response was to decrease it.

Communication—the high volume and a double-triangle pattern, both scheduled and unscheduled—is also the mechanism for creative solutions to the kinds of problems that are detected. Not only must organizational members recognize changes that are occurring— the new product of a competitor, or the disappearance of a kind of client—but they must come forth with an appropriate response. Survival is not only seeing, it is doing and doing the right thing at the right time. High feedback connecting all parts of the organization allows not only for detection but group problem-solving. Here, solution can be understood to mean not only the processes of adjustment and adaptiveness, but the precise variables manipulated. Given a declining demand for courses, one response is to fire teachers, another is to develop new courses. One response might be best in the short run, another in the long run, indicating the complexity of the problem of understanding regulation processes. An extension of the theory is needed to handle the problem of how organizations steer across time in a moving-equilibrium process, whether by adjustment or adaptiveness.

Extending the Control Mechanisms

Although we have considered several other kinds of control processes, there are more than just the two of feedback with socialization and programming with sanctions. The important point is that cybernetic thinking can easily handle coordination and control mechanisms besides those postulated in the premises of the theory.

One possibility is the role of communication specialists. Another possibility is coordination and control specialists. While they are subsumed under the ideas of feedback and socialization, they appear to be qualitatively different from our measure of the volume of horizontal communication. Lawrence and Lorsch (1967a and b) have called attention to the role of the integrator for effecting coordination. Much of the Butler plan called for the addition of specialists in controlling. These are avenues that need more consideration.

Just as we should broaden our concept of regulation to include adjustment and adaptiveness processes, we should begin to look at other kinds of communication pathways. Organizations that are highly adaptive to rapidly changing environments probably establish specialists who monitor the external environment and keep the organization informed about it. Elsewhere, we have called these boundary-spanning roles (Aiken and Hage, 1972) because these specialists spend a good part of their time attending interorganizational committees and communicating in an unscheduled way with members of other organizations. In general, the problem of how much communication flow there is between organizations has not been studied. This would seem to be a key way of understanding how open, to use Buckley's (1967) term, the organizational system is.

Internal communications may not provide a creative solution. If they do not, then the communication links with the outside world may allow for the quick adoption of solutions developed by other organizations. Diffusion is most likely to occur among open and adaptive organizations. Just as the diffusion literature (Rogers, 1962) has placed a great emphasis on the communication behavior of individuals who are early adaptors, we would suggest that the same holds for organizations that are early adaptors. Again, the accent is on the speed with which adaptation occurs by the borrowing from the innovators of techniques, products, or services.

In the first chapter, we noted that social approval might be the middle ground between sanctions and socialization without sanctions. This could be explored in depth. It is difficult to research because it is not necessarily a behavior, as are sanctions, such as praise or criticism, or socialization via communication volume, but it might represent a very important corrective to the present theory.

Even if the cybernetic theory, as postulated and modified, is altered in the future, the concepts of feedback, homeostatic control, and equifinality should remain critical ideas in developing organizational theory. The small shift to feedback leads to the recognition of the importance of socialization and communication. Presumedly this is one reason that cybernetics and communication theory are usually mixed together.

Cybernetics is clearly comprehensive because it includes all parts of the system, by definition, as well as goals and the environment. The old traditions of structural-functionalism, which can be defined as the interrelationships among structure and performances, goal analysis, technological determinism, and size analysis (Hage, 1972: Chapter 8), are all subsumed as different coordinates or problems in the system of the organization (Azuni and Hage: Chapter 7). The research study in Part One indicates how these traditions could be synthesized. It is difficult to see whether any problem is left outside its very general framework. Indeed, its generality has been its biggest handicap. People have had difficulty understanding how the very abstract assumptions and concepts related to organizations. Hopefully, the cybernetic theory and the concern for operationization has helped to indicate how the approach can be fruitfully applied.

Any system of thought that can combine conflict theory and evolutionary theory in the ideas of instability and moving equilibrium is to be recommended. Revolution and evolution become merely different states of the same system described by different combinations of numbers on the same coordinates. Furthermore, the twin notions of equifinality and inherent evolution toward greater differentiation or complexity, which can occur in many ways, give us a much more complex picture of the future than the onward-and-upward notions of old evolutionary theory. In conclusion, cybernetics appears to be a useful candidate as a paradigm in organizational analysis. The best paradigm is one that can handle new problems as well as old ones and synthesize as well as suggest new avenues of research. Cybernetics would seem to have this capacity for growth.

APPENDIX

THE SAMPLING PROCEDURE DIVIDES the organization into levels and departments. Job occupants in the upper levels were selected because they are most likely to be key decision-makers and to determine organizational policy, whereas job occupants on the lower levels were selected at random. The different ratios within departments ensured that smaller departments were adequately represented. Professionals, such as psychiatrists, social workers, and rehabilitation counselors, are included because they are intimately involved in the achievement of organizational goals; nonprofessionals, such as attendants, janitors, and secretaries, are excluded because they are less directly involved in the achevement of organizational objectives.

We stress that in this study the units of analysis are organizations, not individuals in the organizations. Information obtained from respondents was pooled to reflect properties of the 16 organizations, and these properties were then related to one another. Aggregating individual data in this way presents methodological problems for which there are yet no satisfactory solutions. For example, if all respondents are equally weighted, undue weight is given to respondents lower in the hierarchy. Yet those higher in the chain of command, not the lower status staff members, are the ones most likely to make the decisions that give an agency an ethos.

We attempted to compensate for this by computing an organizational score from the means of social positions within the agency. A

244

social position is defined by the level or stratum in the organization and the department or type of professional activity. For example, if an agency's professional staff consists of psychiatrists and social workers, each divided into two hierarchical levels, the agency has four social positions: supervisory psychiatrists, psychiatrists, supervisory social workers, and social workers. A mean was then computed for each social position in the agency. The organizational score for a given variable was determined by computing the average of all social position means in the agency.

The procedure for computing organizational scores parallels the method utilized in selecting respondents—it attempts to represent organizational life more accurately by not giving disproportionate weight to those social positions that have little power and that are little involved in the achievement of organizational goals. Computation of means for each social position has the advantage of avoiding the potential problem created by the use of different sampling ratios. In effect, responses are standardized by organizational location—level and department—and then combined into an organizational score. Computation of means of social position also has a major theoretical advantage in that it focuses on the sociological perspective or organizational reality.

We do not make the assumption that the distribution of power, regulations, or rewards is random within any particular social position. Instead, each respondent is treated as if he provides a true estimate of the score for a given social position. There is likely to be some distortion because of personality differences or events unique in the history of the organization, but the computation of means for each social position hopefully eliminates or at least reduces the variation due to these factors.

Interviews were conducted with 520 staff members in these 16 organizations. Respondents within each organization were selected by the following criteria:

1. All executive directors and department heads;
2. In departments of less than ten members, one-half of the staff selected randomly.
3. In departments of ten or more members, one-third of the staff selected randomly.

Nonsupervisory administrative and maintenance personnel were not interviewed. The number of interviews varied from 11 in the smallest to 61 in the largest.

INDICATORS OF COMPLEXITY

The number of occupational specialties was measured by establishing the number of distinct occupational specialties in the organization. This was done by taking the reports of the executive director and simply counting the number of distinct occupations. A department head, a supervisor, and a social worker were not treated as separate and distinct occupations. Thus this measure is not the same as a count of job titles.

Professional activity was measured as follows:

1. one point for belonging to a professional organization.
2. one point for attending at least two-thirds of the previous six meetings.
3. one point for the presentation of a paper or for the holding of an office.

The number of departments was measured by counting those indicated in the interviews with the executive director and consulting the organizational chart when available. Special charts were made up when not available.

INDICATORS OF STRATIFICATION

The proportion of professional staff who are nonsupervisors was computed by computing the total number of workers interviewed as a percentage of total staff interviewed. It should be remembered that nonprofessional workers were not interviewed.

RESOURCE VARIABLES

Organized size was determined by taking the sum of the number of full-time employees, one-half the number of part-time employees, and one-tenth the number of volunteers. A rank order was used since it was the most conservative measure.

Ecological spread was simply determined by an index of one for a single floor, two for multiple floors, and three for multiple buildings.

Routine technology was based on the following questions:

1. People here do the same job in the same way every day.
2. One thing people like around here is the variety of work (reversed).
3. Most jobs have something new happening every day (reversed).
4. There is something different to do every day (reversed).

Respondents replied differently, true, true, false, or definitely false to each of the questions. (Hage and Aiken, 1967b)

In addition the respondents were asked to describe their work as being very routine, somewhat routine, somewhat nonroutine, or very routine. The answers to thest five questions were averaged.

Client scope was simply determined by an index of one for an hour interview, two for a day's visit, and three for hospitalization for 24 hours.

Client variability was based on the answers of the executive director as to the number of different kinds of clients treated.

INDICATORS OF FORMALIZATION

Presence of job description was measured by asking the respondents whether there were job descriptions. The respondents answered definitely true, partially true, partially false, and definitely false. The index of job specificity was measured by asking the following questions:

1. Whatever situation arises, we have procedures to following in dealing with it;
2. Everyone has a specific job to do;
3. Going through the proper channels is constantly stressed;
4. The organization keeps a written record of everyone's job performance;
5. Whenever we have a problem, we are supposed to go to the same person for an answer.

Respondents gave replies from definitely true to definitely untrue, and then these were averaged to create this scale. The final scale ranged from 1.00 (low specificity) to 4:00 (high specificity). An average score for each respondent was computed.

INDICATORS OF CENTRALIZATION

The index of participation in decision making was based on the following four questions:

1. How frequently do you usually participate in the decision to hire new staff?

2. How frequently do you usually participate in the decisions on the promotion of any of the professional staff?

3. How frequently do you participate in decisions on the adoption of new policies?

4. How frequently do you participate in the decisions on the adoption of new programs?

Respondents were assigned numerical scores from 1 to 5 depending on whether they answered never (1), seldom (2), sometimes (3), often (4), or always (5), to these questions. An average score on these questions was computed for each respondent.

The index of hierarchy of authority was computed by first averaging the replies of individual respondents to each of the following five statements:

1. There can be little action taken here until a supervisor approves a decision.

2. A person who wants to make his own decisions would be quickly discouraged here.

3. Even small matters have to be referred to someone higher up for a final answer.

4. I have to ask my boss before I do almost anything.

5. Any decision I make has to have my boss's approval.

Responses could vary from definitely false to definitely true. An average score for each respondent was computed.

BIBLIOGRAPHY

Aiken, Michael
Jerald Hage
1971   "The Organic Model and Innovation," *Sociology*
                    (March).

Aiken, Michael
Jerald Hage
1972   "Communication Networks and Organizational Innova-
                    tion" unpublished manuscript, University of Wis-
                    consin.

Aldrich, Howard
1972   "Technology and Organizational Structure: A Reexam-
                    ination of the Findings of the Aston Group" *Admin-
                    istrative Science Quarterly* **17** (March): 26–43.

Ashby, W. Ross
1956   *An Introduction to Cybernetics.* New York: Wiley.

Azumi, Koya
Jerald Hage
1972   *Organizational Systems: A Text-Reader in the Sociology
                    of Organizations.* Lexington, Mass.: Heath.

Barton, Allen
1961   *Organizational Measurement and Its Bearing on the
                    Study of College Environments.* New York: College
                    Entrance Examination Board.

249

Barnard, Chester
1946   "Functions and Pathology of Status Systems in Formal
                        Organizations" in William Foote Whyte (ed) *Indus-
                        try and Society*. New York: McGraw-Hill: 46–83.

Bavelas, Alex
1950   "Communication Patterns in Task-Oriented Groups,"
                        Journal of Accoustical Society of America **22**: 725–
                        730.

Berrien, Kenneth
1968   *General and Social Systems*. New Brunswick, N.J.: Rut-
                        gers University Press.

Blalock, Hubert M.
1967   "Causal Inferences in Natural Experiments: Some
                        Complications in Matching Designs," *Sociometry* **30**
                        (September): 300–315.

Blalock, Hubert M.
1972   *Causal Models in the Social Sciences*. Chicago: Aldine.

Blau, Peter M.
1955   *The Dynamics of Bureaucracy: A Study of Interper-
                        sonal Relations in Two Government Agencies*.
                        Chicago: University of Chicago Press.

Blau, Peter M.
1968   "The Hierarchy of Authority in Organizations," *Amer-
                        ican Journal of Sociology* **73** (January): 453–457.

Blau, Peter M.
1970   "A Formal Theory of Differentiation in Organizations"
                        American Sociological Review **35** (April): 201–218

Blau, Peter M.
W. Richard Scott
1962   *Formal Organizations: A Comparative Approach*. San
                        Francisco: Chandler.

Blau, Peter M.
Wolf V. Heydebrand
Robert Stauffer
1966   "The Structure of Small Bureaucracies, "*American So-
                        ciological Review* **31** (April):179–191.

Blau, Peter M.
Richard Schoenherr
1971   *The Structure of Organizations.* New York: Basic Books.

Blauner, Robert
1964   *Alienation and Freedom: The Factory Worker and His Industry.* Chicago: University of Chicago Press.

Brim, Orville G., Jr.
1968   "Adult Socialization," in John A. Clausen (ed.), *Socialization and Society.* Boston: Little, Brown, pp. 182–226.

Bucher, Rue
Anselm Strauss
1961   "Professions in Process," *American Journal of Sociology* **66** (January).

Buckley, Walter
1967   *Sociology and Modern Systems Theory.* Englewood Cliffs, N.J.: Prentice-Hall.

Butler, John
Jerald Hage
1966   "Physician Attitudes Towards a Hospital Program in Medical Education," *The Journal of Medical Education* **41** (October): 913–946.

Burns, Tom
G. M. Stalker
1961   *The Management of Innovation.* London: Tavistock Publications.

Cadwallader, Mervyn
1959   "The Cybernetic Analysis of Change in Complex Social Organizations," *American Journal of Sociology* **65** (September): 154–157.

Cangelosi, Vincent
William R. Dill
1965   "Organizational Learning: Observations Toward a Theory," *Administrative Science Quarterly* **10** (September): 175–203.

Caplow, Theodore
1954   *The Sociology of Work.* Minneapolis: University of
                Minnesota Press.

Chandler, Alfred, Jr.
1962   *Strategy and Structure.* Boston, Mass.: Institute of
                Technology Press.

Coch, Lester
John French, Jr.
1948   "Overcoming Resistance to Change," *Human Relations*
                I (August).

Colombotos, John
1969   "Physicians and Medicare: A Before-After Study of the
                Effects of Legislation on Attitudes," *American Soci-
                ological Review* **34** (June): 318–334.

Corwin, Ronald
1969   "Patterns of Organizational Conflict" *Administrative
                Science Quarterly* **14** (December): 507–521.

Coser, Lewis
1964   *The Functions of Social Conflict.* New York: Free Press.

Crozier, Michael
1964   *The Bureaucratic Phenomenon.* Chicago: University of
                Chicago Press.

Dalton, Melville
1950   "Conflicts Between Staff and Line Managerial Offi-
                cers, *American Sociological Review* **15** (June): 342–
                351.

Davis, James
Kenneth M. Dolbeare
1968   *Little Groups of Neighbors: The Selective Service
                System.* Chicago: Markham.

Duncan, Robert B.
1972   "Characteristics of Organizational Environments and
                Perceived Environmental Uncertainty" *Administra-
                tive Science Quarterly* **17** (September): 313–327.

Durkheim, Emile
1933   *The Division of Labor in Society*, trans. by George Simpson. Glencoe, Ill.: Free Press.

Durkheim, Emile
1951   *Suicide*, trans. by J. Spaulding and George Simpson. Glencoe, Ill.: Free Press.

Etzioni, Amitai
1961   *A Comparative Analysis of Complex Organizations: On Power, Involvement and Their Correlates.* New York: Free Press.

Festinger, Leon
1950   *Social Pressures in Informal Groups: A Study of Human Factors in Housing.* New York: Harper and Row.

Forrester, Jay Wright
1961   *Industrial Dynamics.* New York: Wiley.

Forrester, Jay Wright
1969   *Urban Dynamics.* Cambridge, Mass.: M.I.T. Press.

Frank, Andrew G.
1958   "Goal Ambiguity and Conflicting Standards: An Approach to the Study of Organizations" *Human Organization* 7: 8–13.

Fullan, Michael
1970   "Industrial Technology and Worker Integration in the Organization," *American Sociological Review* 35 (December).

Glaser, Barney
Anselau, Strauss
1967   *Discovery of Grounded Theory: Strategies for Qualitative Research* Chicago: Aldine.

Goode, William J.
1960   "Encroachment, Charlatanism, and the Emerging Profession: Psychology, Sociology, and Medicine," *American Sociological Review* 25 (December): 902–914.

Gouldner, Alvin Ward
1954   *Patterns of Industrial Bureaucracy.* Glencoe, Ill.: Free
                     Press.

Gouldner, Alvin Ward
1970   *The Coming Crisis in Western Sociology.* New York:
                     Basic Books.

Greenblatt, Milton
Richard York
Esther Braun
1955   *From Custodial to Therapeutic Patient Care in Mental
                     Hospitals: Explorations in Social Treatment.* New
                     York: Russell Sage Foundation.

Guest, Robert H.
1962   *Organizational Change: The Effects of Successful
                     Leadership.* Homewood, Ill.: Dorsey Press.

Guetzkow, Harold
1965   "Communications in Organizations," in James March
                     (ed.), *The Handbook of Organizations,* pp. 534–574.

Hage, Jerald
1963   "Organizational Response to Innovation," unpublished
                     Ph.D. dissertation, Columbia University.

Hage, Jerald
1965   "An Axiomatic Theory of Organizations," *Administra-
                     tive Science Quarterly* **10** (December): 289–319.

Hage, Jerald
Michael Aiken
1967a   "*Program Change and Organization Properties: A
                     Comparative Analysis,*" *American Journal of Soci-
                     ology* **72** (March): 503–519.

Hage, Jerald
Michael Aiken
1967b   "Relationship of Centralization to Other Structural
                     Properties," *Administrative Science Quarterly* **12**
                     (June): 72–92.

Hage, Jerald
Michael Aiken
1969   "Routine Technology, Social Structure, and Organiza-
                     tional Goals" *Administrative Science Quarterly* **14**
                     (September): 366–377.

Hage, Jerald
Michael Aiken
1970   *Social Change in Complex Organizations.* New York:
                        Random House.

Hage, Jerald
Michael Aiken
Cora B. Marrett
1971   "Organizational   Structure   and   Communications,"
                        American Sociological Review (October): 860–871.

Hage, Jerald
1972   *Techniques and Problems of Theory Construction.*
                        New York: Wiley Interscience.

Hagstrom, Warren O.
1965   *The Scientific Community.* New York: Basic Books.

Hall, Richard H.
J. Eugene Haas
Norman J. Johnson
1967a   "An Examination of the Blau-Scott and Etzioni Typol-
                        ogies," *Administrative Science Quarterly* **12** (June):
                        118–139.

Hall, Richard H.
J. Eugene Haas
Norman J. Johnson
1967b   "Organizational Size, Complexity and Formalization,"
                        American Sociological Review **32** (December): 903–
                        912.

Hickson, David J.
D. S. Pugh
Diaria C. Pheysey
1969   "Operations Technology and Organizational Structure:
                        An Empirical Reappraisal," *Administrative Science
                        Quarterly* **14** (Sept.): 378–397.

Homans, George C.
1961   *The Elements of Human Behavior.* New York: Har-
                        court, Brace.

Jeghers, Harold
John O'Brien
John Butler
1956   "An Experiment in Making the Hospital a Graduate
                        Medical Center," *Journal of the American Medical
                        Association* **58**.

Julian, Joseph
1966   "Compliance Patterns and Communication Blocks in
                        Complex Organizations," *American Sociological Re-
                        view* **31** (June): 382–389.

Kahn, Robert
Donald Wolfe
Robert Quinn
J. D. Snoek
1964   *Organizational Stress: Studies in Role Conflict and
                        Ambiguity.* New York: Wiley.

Katz, Daniel
Robert L. Kahn
1966   *The Social Psychology of Organization.* New York:
                        Wiley.

Kaufman, Herbert
David Seidman
1970   "The Morphology of Organizations" *Administrative
                        Science Quarterly* **15** (December): 439–452.

Kendall, Patricia
n.d.   A large survey of interns and residents conducted at the
                        Bureau of Applied Social Research, New York:
                        Columbia University, unpublished data.

Kuhn, Thomas
1962   *The Structure of Scientific Revolutions* Chicago: Uni-
                        versity of Chicago Press.

Landsberger, Henry A.
1961   "The Horizontal Dimension in Bureaucracy," *Admin-
                        istrative Science Quarterly* **6** (December): 299–332.

Lawrence, Paul
Jay Lorsch
1967a   "Differentiation and Integration in Complex Organiza-
                     tions," *Administrative Science Quarterly* **12** (Septem-
                     ber): 1–47.

Lawrence, Paul
Jay Lorsch
1967b   *Organizations and Environment: Managing Differen-
                     tiation and Integration.* Cambridge, Mass.: Harvard
                     Business School.

Lefton, Mark
William R. Rosengren
1966   "Organizations and Clients: Lateral and Longitudinal
                     Dimensions," *American Sociological Review* **31** (De-
                     cember): 802–810.

Levine, Sol
Paul E. White
1961   "Exchange as a Conceptual Framework for the Study
                     of Interorganizational Relationships," *Administrative
                     Science Quarterly* **7** (December): 349–364.

Litterer, Joseph A.
1963   *Organizations: Structure and Behavior*, vol. II. New
                     York: Wiley.

Loy, John W. Jr.
1969   "Social Psychological Characteristics of Innovators,"
                     American Sociological Review **34** (February): 73–81.

March, James G.
Herbert A. Simon
1958   *Organizations.* New York: Wiley.

March, James G.
1965   *Handbook of Organizations.* Chicago: Rand McNally.

Marwell, Gerald
Jerald Hage
1970   "The Organization of Role Relationships: A Systematic
                     Description," *American Sociological Review* **35**
                     (October): 884–900.

McCleery, Richard
1957
    Policy Change in Prison Management. East Lansing, Mich.: Government Research Bureau, Michigan State University.

Meadows, Donella H.
Jorgen Randers
William W. Behrens III
Dennis L. Meadows
1972
    Limits to Growth: A Report for the Club of Rome's Project on the Predicament of Mankind. New York: Universe Books.

Mechanic, David
1962
    "Organizational Power of Lower Participants," *Administrative Science Quarterly* **7** (December): 349–364.

Merton, Robert K.
1957
    Social Theory and Social Structure, rev. ed. Glencoe, Ill.: Free Press.

Michels, Robert
1949
    Political Parties. Glencoe, Ill.: Free Press.

Miller, Daniel R.
Guy E. Swanson
1958
    The Changing American Parent. New York: Wiley.

Morse, Nancy
Everett R. Reimer
1956
    "The Experimental Change of a Major Organizational Variable," *Journal of Abnormal and Social Psychology* **52**: 120–129.

Nisbet, Robert A.
1970
    The Social Bond: An Introduction to the Study of Society. New York: Knopf.

Palumbo, Dennis
1969
    "Power and Role Specificity in Organization Theory," *Public Administration Review* **29**, No. 3 (May–June).

Parsons, Talcott
1951
    The Social System. Glencoe, Ill.: Free Press.

Parsons, Talcott
1966

Societies: Evolutionary and Comparative Perspectives. Englewood Cliffs, New Jersey: Prentice-Hall.

Peabody, Robert L.
1962

"Perceptions of Organizational Authority," *Administrative Science Quarterly* **6** (March): 463–482.

Perrow, Charles
1963

"Goals and Power Structures—A Historical Case Study," in Eliot Freidson (ed.), *The Hospital in Modern Society.* New York; Free Press, pp. 112–146.

Perrow Charles
1965

"Hospitals: Technology, Structure and Goals," in James March (ed.), *Handbook of Organizations*, pp. 910–971.

Perrow, Charles
1967

"A Framework for the Comparative Analysis of Organizations," *American Sociological Review* **32** (April): 193–208.

Perrow, Charles
1968

"Organizational Goals," in *International Encyclopedia of the Social Sciences*, vol. 11, New York: Macmillan, pp. 305–311.

Perrow, Charles
1970

Organizational Analysis: A Sociological View. Belmont, Cal.: Wadsworth.

Peterson, Osler
1956

"An Analytical Study of North Carolina General Practice, 1953–1954," *Journal of Medical Education* **31**, No. 12, Part 2.

Poudy, Louis R.
1967

"Organizational Conflict: Concepts and Models" *Administrative Science Quarterly* **12** (September): 296–321.

Price, James
1967

Organizational Effectiveness: An Inventory of Propositions. Homewood, Ill.: Irwin.

Price, James
1972   The Handbook of Organizational Measurement. Lex-
                    ington, Mass.: Heath.

Pugh, Derek S.
David Hickson
C. R. Hinings
K. M. Macdonald
C. Turner
T. Lupton
1963   "A Conceptual Scheme for Organizational Analysis,"
                    Administrative Science Quarterly 8 (December):
                    289–315.

Pugh, Derek S.
David Hickson
C. R. Hinings
C. Turner
1968   "Dimensions of Organizational Structure," Administra-
                    tive Science Quarterly 13 (June): 65–105.

Pugh, Derek S.
David Hickson
C. R. Hinings
C. Turner
1969a   "The Context of Organizational Structures," Adminis-
                    tative Science Quarterly 14 (March): 91–114.

Pugh, Derek S.
David Hickson
C. R. Hinings
1969b   "An Empirical Taxonomy of Structures of Work Organ-
                    izations," Administrative Science Quarterly 14
                    (March): 115–126.

Ronken, Harriet
Paul Lawrence
1952   Administering Changes: A Case Study of Human Rela-
                    tions in a Factory. Boston: Harvard University, Divi-
                    sion of Research, Graduate School of Business Admin-
                    istration.

Rogers, Everett M.
1962   Diffusion of Innovation. New York: Free Press.

Rosengren, William R.
Spencer De Vault
1963   "The Sociology of Time and Space in an Obstetrical
                    Hospital," in Eliot Friedsen (ed.), *The Hospital in
                    Modern Society*. New York: Free Press.

Samuel, Yitzhak
Bilka F. Mannheim
1970   "A Multi-Dimensional Approach Toward a Typology
                    of Bureaucracy," *Administrative Science Quarterly*
                    15 (June): 216–228.

Schmidt, Stuart M.
Thomas A. Kochan
1972   "Conflict: Toward Conceptual Clarity" *Administrative
                    Science Quarterly* **17** (September): 359–370.

Scott, John Finley
1971   *Internalization of Norms: A Sociological Theory of
                    Moral Commitment*. Englewood Cliffs, N.J.: Prentice-
                    Hall.

Seashore, Stanley
David G. Bowers
1963   *Changing the Structure and Functioning of an Organi-
                    zation*, Monograph 3. Ann Arbor: University of
                    Michigan, Institute for Social Research.

Seeman, Melvin
John Evans
1961   "Stratification and Hospital Care: I. The Performance
                    of the Medical Intern," *American Sociological Re-
                    view* **26** (February): 67–80.

Smith, Clagett G.
1966   "A Comparative Analysis of Some Conditions and Con-
                    sequences of Intraorganizational Conflict," *Admin-
                    istrative Science Quarterly* **10** (March): 504–529.

Smith, Clagett G.
1970   "Consultation and Decision Processes in a Research
                    and Development Laboratory," *Administrative Sci-
                    ence Quarterly* **15** (June): 205–215.

Spencer, Herbert
1898   *Principles of Sociology*. New York: Appleton-Century.

Starbuck, William H.
1965   "Organizational Growth and Development," in James
                       March (ed.), *Handbook of Organizations*: 451–533.

Tannenbaum, Arnold S.
        (ed.)
1968   *Control in Organizations.* New York: McGraw-Hill,
                       Chapters 1, 2, 3.

Terreberry, Shirley
1968   "The Evolution of Organizational Environments,"
                       Administrative Science Quarterly **12** (March): 590–
                       613.

Thompson, James D.
1967   *Organizations in Action.* New York: McGraw-Hill.

Thompson, Victor
1961a   "Hierarchy, Specialization, and Organizational Con-
                       flict," *Administrative Science Quarterly* **5** (March).

Thompson, Victor
1961b   *Modern Organization.* New York, Knopf.

Toffler, Mark
1970   *Future Shock.* New York: Bantam.

Trussel, Ray
Mildred Morehead
June Erlich
1961   The Quantity, Quality, and Costs of Medical and Hos-
                       pital Care Secured by a Sample of Teamster Families
                       in the New York Area. New York: Columbia Univer-
                       sity School of Public Health.

Walton, Richard
John Dutton
1969   "The Management of Interdepartmental Conflict: A
                       Model and Review *"Administrative Science Quarterly*
                       14 (March): 73–90.

Warren, Donald I.
1968   "Power, Visibility, and Conformity in Formal Organizations," *American Sociological Review* (December): 951–971.

Warren, Donald I.
1969   "The Effects of Power Bases and Peer Groups on Conformity in Organizations," *Administrative Science Quarterly* **14** (December): 544–556.

Weber, Max
1947   *The Theory of Social and Economic Organization,* trans. by A. M. Henderson and Talcott Parsons. Glencoe, Ill.: Free Press.

White, Harrison
1961   "Management Conflict and Sociometric Structure" *American Journal of Sociology* **67** (September): 185–199.

Wonnacott, Ronald
Thomas Wonnacott
1970   *Econometrics.* New York: Wiley.

Woodward, Joan
1965   *Industrial Organization: Theory and Practice.* London, N.Y.: Oxford University Press.

Zald, Mayer
1963   "Comparative Analysis and Measurement of Organizational Goals: The Case of Correctional Institutions for Delinquents," *Sociological Quarterly* **4** (Summer): 206–230.

Zelditch, Morris Jr.
Terence K. Hopkins
1961   "Laboratory Experiments with Organizations," in Amitai Etzioni (ed.), *Complex Organizations: A Sociological Reader.* New York: Holt, Rinehart and Winston.

Zetterberg, Hans
1963   *On Theory and Verification in Sociology,* rev. ed. N.J.: Bedminister Press.

INDEX

in Community Hospital, 71–72, 76
and complexity, 61
and conflict, social, 78, 87–88, 96–97, 99
continuous, 35
and control, cybernetic, 10–11, 13, 15, 19
and control, social, 20
as critical aspect of cybernetics, paradigm, 37–38, 74–75, 242
definition of, 29
difference from cause and effect, 10–11
and diversity, 34, 187
evolution of, 187–189
and instability, 97, 143
as mechanism of coordination and control, 13, 15, 19, 21, 29–30
and morale, 72
and programming, 47
and social change, 76, 86, 87–88, 122–123
and socialization, 5, 25, 28, 36, 37–39, 42, 102
and survival, 241
see also Control, cybernetic; Cybernetics, paradigm of; Homeostatic control
Festinger, 218, 253
Formalization, and centralization, 204–205, 229
and communication, task, 28, 191, 195–198, 208–212
and complexity, 204–205
definition of, 40, 191
and ecological spread, 218
and evolution, 43–45
measures of, 195–196, 247–248
and programming, 40
and punishments, 42
and rewards, 42
and stratification, 204–205, 229
Forrester, 4, 11, 26, 253
Frank, 40, 253
French, 20, 83, 252
Fullan, 105, 215, 253

Glazer, 6, 253
Goals, collective, 117, 140
in Community Hospital, 73–74, 137–144
and complexity, 117
conflicts in, 74, 140

consensus about, 139–140, 142
and evolution, 117
Goode, 77, 253
Gouldner, 4, 58, 254
Greenblatt, 83, 254
Guest, 58, 254
Guetzkow, 38, 254

Haas, 230, 255
Hage, 3, 4, 17, 18, 27, 28, 43, 48, 53, 59, 72, 77, 103, 105, 106, 120, 144, 147, 150–151, 157, 191, 198, 201, 203, 204, 215, 220, 226, 230, 239, 242, 249, 255, 257
Hagstrom, 254
Hall, 4, 230, 255
Heydebrand, 250
Hickson, 18, 105, 220, 255, 260
Hierarchy, of authority, and communication task, 166–167, 177, 199–201
in Community Hospital, 46, 66–67, 71, 74
standardization of, 157–158
Hinnings, 260
Homans, 136, 158, 255
Homeostatic control, 13, 238
conflict, social as, 143
and control, cybernetic, 10, 15–16, 43
deviance as, 143
difference from adaptive control, 16, 24 238–240
difference from equilibrium, moving, 11, 24, 143–144
and equilibrium, moving, 24, 187–189
see also Control, cybernetic; Cybernetics, paradigm of; Feedback, of information
House staff, definition of, 62, 63
Hopkins, 60, 263
Human relations, 83, 99

Ideology, measure of, 115
and work style, 115–119
Input, 3, 8–10, 19
Instability, states of, 43–45
causes of, 47–48, 76–77, 99, 143
and communication, task, 143, 187–189
and equifinality, 99–100, 125–126
and feedback, of information, 97, 143
and stability, 16, 42–45
as a test of theory, 44–45, 143
see also Equilibrium; Disequilibrium; Stability